JERUSALEM PRAYER TEAM

"Pray for the Peace of Jerusalem..."

www.jerusalemprayerteam.org

DR. MICHAEL D. EVANS

MIKE EVANS

PERSIA

THE FINAL JIHAD

TimeWorthy
BOOKS

P.O. Box 30000, Phoenix, AZ 85046

Persia: The Last Jihad
Copyright 2013 by Time Worthy Books
P. O. Box 30000
Phoenix, AZ 85046

Front Cover Photos: ShutterStock & AFP/Getty Images

Cover Design: Lookout Design, Inc.

Hardcover ISBN: 978-0-935199-66-6
       US ISBN: 978-0-935199-67-3
   Canada ISBN: 978-0-935199-68-0

Unless otherwise indicated, all scripture quotations are taken from *The New King James Version* of the Bible. Copyright© 1979, 1980, 1982, 1983, 1984 by Thomas Nelson, Inc. Publishers. Used by permission.

Scripture quotations marked NIV are taken from *The Holy Bible: New International Version*® NIV ®. Copyright © 1973, 1978, 1984 by International Bible Society. Used by permission of Zondervan Publishing House. All rights reserved.

Scripture quotations marked NLT are taken from the *New Living Translation*, copyright © 1996, 2004 by Tyndale Charitable Trust. Used by permission of Tyndale House Publishers.

Scripture quotations marked ESV are taken from *The Holy Bible, English Standard Version. Containing the Old and New Testaments*. J. I. Packer, ed. Wheaton, Illinois: Crossway Bibles (a division of Good News Publishers), 2001.

This book is dedicated to

Dr. Mike Atkins,

one of the greatest men I've ever had the privilege
of knowing. He is a man of impeccable integrity,
humility, and compassion and is brilliant.
In the Middle East, a word is used as a term
to describe a very significant person. It is "honorable."
There is no higher expression than,
"that man is an honorable man."

Those are the words I can truly say describe Mike Atkins.
It's easy for me to say that about him; he is my best friend.
As such, I know he is a man who is trustworthy, loyal, a servant.
Seldom in one's life does a person find an individual who is truly
a best friend. I can say in all sincerity that is true of Mike.

He has been with me during every conceivable situation,
and has inspired me to be a better man. Probably the best way
to describe Mike Atkins is by relaying this to you:

_One day while driving to the venue where the mayor of Jerusalem
and I would speak to several thousand people, Mike and I were within
two exits of arriving. Suddenly, something fell from my mouth into
my hand. It was the cap off my front tooth. I turned toward Mike.
He smiled and started singing, "When the tooth falls out and you
don't know what to do, go to Eckerd's and buy some superglue." At the
next exit was an Eckerd's. We ran inside, grabbed a tube of superglue,
went directly to the restroom, and opened the package. I applied glue
to the cap and secured it to my front tooth. We used the hand dryer
to insure that the glue was dry. We then walked up to the cashier and
paid for the package of superglue._

Rather than offering a negative response to the situation,
Mike's silly jingle took the stress away, and we were able to enjoy
a great night with the mayor and those in attendance.

C. S. Lewis said: "Friendship is born at that moment when one person
says to another: 'What! You too? I thought I was the only one.'"

— 1 —

ANCIENT PERSIA

"No one is fool enough to choose war instead of peace—
in peace sons bury their fathers but in war fathers bury sons."
—CROESUS[1]

PERSIA. THE VERY WORD EVOKES IMAGES OF KINGS AND PRINCES and tales of Arabian nights, of Scheherazade, the teller of 1001 stories of cunning and derring-do in an attempt to save her own life. As the daughter of the grand vizier, she caught the eye of Shahryar, who was known for marrying a new virgin every morning and sending the previous day's wife to be beheaded. He was betrayed by his first wife and felt he had devised a means to ensure it would never happen again.

Knowing there had been some three thousand wives before her, Scheherazade was determined not to be number 3001. She studied the books of Persian history and legends in order to prepare for her "night with the king." Having enlisted the help of her sister beforehand, the new queen made a final request of Shahryar before being led away to the chopping block: She asked to say goodbye to her sibling.

Dinazade, her sister, asked Scheherazade to tell her a story before being dragged away. The gifted storyteller spun a tale that so intrigued the king, he spared her night after night until Scheherazade had told 1001 tales, the next one more exciting and spellbinding than the last. The king became so enchanted with his wifely entertainer that he made her Queen Consort. Legend has it she bore the king three sons.

However, Persia was not solely acclaimed for the tales of *1001 Arabian Nights*. Among other things, her citizens achieved mind-boggling feats including creating the first postal system. While chess was initially introduced in India, it is the Persians who are recognized as having perfected and promulgated the brainy game. With design assistance from Greek architects, the Persians helped fashion one of the Seven Wonders of the World, the Mausoleum of Maussollos in modern-day Bodrum, Turkey.

The kingdoms of Persia and Babylonia inhabited the region that played host to the world's earliest civilizations. They are thought by most archaeological scholars to contain the site named in the Old Testament book of Genesis as the Garden of Eden. Ur of the Chaldeans, the home of Abraham, was also a part of the region that was once Babylonia—later controlled by the Persians.

At its zenith the Empire encompassed the landmass from India to Greece, from the Caspian Sea to the Red Sea, and included the Arabian Sea. Its modern-day equivalent would be the countries of Pakistan, a portion of India, Afghanistan, Iran, Iraq, Syria, Turkey, Jordan, Israel, and Egypt—all combined into one vast empire.

For three millennia Iran has maintained its existence as an autonomous territory. It was the first Pahlavi, Reza Shah Pahlavi the Great, who in 1935 asked the world to stop referring to his nation as Persia and to use the name Iran instead. Iran means "land of the Aryans" and was the name the natives used in referring to their country.[4]

Unlike its neighbors, Iran is not Arab—it is Persian, or more correctly, Indo-European. While the Iranians use Arabic script to write, the official language of the nation is not Arabic but Farsi. Unlike its neighbors, Iran's history is not rooted in Islam but rather in the time when kings were treated as gods and massive structures were erected in their honor. Even today Iranians celebrate *No Ruz* (meaning "new day" or "New Year"). This is not a tradition of Islam but was established before Islam conquered Persia.

Cyrus the Great, the first Achaemenid emperor—and incidentally, the first king to add "Great" to his title—established the Persian Empire by uniting two of the earliest tribes in Iran, the Medes and the Persians. He ruled the extensive empire from 550–529 BC.

Within four years of his ascension to the throne, Cyrus subjugated Croesus, the king of Lydia (of "rich as Croesus" fame), and controlled the Aegean coast of Asia Minor, Armenia, and the Greek colonies along the Levant (a large area in the Middle East bordered by the Mediterranean, the Arabian Desert, and Upper Mesopotamia). Turning eastward, Cyrus seized Parthia, Chorasmis, and Bactria. He ruled over one of the largest empires of early-recorded history. Although he conquered people after people, he was known for his unparalleled forbearance and charitable posture toward those whom he subjugated.

Cyrus and his troops marched into Babylon on October 12, 539 BC and without shedding a drop of blood apprehended Nabonidus, king of Babylon. Cyrus took the title of "King of Babylon, King of Sumer and Akkad, King of the Four Corners of the World....The Iranians regarded him as 'The Father'; Babylonians as 'The Liberator'; the Hellenes as 'Law-Giver'; and the Jews as 'The Anointed of the Lord.'"[2]

He was greeted by roars of welcome from the Jews who had been carried captive to Babylon by Nebuchadnezzar. Following his conquest of that great city, Cyrus permitted some forty thousand Jews to return to their homeland in Canaan. With such an unprecedented move Cyrus displayed great deference toward the religious tenets and social mores of other peoples.

Twenty-three times in the Old Testament we find references to Cyrus, many of them in the book of Ezra. He is praised as the king who assisted the Jews in rebuilding the Temple in Jerusalem. He sent Ezra and Nehemiah to oversee reconstruction of the Temple, as well as sending caravans of materials to aid in the building. When Nebuchadnezzar captured Jerusalem in 604 BC, every precious vessel was looted from the temple and carried away to Babylonia.

When nations were conquered by the Babylonians, the idols worshiped by that people were placed in a position of subservience to Marduk, the god worshiped by the Babylonians. The Israelites were an exception. They did not worship graven images; therefore, the vessels taken from Solomon's temple were likely placed in close proximity to but not in subservience to Marduk. Cyrus authorized the return of many of the golden vessels used in Temple observances that had been taken by Nebuchadnezzar and carried off to Babylon.

Cyrus is first mentioned in 2 Chronicles 36:22-23 and then in Ezra 1:1-3. Both passages record that God "moved the heart of Cyrus king of Persia" in order to fulfill "the word of the Lord spoken by Jeremiah":

> In the first year of Cyrus king of Persia, in order to fulfill the word of the Lord spoken by Jeremiah, the Lord moved the heart of Cyrus king of Persia to make a proclamation throughout his realm and to put it in writing:
> "This is what Cyrus king of Persia says:
> 'The Lord, the God of heaven, has given me all the kingdoms of the earth and he has appointed me to build a temple for him at Jerusalem in Judah. Anyone of his people among you—may his God be with him, and let him go up to Jerusalem in Judah and build the temple of the Lord, the God of Israel, the God who is in Jerusalem.'"[3]

Cyrus was unique, not only because he allowed the Jews to return to Israel, but also because the prophet Isaiah foretold his birth and his name almost one hundred fifty years before he was born. God also revealed Cyrus' mission to the prophet. Isaiah recorded that Cyrus would accomplish specific tasks under God's direction during his lifetime. King Cyrus was destined to carry out God's plan as it related to His chosen people. It was through Cyrus that the Babylonian Empire and seventy years of Jewish captivity came to an end. The prophet Isaiah wrote:

> "Who says of Cyrus, He is my shepherd and will accomplish all that I please; he will say of Jerusalem, 'Let it be rebuilt,' and of the temple, 'Let its foundations be laid.'"[4]

In 1878 AD archaeologist Hormuzd Rassam uncovered what has come to be called the Cyrus cylinder at a dig near ancient Babylon. Written in Akkadian cuneiform and now in the British Museum, the cylinder describes Cyrus' invasion of Babylon and the ensuing treatment of the Babylonian people. The cylinder has been touted as the first known pronouncement of human rights.

The cylinder seems to confirm Cyrus' humanity. He is said to have "allowed many of the nations he conquered to practice their various religious beliefs...even actively assisted captive peoples, including the Jews, to return to their lands of origin. This support was not only political but even financial—as he gave grants both from the Imperial treasury and also from his own personal fortune."[5]

The historian Herodotus records that Cyrus fell while in a battle to defend his northeastern borders from Tomyris, Queen of the Massagetae, a warrior tribe of Iranian people. It is also recorded that Tomyris was so devastated at the loss of her son, Spargapises, during the battle that upon finding Cyrus' body, she had his head immersed in a wineskin filled with blood.

Cyrus was succeeded by his son Cambyses II, who attacked the Massagetae, recovered his father's body, and buried it in the city of Pasargadae. Cambyses II reigned only one year but was able to do what Cyrus could not—conquer Egypt. The Persians would rule the land of the Pharaohs for 193 years, until Alexander the Great defeated Darius III in 332 BC.

In 522 BC Darius I wrested the Persian kingdom from the descendants of Cyrus the Great, but the establishment of his rule was fraught by skirmishes with the surrounding provinces. Darius proved to be quite the tactician. His trusted generals used the small army of Medes and Persians to great advantage and were able to solidify Darius' rule over the entire Persian Empire.

Darius was a forward-thinking ruler whose legal expertise produced the "Ordinance of Good Regulations" used to create a uniform code of law throughout the empire. He followed in the steps of Cyrus as a benevolent leader who hailed the rights of all people to co-exist under his leadership. It was Darius who instituted the satrap—or governor—system of rule throughout the empire. He directed the building of roads, seaports, banks, and canals. It was he who oversaw the construction of the waterway from the Nile to the Red Sea.

An inscription that was discovered in Egypt reads: "I am a Persian. I commanded to dig this canal from a river by the name of Nile which flows in Egypt.... After this canal was dug, ships went from Egypt through this canal to Persia, thus as was my desire."[6]

Darius, succeeded by his son Xerxes I, was also responsible for the building of a fifteen-hundred-mile long paved road from Sardis in Turkey to Shustar (the site of the Prophet Daniel's overnight visit to the lions' den). The roadway allowed the postal service to deliver mail in six to nine days—unlike the era's normal three-month timeframe. This was the prototype for the Pony Express. It was from Darius' era that the US Postal Service got its unforgettable motto: "Neither snow nor rain nor heat nor gloom of night stays these couriers from the swift completion of their appointed rounds."[7]

— 2 —

BIBLICAL HISTORY

The nation that attempts to destroy the Jews, will itself,
be destroyed in exactly the same way that it
attempted to perpetrate that destruction.
—GARY STEARMAN[8]

IRAN HAS AN EXTENSIVE AND OPULENT ANTIQUITY. The region has been inhabited almost since the end of the flood. It was in about 2,000 BC that the Aryan people appeared on the scene and then broke into two basic factions—the Medes and Persians. The Aryan influence would be felt not only in Persia, but much later in European countries.

Before the area we know today as Iran was ruled by the Medes and Persians, it was first under the control of the Elamites, Assyrians, and Babylonians. The Elamites, a fierce warrior tribe, were the initial rulers over the region. Elam, the progenitor of the band, was the son of Shem and the grandson of Noah. The capital city of the ancient kingdom was Shushan or Susa. It was the jewel in the crown of the Elamites and stood proudly until razed by the Mongols under the leadership of Genghis Khan in 1218 BC.

Historical records indicate that the Elamites were constantly engaging in wars with Assyria and Babylonia in an attempt to control the Mesopotamian plateau. Following centuries of conflict, the Elamites allied themselves with armies from the Susiana Plain and overran Ur of the Chaldeans. The fierce tribe and its allies also subjugated many of the lands that had been dominated by the Babylonians before setting its sights on the kingdom of Babylonia.

Elam first appears in Genesis 10 in the lineage of Noah. The second instance is in chapter 14 when Chedorlaomer, the king of the Elamites, joined forces with five other Mesopotamian leaders in the region, including the kings of Sodom and Gomorrah. Together they launched a campaign to attack and subdue the territory, and after having put them to flight, they sacked the cities and carried off the inhabitants, among them Abraham's nephew, Lot, and his family. Abraham and his three hundred trained warriors then set out to successfully rescue his family members—not by their own might, but by the hand of God.

The prediction of the downfall of the ferocious army of Elam can be found in the books of Jeremiah and Ezekiel in the Old Testament. In Jeremiah 49, God pronounces judgment upon Elam:

> This is what the Lord Almighty says: "See, I will break the bow of Elam, the mainstay of their might. I will bring against Elam the four winds from the four quarters of heaven; I will scatter them to the four winds, and there will not be a nation where Elam's exiles do not go. I will shatter Elam before their foes, before those who want to kill them; I will bring disaster on them, even my fierce anger," declares the Lord. "I will pursue them with the sword until I have made an end of them.[9]

Jeremiah prophesies that the Elamite armies will be reduced to nothing—unable to effectively sustain superiority in battle. Famous for their archers, it was predicted that the bows of the troops would be, not just ineffective, but broken, useless. The populace would then be driven out by fear of their conquerors and scattered throughout the kingdoms of their enemies. If that were not a sufficient pronouncement, the Elamites would be fleeing those whose only intent was to inflict evil.

Elam is mentioned only once in the New Testament in Acts 2:9. On the Day of Pentecost, descendants of the Elamites were in Jerusalem as the disciples began to preach to those in the streets.

As we saw in chapter one, the Elamites gave way to the Assyrians and then the Babylonians before the Medes and Persians subjugated the peoples in the region. It has been conjectured that the Persian people originated in Media, which today is found in southern Azerbaijan and western Iran. The group established a base on the Persian Gulf.

The prophet Ezra recorded:

> In the first year of Cyrus king of Persia, in order to fulfill the word of The Lord spoken by Jeremiah, The Lord moved the heart of Cyrus king of Persia to make a proclamation throughout his realm and to put it in writing: This is what Cyrus king of Persia says: "The Lord, The God of heaven, has given me all the kingdoms of the earth..."[10]

Biblical history was also shaped by ancient empires that included the Egyptians, Assyrians, Babylonians, Persians, and the Romans. It was the Persians under Cyrus who allowed Ezra and Nehemiah to rebuild the Temple:

> "And He has appointed me to build a Temple for Him at Jerusalem in Judah. Anyone of his people among you - may his God be with him, and let him go up to Jerusalem in Judah and build The Temple of The Lord, The God of Israel, The God who is in Jerusalem."[11]

Seventy years after King Nebuchadnezzar had razed Jerusalem, looted the Temple, and carried the Israelites captive to Babylon, Cyrus granted permission for them to return to their homeland. One can but wonder how much history the descendants of the Persians (today's Iranians) have had to rewrite in order to erase the move that returned the Jewish people to the land the Palestinians now claim belongs to them.

Other books in the Old Testament—II Chronicles, Ezra, Nehemiah, Esther, Ezekiel, Daniel, Haggai, Zechariah, and Malachi—include mentions of the Persians in their texts. The empire played an important part in the diaspora of the Jews and in their restoration. Simply stated, the ancient Persians believed in grandeur and practiced it accordingly. Their history and culture reflect that it was one of the grandest kingdoms of all.

Over twenty-five hundred years ago, the Hebrew prophet Daniel was taken captive to Babylon. He was near the palace on the night King Darius and his troops rerouted the Euphrates River and entered Belshazzar's stronghold. The king and his courtiers had spent the night in drunken revelry—up to the moment God had captured their attention:

> While Belshazzar was drinking his wine, he gave orders to bring in the gold and silver goblets that Nebuchadnezzar his father had taken from the temple in Jerusalem, so that the king and his nobles, his wives and his concubines might drink from them. So they brought in the gold goblets that had been taken from the temple of God in Jerusalem, and the king and his nobles, his wives and his concubines drank from them. As they drank the wine, they praised the gods of gold and silver, of bronze, iron, wood and stone. Suddenly the fingers of a human hand appeared and wrote on the plaster of the wall, near the lampstand in the royal palace. The king watched the hand as it wrote. His face turned pale and he was so frightened that his legs became weak and his knees were knocking.[12]

Belshazzar was terrified and called for his diviners to determine the meaning of the message. The queen reminded her husband of Daniel who was "found to have a keen mind and knowledge and understanding, and also the ability to interpret dreams, explain riddles and solve difficult problems."[13]

The king quickly sent a servant to fetch Daniel to the banqueting room where he was asked to explain to Belshazzar what had just happened and why:

"You had the goblets from his temple brought to you, and you and your nobles, your wives and your concubines drank wine from them. You praised the gods of silver and gold, of bronze, iron, wood and stone, which cannot see or hear or understand. But you did not honor the God who holds in His hand your life and all your ways. Therefore He sent the hand that wrote the inscription. This is the inscription that was written: mene, mene, tekel, parsin. Here is what these words mean:

> *Mene*: God has numbered the days of your reign and brought it to an end.

> *Tekel*: You have been weighed on the scales and found wanting.

> *Peres*: Your kingdom is divided and given to the Medes and Persians."[14]

That very night, the Babylonian ruler was slain. Darius, the king of the Medes, became lord of the land and Nebuchadnezzar and his offspring became ancient memories to the inhabitants. Persia had stepped onto the stage of powerful players. Some scholars believe that:

> The name Darius was not a proper name at all, but a title of honor meaning "Holder of the Scepter." In other words "The Scepter Holder (King) of the Medes." The Jewish historian Josephus also recorded that: "Darius the Mede, who along with his relative, Cyrus the King of Persia, brought an end to the Babylonian empire. Darius was the son of Astyages."[15]

After Darius swept through Babylon and took control, he erected a resplendent citadel in the city of Shushan. It later became the home of

Ahasuerus (aka, Artaxerxes II) the king who took Esther as his queen. Islamic tradition intimates that the tomb of the prophet Daniel is also located in the present-day town of Shush located in southwestern Iran near the Iraqi border.

The Bible contains many references to the rulers of Persia, but not all refer to Cyrus, Darius, or Ahasuerus.   Daniel, after having been carried captive from Jerusalem to Babylon, turned to the Lord and repented for the sins of his nation. He asked for forgiveness on their behalf, and prayed God's Word and His will concerning them would be fulfilled.[16] Daniel was told that his prayer had been heard from the moment it was uttered, but the "prince of Persia" (a demonic being such as those mentioned in Ephesians 6:12) resisted Gabriel for twenty-one days. He was also told that Michael the arch-angel had joined Gabriel in battling this demonic power.[17]

What was the result of Daniel's steadfastness in prayer? Deliverance! Daniel knew his most important assignment was prayer. That was confirmed to him by the battle in the heavenlies between demons and angels, between good and evil. The city of Babylon was one of the Seven Wonders of the Ancient World. It was considered impregnable, but Daniel, through the power of prayer, was able to "be strong, and carry out great exploits."[18]

It is puzzling that, with such a rich history and the witness of devout followers of the God of the Bible— Esther, Mordecai, Daniel, Shadrach, Meshach, Abednego—the Iranians are not worshippers of Yahweh. This concept is supported by the contents of museums, textbooks, and even the universities in the country. And yet, 99 percent of Iran's inhabitants are prac-ticing Muslims—followers of Mohammad and worshippers of Allah. They adhere to the teachings, not of the Bible, but of the Koran. Christians and Jews are met with increasing hatred and antagonism.

As offspring of the early Persian people, Iran has a significant role in Bible prophecy and end-time events. The prophet Ezekiel envisioned a war against Israel launched by what many have determined to be Russia, Iran, and a multi-national coalition.

Many evangelical Christians see this as an alliance formed between Russia and Iran for the purpose of attacking the Jews in the Middle East.

The war of Gog and Magog was predicted to hit Israel after the Jews returned to their homeland. The prophecy also speaks of this as a time when Israel is "brought back from the sword." In other words, the war will occur when Israel is at peace.[19]

As the nuclear crisis with Iran deepens, millions of Christians worldwide are consulting their Bibles and praying to sort out how current world events fit into "last days" prophecies. Ezekiel 38:21-22 predicts massive human carnage as a result of the war. That Israel will win this Great War is little consolation given the mammoth number of deaths Ezekiel predicts as a result of the conflict.

— 3 —

RISE OF MOHAMMAD — DOWNFALL OF PERSIA

"If the teacher be corrupt, the world will be corrupt."
—A PERSIAN PROVERB

THE PERSIAN EMPIRE MET ITS DEMISE at the hands of Alexander the Great. However, he adopted many Persian customs, married Roxana, a Persian woman, and ordered his troops to take Persian wives in what might have resembled one of Rev. Sun Myung Moon's mass weddings.[20] Despite his legacy of raping the inhabitants, plundering the countryside, and destroying the city of Persepolis by fire, Alexander is credited with having exported the principles of law formulated under Cyrus and Darius that were later implemented throughout the Roman Empire. The rule of Alexander the Great over Persia was followed by the Parthians and the Sasanians.

In 570 AD an event took place that would forever change, not only the remaining once-great Persian Empire, but the entire world: The Prophet

Mohammad was born. The rise of Islam—the religion founded by Muhammad ibn Abdullah, regarded by the Muslim world as a messenger and prophet of God—would result in Persia being conquered by nomads armed with a totally different weapon—a new religion. The Persian people would welcome new leadership and embrace Islam's five pillars of faith: 1) "There is no god but Allah, and Mohammad is the Prophet of Allah; 2) Prayer (to always be in touch with God); 3) Pilgrimage to Mecca; 4) Fasting in order to feel the pain of the disadvantaged and to develop self-discipline; and 5) Alms or charitable contributions."[21]

The Persian population would eventually learn that it had exchanged one tyrannical ruler for another. Under Islamic rule the people would be forced to forsake the Persian language in favor of Arabic, which would become the sanctioned tongue of the Muslim world.

Many empires fall prey to the march of time; however, in Persia—or Iran—the Arab onslaught produced a cultural mix that was unique. Persia would be dramatically influenced by the armies of Muhammad, but the conquerors would be influenced by the conquered. Arabic became the new language, Islam became the new religion, mosques were built, and Islamic customs became the norm for the people of Persia.

It may surprise you to know that political correctness is not an invention of modern-day America; it has dictated the actions of people from the beginning of time. For many Iranian nobles, conversion to Islam was a politically correct move that enabled them to keep their vast holdings and coveted social position. For others, the impetus for conversion was tax evasion. Their Muslim superiors had levied an exorbitant tax against all non-Muslims, which they wished to avoid. Some Jews living in Iran were forced, on forfeiture of their lives, to convert to Islam. Zoroastrian priests simply fled the country.

The predominant Iranian culture is Persian, not Arabian. The Persians consider Arabs in an uncomplimentary sense, thinking of them as desert nomads. To many Persians, Arabs are mere "Bedouins," a migratory people known for packing their tents and moving across the sands on camels.

The Persian people by comparison think of their culture as more elevated. The Persians of history lived along the ancient silk routes. They were traders who established shops, in a tradition of entrepreneurial "bazaars." The traditional religion of the Persian people was Zoroastrianism, which some claim traces back 600 BC. Zoroaster preached monotheism. While few Americans know much about this religion, Zoroastrianism was one of the first religions to identify a duality between good and evil.

Theologians argue that Jewish and Christian ideas of God and Satan, as well as Heaven and Hell, trace back to Zoroastrianism. Islam was founded in what is now Saudi Arabia by Mohammed, who was born in 570 AD and received his first revelation of Allah in 610 AD. For the Persians, Islam is an Arab religion, not a Persian religion.

The Arabs invaded Persia around 650 AD, bringing with them Islam. Over time, Islam supplanted Zoroastrianism as the predominant religion of Persia. Many Zoroastrians fled to India when the Arabs invaded, introducing their religion. These distinctions are well-appreciated in the Middle East, even today. To call a Persian an "Arab" may be taken as an insult. That Islam is not the original religion of Iran remains a tension even today just below the surface.

Although the conquest of Iran by the Arab hordes was relatively violence-free, the ensuing struggle for leadership culminated in a bloody and lopsided battle. Hussein, the grandson of the Prophet Muhammad, and forces loyal to Caliph Yazid met on the plains of Karbala—today one of the holiest cities in Iraq. (It was to be a watershed event in Islam, for it was here that the grandson of the prophet Muhammad was beheaded. Also, it was here that the irreparable division between the Sunnis and the Shi'ites began.)

From 820 AD until 1220 AD under various rulers the Persians were to see a resurgence of their culture. The Persian language was revived, as were customs and mores. Scholars would discover the medicinal use of alcohol and write tomes dedicated to medicine. There was a rebirth of Persian poetry and writings, the decimal system was perfected and algebra defined, and Omar Khayyam would be born. He would pen the Rubaiyat, a definitive work of poetry that has subsequently been translated into numerous languages and has sold millions of copies.

Just as the name Omar Khayyam brings to mind poems of love and life, so the name of the next conqueror of Persia will forever be linked to brutality and heinous crimes against humanity—Genghis Khan. He and his horde of over seven hundred thousand fighting men invaded Persia with unequaled cruelty. His intent was to conquer the known world.

Upon his death his kingdom was divided among his male heirs. One vicious descendant, Hulagu Khan, destroyed nearly all the major cities, decimated libraries and hospitals, and massacred the inhabitants. The carnage was estimated in the range of millions of people. In 1271 Marco Polo traversed Persia on his journey to China. He wrote: "How sad it is, the destruction, waste and death inflicted on this once mighty, prosperous, and beautiful Persia."[22]

Persia would remain under Mongol influence until the beginning of the Safavid Dynasty in 1501. After nine centuries of a fragmented Persia, Shah Ismail I, a Shi'a Muslim, would gather the disjointed peoples together under the banner of Shiism. It would separate them from the Sunni Muslims of the Ottoman Empire. He would be succeeded by Shah Abbas who would fashion a fighting force from the rag-tag army of Ismail I. His troops engaged and defeated the Ottomans. He was instrumental in rebuilding the infrastructure of the country and encouraging Persian artisans to ply their trade. The results included fine Persian rugs (still prized today). Persian arts and crafts were in demand worldwide for their beauty.

In 1722, Mahmoud Khan, an Afghan tribal chief, invaded Persia. His rule lasted until he was expelled by Nadir Shah. Nadir's claim to fame was the invasion of India and the capture of two of the world's most coveted diamonds. They were the Sea of Light (housed in Iran), and the Kohinoor Diamond (Mountain of Light) worn by British queens for decades. Today the diamond—all 108.93 karats—embellishes the crown of Queen Elizabeth II, accompanied by 2,800 smaller diamonds.

After Nadir Shah died in 1747, his army collapsed and the country was taken by Karim Khan Zand. His dynasty lasted a mere thirty-two years before the Qajar Dynasty assumed rule of the land. Noted as being weak and ineffectual rulers, leaders under the Qajar Dynasty signed treaties with Russia, which gave away Georgia, Armenia, and Azerbaijan. Soon after, the Persians were forced to relinquish the area known as Afghanistan to the British.

Corruption within the dynasty ultimately led to the formation of the Majlis—Persia's first parliament-style government. The dream of establishing a constitutional monarchy such as the one in England was never realized. The nation would ultimately be divided between two early twentieth century superpowers—Russia in the north and Britain in the south and east. In 1921, following World War I, the country that would become Iran fell into chaos.

Stepping to the forefront to lead a coup against the Qajar Dynasty and its corrupt rule was Reza Khan, an army officer, who was crowned Reza Shah Pahlavi by the Majlis in April 1926. His rise to a monarchial position in Iran might be equated to the rise of Napoleon in France. The "Little General" of French fame had, at least, military training. Khan was a totally self-made man with no formal education. It is said, however, that he was an intelligent leader:

> [Reza Shah] created an extensive system of secular primary and secondary schools and, in 1935, established the country's first European-style university in Tehran. These schools and institutions of higher education became training grounds for the new bureaucracy and, along with economic expansion, helped create a new middle class. The Shah also expanded the road network, successfully completed the trans-Iranian railroad, and established a string of state-owned factories to produce such basic consumer goods as textiles, matches, canned goods, sugar, and cigarettes.
>
> Many of the Shah's measures were consciously designed to break the power of the religious hierarchy. His educational reforms ended the clerics' near-monopoly on education. To limit further the power of the clerics, he undertook a codification of the laws that created a body of secular law,

applied and interpreted by a secular judiciary outside the control of the religious establishment. He excluded the clerics from judgeships, created a system of secular courts, and transferred the important and lucrative task of notarizing documents from the clerics to state-licensed notaries. The State even encroached on the administration of *vaqfs* (religious endowments) and on the licensing of graduates of religious seminaries.[23]

When World War II began, Reza Shah declared Iran to be a neutral nation. Despite the declaration of neutrality, the country was soon invaded by both Britain and the Soviet Union. The two Allies had been frustrated after the Shah rebuffed an ultimatum calling for the expulsion of all Germans from Iran. Fearing that the Shah might side with the Germans and having itself been invaded by Hitler, the Soviet Union desperately required a route by which to move war materiel. The Soviets and British allied to invade Iran in a joint attack on August 26, 1941.

Reza Khan, somewhat like Belshazzar before him, saw the handwriting on the wall. He knew the Allied Forces would quickly remove him from power. In an attempt to preserve Iran he abdicated in favor of his twenty-two-year-old son. Reza Shah was deported to the Island of Mauritius and later to Johannesburg, South Africa. He died there in July 1944. His body was later transported to Egypt where it was embalmed and placed in the Al-Rifa'i Mosque, to be joined years later by his son, Mohammad Reza Shah Pahlavi, also a king in exile.

The young Shah was charged with guiding Iran through the war years and ultimately joined the Allies, thus giving him entry into the United Nations. As we will see in later chapters, the Shah faced his first major challenge when Prime Minister Mohammad Mossadegh took control of the nation's government and forced the Shah into a brief exile.

As noted earlier, the Iranian people are principally followers of Shi'a Islam, founded in 661 AD by Ali ibn Abi Talib. It was from his name that Shi'a evolved. It is literally a derivation of *Shi'at Ali*—"partisans of Ali." As a descendant of Muhammad, Ali was thought to be the last of the true caliphs. He was wildly popular until he came face-to-face in a battle with the army of the governor of Damascus in 661 AD. It is said that the Damascene soldiers attached verses from the Quran to the tips of their spears. When faced with fighting a force hiding behind the words of Muhammad, Ali's army declined to fight. Ali, left only with the option of negotiating with his enemy, sought appeasement. While he escaped death at the hands of his enemy in open combat, Ali was eventually killed by one of his own rabid followers.

When Ali died, the governor of Damascus, Mu'awiya, anointed himself caliph. Ali's son, Hassan, the rightful heir to the caliphate, died under suspicious circumstances, while the next in the line of succession, Hussein, agreed to do nothing until Mu'awiya died. He was soon disappointed yet again, however, when Mu'awiya's son, Yazid, appropriated the position of caliph and went to war against Hussein. The bloody battle resulted in the deaths of Hussein and his army. Only Hussein's baby boy survived the carnage, and he became the hope of reestablishing Ali's claim to the caliphate.

With the more recent ascension of Mahmoud Ahmadinejad to the position of power in Iran, we have heard much about the last known descendant of Hussein, Muhammad al-Mahdi, or the Mahdi. Al-Mahdi was the Twelfth Imam in the line of Ali, who disappeared down a well at the age of five. Refusing to believe that he was dead, his followers imbued him with timelessness. They declared him to be merely "hidden," and that on some future date he would suddenly appear to reestablish an Islamic caliphate worldwide. Their eschatology, however, proved problematic; it espoused an apocalyptic upheaval in order for the Mahdi, or Hidden Imam, to ascend to his rightful place of leadership. These "Twelvers" championed the idea that every individual, regardless of his religious belief, would one day bow to Islam—or die.

As time passed and the Mahdi failed to make an appearance, authority passed to the *ulema*, a body of mullahs endowed with the power to appoint a supreme leader. Perhaps one of the best-known imams was Grand Ayatollah Ruhollah Khomeini.

It was under the Safavid dynasty (1501-1736) that Shi'a Islam became Iran's official religion. It was also during this time that Persia was united as a single sovereignty and became the precursor to what we now know as Iran.

During more than twenty-five centuries of history, Persians have maintained their unique sense of identity. Though they converted to Islam, they have not always followed the accepted views of the religion. To an extent, Zoroastrianism, that religion of the early Persians, colors the Iranian variety of Islam.

Iran is now not only one of the largest countries in the Middle East but also in the Islamic world. Because of past experiences, Iran has developed a thorny separatism. Invaded during both World Wars and later set upon by Iraq, Iran has reason to fear foreign influence.

The borders of Iran have remained largely unchanged during the twentieth century, but the desire to recapture the glory of the vast Persian Empire has until now lain dormant. Perhaps this pragmatism is the driving force behind Iran's seemingly sudden emergence as a budding player in the world's nuclear superpower game.

The Shah began to amass materials to build twenty nuclear reactors during his reign. Only two were started in Bushehr on the Persian Gulf. They were damaged by bombs during the Iran/Iraq war and were left unfinished. After Khomeini assumed power in 1979, the Ayatollah halted all work on the nuclear sites. Work was eventually resumed, though on a much more modest scale.

Iran's current leader, President Mahmoud Ahmadinejad has, with the blessing of Supreme Leader Ali Khamenei, launched today's full-scale nuclear program much to the chagrin of the Western world.

— 4 —

A SHAH IS
CROWNED

*"As nightfall does not come all at once; neither does oppression.
In both instances, there is a twilight when everything
remains seemingly unchanged. And it is in such twilight that
we all must be aware of change in the air however slight,
lest we become unwitting victims of the darkness."*
—JUSTICE WILLIAM O. DOUGLASS[24]

IN 1953 THE US HAD BACKED A COUP IN FAVOR OF THE SHAH and against Prime Minister
Dr. Mohammad Mossadegh. While in ofice, Mossadegh made a commitment
to establish a constitutional monarchy, promote democracy, and nationalize
the Iranian oil industry, then under the control of Britain. When Mossadegh
ejected Anglo-Iranian Oil, the British determined that he must be removed
in any way possible and enlisted the aid of the United States to achieve the
goal. Mossadegh had believed the US would back his plan.

Kermit "Kim" Roosevelt Jr., grandson of Theodore Roosevelt and a CIA
agent, covertly joined hands with the British and military forces loyal to the
Shah in "Operation Ajax" to remove Mossadegh and restore the monarchy of
Reza Pahlavi. The coup attempt initially failed and the Shah fled to Rome.

Kim Roosevelt was so determined to overthrow the prime minister that he ignored communiqués sent from CIA headquarters and launched a second successful coup.

Kermit Roosevelt dispatched US Army General Norman Schwarzkopf Sr., who had from 1942-1948 trained and commanded the Iranian Gendarmerie, to Rome to try to persuade the Shah to adopt the "Operation Ajax" plan, but the Shah declined to commit to the CIA plot. Reportedly, the general carried several bags filled with millions in currency with which he paid members of the covert operation and enticed politicos, clerics, the media, and gangsters to support the overthrow of Mossadegh's government. After meeting with the Shah, the general advised President Eisenhower to approach the Shah to secure his cooperation. Pahlavi eventually agreed, but only after he was assured that both Britain and the US were officially part of the plot to over-throw Mossadegh.

Author Manucher Farmanfarmaian wrote of the Shah's acquiescence to Kermit Roosevelt's plan:

> A man whom I did not recognize appeared from behind the plane. He was dressed neatly in a dark suit...presented him [the Shah] with a document... the messenger was sent by Kermit Roosevelt and the document the Shah had signed appointed General [Fazlollah] Zahedi prime minister. Mos-sadegh's fall was imminent.[25]

On August 19, Zahedi formally claimed the title "Prime Minister." The following day Mossadegh surrendered. The US immediately stepped forward and promised the new prime minister the funds necessary to untangle the Iranians from their ongoing oil disagreement with Great Britain, a total of approximately $150 million.

In 1977 Kermit Roosevelt approached the Shah to discuss his plans to write a book on the "Operation Ajax" plot. Assadollah Alam, the Shah's con-fidant, wrote of that audience:

I reported that I've now examined the book and found it most undesirable. It portrays HIM [His Imperial Majesty] as a waverer, forced into various crucial decisions, for example the appointment of General Zahedi as Prime Minister, by pressure from Roosevelt. The man is...hoping to present himself as a hero. HIM said he had no idea the book contained so much nonsense.[26]

In an interview by Amir Taheri with the Shah's former son-in-law, Ardeshir Zahedi, he patently denies that the overthrow of Mossadegh was a direct result of CIA plotting:

They (the US) may have plotted that. But what is important is to ascertain whether Mossadegh fell because of American plotting or as a result of other factors. What I can say with confidence is that the fall of Mossadegh was not a result of any CIA plot. Victory, of course, has a thousand fathers while defeat is always an orphan. Had the August 1953 efforts to remove Mossadegh from power failed, there would have been no CIA "heroes" claiming the credit. There is a mass of evidence, including US, Iranian, British, and Soviet official documents and testimonies by people who played a role in the events that give the lie to the CIA operatives' claims.[27]

Manucher and Roxane Farmanfarmaian wrote of the Mossadegh affair:

Had Churchill not won the election in England or had Truman run again in the United States; had Stalin not died or the Korean War not wound down when it did; had Senator Joseph McCarthy been silenced just a bit sooner or Congress not been rocked by a Carter oil scare—history would have been different. Most bizarre of all, had the CIA not had an operative named Kermit Roosevelt...Mossadegh might

have at last won. There are still many mysteries. The greatest
is the resonant silence of the Soviet Union, which was fighting the United States and the rest of the UN on its eastern
flank in Korea yet remained mute about Washington's fla-
grant activity on its southern border in Iran. History books
ignore this detail, and the British archives on the subject are
closed until 2050. No doubt there is much to hide.[28]

President Eisenhower remembered the joy with which the Shah returned
to Iran following the coup:

> The Shah is a new man. For the first time, he believes in
> himself because he feels that he is the king of his people's
> choice and not by arbitrary decision of a foreign power.[29]

On March 17, 2000, the Clinton administration gave the nod to Secretary
of State Madeleine Albright who delivered a cleverly phrased apology to Iran
for the role of the US in the Mossadegh affair:

> The United States played a significant role in orchestrat-
> ing the overthrow of Iran's popular Prime Minister Moham-
> med Mossadegh. The Eisenhower administration believed its
> actions were justified for strategic reasons. But the coup was
> clearly a set-back for Iran's political development, and it is
> easy to see why so many Iranians continue to resent this
> intervention by America in their internal affairs.[30]

Just weeks later President Clinton went one step (or perhaps two) further than his secretary of state; he spoke to a group assembled for a Millennial
Evening in the White House East Room. Clinton all but grovelled at the feet
of the mullahs controlling Iran:

> "I think it is important to recognize...that Iran, because
> of its enormous geopolitical importance over time, has been

the subject of quite a lot of abuse from various Western nations. And I think sometimes it's quite important to tell people, look, you have a right to be angry at something my country or my culture or others that are generally allied with us today did to you fifty or sixty or one hundred or one hundred fifty years ago...So we [the US] have to find some way to get dialogue—and going into total denial when you're in a conversation with somebody who's been your adversary, in a country like Iran...is not exactly the way to begin."[31]

It was quite obvious to all but Albright and Clinton that the two had chosen to ignore the indignities committed against the hostages taken from the US Embassy and held for 444 days, or that the Iranian-sponsored Hezbollah in Lebanon had murdered Dr. Malcolm Kerr, William Buckley, and Lt. Colonel Robert Higgins—Americans all.

Imagine the impact that Clinton's words had on the people in Iran: A US president was, for all practical purposes, apologizing not only for his country but for the actions of other countries. Clinton went a bit overboard in describing Iran as "a true democracy" and "one of the most stable countries" in the Middle East.[32]

Following the coup to unseat Mossadegh, an international consortium was formed to oversee the petroleum industry in Iran. Dr. Parviz Mina, director, National Iranian Oil Company, related to me the breakdown of the members:

"Five major Americans [Mobil, Exxon, Gulf, Chevron, and Standard Oil of California], seven independents, British Petroleum, Shell, and *Compagnie Francaise des Petroles* formed the group... 40 percent belonged to British Petroleum, 14 percent to Shell, 6 percent to the French company."[33]

Over time Iran exported $5.2 million in oil daily to the world market, the majority to Western Europe and the United States. The country was second only to Saudi Arabia as the largest exporters of crude. In 1971 the

Shah hosted an OPEC conference in his country. He became an instant media target when he spoke in favor of OPEC's demanding the right to control production and oil prices. Pahlavi asked why the OPEC members should not get a higher price for their commodity in relation to rising prices for other commodities worldwide. Newspapers dubbed him a monster and began to blame the Shah for economic problems suffered by the West. According to Mina, the press used the fact that the conference was held in Iran to put pressure on the monarch.

By 1973 the Iranian National Oil Company (INOC) would rank 28th worldwide; in 1974 it had captured the third spot and would be on its way to an output of six and a half million barrels daily. Iran in 1977 boasted an export figure of two hundred seventy million tons of oil products and had captured second place. The Iran-owned oil terminal on Kharg Island boasted the largest tanker port in the entire world.[34] The land of the Shah was a shining star in OPEC.

— 5 —

LAVISH LIFESTYLE CAUSES COLLAPSE

"The lavishness and the emphasis on Western taste turned out to be a major mistake…we reporters didn't know that the Persepolis indulgences would become a major milestone in the Shah's eventual downfall…. We were there to cover a party."
—BARBARA WALTERS[35]

ANOTHER EVENT IN 1971 WOULD GARNER intense dislike for Reza Pahlavi. It began with a desire to pay homage to Cyrus, the founder of the Iranian Empire, on its 2500th anniversary; the event escalated to what was likely the largest gathering of heads-of-state in modern history. Such was the magnitude of the celebration that a spokesperson for the Iranian government declared, "During these unforgettable days, this august assembly will make Persepolis [the site of the magnificent party] the centre-of-gravity of the world."[36]

Initially the celebration was to have been a national event for the Iranian people. It escalated to the point that multiplied-millions of dollars were spent to create a field of sixty-eight fireproof tents set on concrete slabs, with every possible amenity for the comfort of the guests. Each tent was resplendent with silk and velvet walls, gold-leaf furnishings, and Persian

35

carpets specially woven for the guests. China and crystal came from the French house of *Baccarat*. Male and female escorts were clad in French-designed dress. Guests were given a collection of gift products by *Elizabeth Arden* named after the Empress Farah. Mercedes 280-SEs transported visitors to and from the elaborate setting on the site of ancient Persepolis. The fact that cost was no object ignited the ire of many Iranians, few of whom were allowed to see inside the "city."

The five hundred guests ranged from Vice President Spiro Agnew to Emperor Haile Selassie; from Kings and Queens of Belgium, Denmark, Jordan, Morocco, Norway, Thailand, and Nepal, to Prince Rainer and Princess Grace of Monaco, Prince Philip and his daughter, Princess Anne of Great Britain; from Marshal Tito and Aga Khan to the socialite, Charlotte Ford. Despite a tiff with Georges Pompidou, the president of France, the country was duly represented by its Prime Minister Jacque Chaban-Delmas. Could it have been the French president's childish insistence that he be seated during the banquet higher-up in the pecking order than any other French-speaking head of state that shaped France's future relationship with the Shah?

The New York Times journalist Neil Farquhar wrote:

> Historians tend to point to the estimated $200 million fete as the beginning of the end for the Shah, a breathtaking symbol of just how out of touch he was with ordinary Iranians, none of whom were allowed within miles of the place during the party.
>
> The festivities ignored centuries of Islamic rule in Iran, provoking scorn from Ayatollah Ruhollah Khomeini, patriarch of the revolution that toppled the Shah.[37]

This was only another nail in what was to become Pahlavi's political coffin. With three groups in Iran swiftly aligning against him, the National Front, the *Mujahedeen*, and the clerics, the Shah would ultimately fall victim to President James Earl "Jimmy" Carter's human rights agenda of change. Change for the sake of change is not always the most productive path to take, however. Once in office, Carter antagonistically tackled the agenda that had been proposed by President Richard M. Nixon and his National Security Advisor (and later Secretary of State) Henry Kissinger. Nixon's plan covered the next several decades. Kissinger believed:

> It was dangerous for us to make the domestic policy of countries around the world a direct objective of American foreign policy... The protection of basic human rights is a very sensitive aspect of the domestic jurisdiction of... governments.[38]

Nixon adopted the purview that his administration would ignore a nation's human rights history if necessary to secure a geographical edge. He had to look no further than Iran, the strong US ally. Mr. Kissinger, who enjoyed a close, personal relationship with the Shah, labeled Reza Pahlavi of Iran "the rarest of leaders, an unconditional ally."[39]

During Richard Nixon's White House, the relationship between the Shah of Iran and the US was at its apex. The two men first met while Nixon was vice president under Dwight Eisenhower. As president, Nixon appointed Henry Kissinger as secretary of state, and the two men quickly determined the Shah just might fulfill a major need in the Persian Gulf region—that of staunch political ally. Unable to police the area due to the war in Vietnam, it seemed that the Shah was an answer to a genuine need for a proxy to provide power and influence in the region. Nixon and Kissinger flew to Tehran to meet with the Shah and to ink an agreement outlining a new military pact between the two countries—Iran would become a "regional superpower" under the auspices of the US:

> The deal's principle feature was an unprecedented directive from the president of the United States ordering his government to sell the Shah virtually any kind of military hardware he wanted, short of nuclear weapons. No foreign government had ever been given such a shopping spree in the history of American military sales.[40]

How did US foreign relations transition from the glory days of the Richard Nixon administration to the morass reached in 1979? It would turn on the dime of a presidential campaign. The Shah's friend, Richard Nixon, would leave the White House in ignominy. His successor Gerald Ford would serve just over twenty-nine months before being defeated in his bid for election. (Gerald Ford had never been elected, but had ascended to the office of president upon the resignation of President Richard Nixon.)

No one knew, and especially not the Shah, just how directly Iran would be affected by the winds of political change in the United States when the peanut farmer from Georgia entered the presidential campaign in 1976. The Liberal Left wanted a strong plank in the Party platform that supported leftist regimes and virtually ignored right-wing allies. This seemed to appeal to the president, as it fed his desire to see the world's poor elevated from abject poverty, disease, and war to a state of plenty. It appealed to his crusade for morality, his sense of community, and his ongoing battle against elitism. To reach his goal Washington would have to be rid of former Nixon and Ford insiders and replacee them with new names and faces.

Some Congressional leaders and many Americans felt that US policy abroad should reflect its policy at home, thus the birth of the human rights agenda. The decision would deeply affect the Shah of Iran and ultimately decimate his regime. Members of the committee determined that human rights issues should be given precedence when deciding foreign policy. A law was passed that established an official prerequisite for the limitation or rejection of assistance for a nation or nations that repeatedly denied basic civil liberties for people. The law was an attempt to dissociate the US from the unethical and abusive actions of beneficiaries of foreign assistance. Aid would no longer be dependent on a seeming pro-American stance; it would be given to those nations that valued human rights and self-determination.

The Foreign Assistance Act was made for the new chief executive. In her treatise on human rights, Clair Apodaca wrote:

> There existed a coalition of those concerned with human
> rights, those that were looking for any reason to cut the

foreign aid budget and foreign commitments, and those that
simply wished to attack the Republican Party.[41]

What made the Act even more attractive was a congressional amend-
ment in 1976 that made the president responsible for the determination
of which countries were guilty of abusing the human rights of its citizens.
The escape clause giving the president more decision-making latitude came
in the words "extraordinary circumstances exist, which necessitate a con-
tinuation of security assistance for such country." This allowed the sitting
president the leeway to determine what aid to which countries was in the
national interest of the US. Such wording made it possible for a campaign
to be launched against the Shah of Iran while simply ignoring other abusive
regimes such as the one in Indonesia.

Countries that were particular targets for human rights violations were
El Salvador, Nicaragua, South Korea, and, of course, Iran. Apparently, it did
not occur to anyone in the new administration that the US must be prepared
for what might happen if the Shah's monarchy were to fall. As a result, no
one was equipped for what the end result of such failure might mean to the
United States in particular and the world in general. US leaders were not
alone in their inability to comprehend the state of affairs in Iran; other countries with strong ties to the Pahlavi monarchy, i.e., France, Britain, and Israel
either did not count the cost of an Iran without the Shah or simply waited
too long to act.

When Jimmy Carter took office in January 1977, he inherited the estab-
lished Iran policies of numerous presidents before him, including Richard
Nixon and Gerald Ford. President Nixon had instituted what became known
as the "Twin Pillar Doctrine." His approach was to establish US military substitutes in various regions, especially in Iran and Saudi Arabia, to deter the
Soviet Union and provide protection for US interests. Thus, it behooved
Nixon to see that the Shah was adequately supplied with military arms.
Following the debacle in Vietnam, Nixon determined to anoint proxies to
act on behalf of the United States within their region. Iran received such a
designation and was thus guaranteed access to US arms in abundance.

Having Iran in his corner would give Nixon a deterrent against the Soviets in the Persian Gulf and would insure a virtual unending supply of Gulf oil. Pahlavi had no way of knowing that he was creating "a system capable only of defending itself but incapable of satisfying the people [of Iran.] This was its greatest weakness and the true cause of its ultimate defeat."[42]

Prior to a visit to Iran by President Nixon in May 1972, the Shah called on his friend and former son-in-law, Ambassador Ardeshir Zahedi,[43] who had left Iran for Montreaux, Switzerland. The Shah requested that Zahedi make a trip to Pakistan and Afghanistan before the president's arrival in Tehran in order to promote peace between the two neighbors. Zahedi's long-standing friendship with Pakistani Prime Minister Zolfaghar-Ali Bhutto and Afghanistan Prime Minister Mohammad-Musa Shafiq made him the logical choice for the mission. (He was excuted by the Soviets when Afghanistan was invaded in 1978.) The Shah was most interested that these two countries co-exist peacefully in order to deter Soviet expansion in the region.[44]

Zahedi, who had known Nixon since his days as vice president, provided the background for the president's visit to Iran and for what eventually became known as the "Nixon Doctrine." The ambassador was in New York for UN discussion regarding the Six-Day War. He and Nixon met for dinner at Club 21 in Manhattan. Zahedi remembered:

"In those days nobody believed in a Nixon comeback, not even the Shah. On his return from a Vietnam trip in 1967, he stopped over in Tehran as my personal guest. I arranged an audience with His Majesty, which was supposed to be short but lasted several hours. I [invited] Mr. Nixon to dinner in my residence at Hesarak with Armin Meyer, then the US ambassador in Tehran, and my deputy, Amir-Khos-row Afshar. When these two men left, we chatted until the early hours of the morning. We discussed the problems of the region, specifically Iraq, Oman, and South Yemen, which was on the verge of gaining independence... I also arranged for Nixon to travel to Romania, especially as he had not been well-received by the Soviet leaders during a recent trip to Moscow. [The trip was arranged] through my friend Corneliu Mănescu [who later became the UN Secretary General.]

"When Nixon became president in 1969, he was anxious to further develop his ties with Iran. He sent Elliot Richardson and Governor Harold Stassen to Tehran." [The Shah made a reciprocal visit to Washington, D.C. accompanied by Mr. Zahedi.]

"When I look back at that visit, I think probably the most significant point which was made was related to China. At that time, Nixon's policy toward China had not yet been developed. Poland was acting as the go-between with China. I advised Secretary of State William P. Rogers to use Pakistan more as go-between; Rogers took that advice. (When Henry Kissinger went to China in 1971, he pretended to be in Pakistan.)

"We raised a second point with Nixon and Rogers about Iraq...over close ties between Iraq and the USSR, especially when...Saddam Hussein came to power. Looking back, I can say that these events played an important role and were the roots of the policies that President Nixon and His Majesty developed in 1972. They wanted Iran to assure the security of the Persian Gulf and this was what the Nixon Doctrine was about.

"American military sales to Iran began much before Nixon; but once Nixon and the Shah agreed on the role Iran should play in ensuring the security of the Persian Gulf, it was natural that Iran would receive the best military equipment. Nixon gave the Shah full assurance and *carte blanche* in that respect."[45]

Reza Pahlavi was only too eager to ally Iran with the United States, and he was quite vocal about his vision for the Persian Gulf region: "My policy is honest and straightforward, and I have no hidden agenda," he told Nelson Rockefeller. "I say quite openly that I wish Iran to play a role in the Indian Ocean. I have no objection to America being present; indeed, I shall actively defend your interests."[46]

In a memo to Secretary of State William Rogers and to Secretary of Defense Melvin Laird, Henry Kissinger forwarded the president's approval of a conversation Nixon had with the Shah. According to Kissinger, "The president has also reiterated that, in general, decisions on the acquisition of military equipment should be left primarily to the government of Iran. If the government of Iran has decided to buy certain equipment, the purchase of US equipment should be encouraged tactfully where appropriate, and technical advice on the capabilities of the equipment in question should be provided."[47]

In an interview several years ago with Major General George J. Keegan, air force chief of intelligence from 1972 to 1977, he told me of documents secured near the end of World War II. The documents outline exactly what the Shah and Nixon were trying to prevent:

> "Russia's desire to dominate the Persian Gulf is long-standing and well-documented. In 1945 our boys managed to capture records of the German Foreign Office... One of the files deals with the Soviet-Nazi Non-Aggression Pact signed by Hitler and Stalin in the late 1930s. Right there in black and white is the Soviets' clear statement of their desire to be the dominant force in the Persian Gulf."[48]

Nixon was the beneficiary of President Lyndon Johnson's attempts to encourage the Shah to continue his efforts to modernize Iran, but at a steady pace. It was Johnson who declared Pahlavi a model monarch. "What is going on in Iran is about the best thing going on anywhere in the world," said Johnson.[49] The Shah was advised, however, not to overwhelm his people with an excessive number of proposed changes. When Jimmy Carter took office Iran was well-supplied with US military equipment, it was decidedly pro-American, and it would relieve the US of having an overt presence in the Persian Gulf.

During the five years preceding the president's inauguration, the Shah of Iran had purchased some $10 billion in US military materiel. The US government's presence in the Persian Gulf region and its supply of oil from that area were contingent on the goodwill of the Shah. The United States looked to Pahlavi for the economic survival of Western industry and he, in turn, relied on the United States for the arms and assistance to implement his vision for Iran's future. Failure on the part of either nation could cause unimagined economic and political upheaval.

Liberal Left leanings dovetailed perfectly with those inhabitants of "Foggy Bottom," the area in Washington where the State Department is located. The organization was composed of decidedly Left-leaning Arabists with views contrary to most Israel-supporting US presidents. Their grasp of foreign policy often tended to favor accommodation rather than confrontation. This was especially true during the late 1970s; the attitude at State was anti-Shah and anti-Iran. This divisive position would haunt US interests abroad for decades to come. It would open the door for the fanatical Ayatollah Khomeini and his Islamic revolution.

By the mid-70s the Shah changed from an insecure young leader to one fully in control of Iran's bureaucracy. Pahlavi was working to drag the country into the twentieth century and was not seeking advice or direction, not even from his mentor, the United States government. How did the Shah make the transition from a retiring young man to the grandiose ruler?

Marvin Zonis writes in *Majestic Failure: The Fall of the Shah* that Pahlavi "relied on four principal sources of…support to maintain his capacity to act as Shah…the admiration he received from others [i.e., the people of Iran]… strength he received through a very small number of close personal associates…a life-long belief in a watchful and protecting God who had decreed his success in carrying out a divine mission…important diplomatic and personal psychological ties with the United States."[50] Perhaps there was one other well of adulation for the Shah that, when it had run dry, contributed to his unpopularity: the support of the mass media. It is likely that the failure of these five sources of support for Pahlavi led to his downfall.

The liberal media in America became obsessed with turning the Shah from the champion of modernization into the monster of human rights violations. One mass market paperback fiction writer of the times wrote a novel entitled, *A Bullet for the Shah: All They Had to Do Was Kill the World's Most Powerful Man.* In an interview with a former US joint chief of staff, I asked the question, "Who determines when wars are won or lost?"

He replied, "If you will commit not to divulge that I told you, I will tell you the truth." I affirmed my commitment to keep his identity secret. His response: "The media. Take Somalia. Why did we go there? We went there because of the media's obsession. Why did we leave? For the same reason! This is why we lost the Vietnam War and Cambodia." I was stunned at his revelation. However, in looking back over the life of the Shah of Iran it was confirmed that he was riding high when Carter took office. Three years later he was, as Henry Kissinger asserted, "a flying Dutchman looking for a port."[51] He was a ruler without subjects, a king without a throne, a man without a country, a long-time ally bereft of his partner, the United States.

Decisions made between 1977 and 1981 which relegated the security of one of the world's richest regions into the hands of a monarch whose determination to bring social and economic change to Iran did not take into account the smoldering fire of Islamic instability that would soon explode.

The Shah had enjoyed a prolonged political association with the Republican administrations of Presidents Richard Nixon and Gerald Ford. Under Nixon the Shah purchased vast supplies of military equipment, grew his army to the point that it had doubled the size of British forces, and increased his military budget from $293 million in 1963 to $7.3 billion in 1977.[52] The enormous amount the Shah spent on the purchase of arms was unquestionably a boon to the US economy during the oil crisis of the Nixon presidency.

Pahlavi was understandably wary of Jimmy Carter, whose campaign platform stressed both human rights issues and a reduction in arms sales. The Shah was concerned that he would be viewed not as a progressive ruler but rather as tyrannical. This was of major concern because the Shah's regime had been criticized for the actions of its secret police, SAVAK, and had a long-standing and lucrative relationship with US arms suppliers.

Asadollah Alam, appointed prime minister by the Shah in July 1962, was Pahlavi's personal confidant. Alam and the Shah had been classmates at the exclusive Swiss boarding school, *Institut Le Rosey*. He remained in office through major industrial and social reforms implemented by the Shah, sometimes referred to as the "White Revolution." Alam wrote of the Shah's concerns over Carter's election in his diary: "Who knows what sort of calamity he may unleash on the world?"[53] He also wrote that the newly installed president was "a political lightweight. He's managed to duck out of any clear statement policy issues."[54]

In September of 1976 Alam met with Ambassador Uri Lubrani, Israel's representative in Iran, and asked for his assistance to help improve the Shah's image with the American people. (It was Lubrani who co-authored, along with Mossad member Reuven Merhav, one of two reports that predicted the overthrow of the Shah within twelve months. Lubrani's report was so persuasive that Iranian Jews were cautioned to flee the country and seek refuge elsewhere.) Gholam-Reza Afkhami, an advisor to Pahlavi, felt, "No one could match Iran's power, Iran's culture, or Iran's history…It's important to realize this in order to understand why [the Shah] did what he did…And also why everyone else in the world said that he was arrogant."[55]

On November 4, 1979, the US Embassy in Tehran would be overrun by fanatical Muslims. The administration would support the deposing of the Shah of Iran, who would be ousted in favour of the religious cleric, Ayatollah Ruhollah Khomeini.

— 6 —

REVOLUTION ERUPTS

*"Power is not a means; it is an end. One does not establish
a dictatorship in order to safeguard a revolution; one makes
the revolution in order to establish the dictatorship."*
—GEORGE ORWELL

REVOLUTION WAS BUBBLING BENEATH THE SURFACE in Iran. Many US government leaders seemed determined to strip the Shah of power. Little did they know that foreign policy initiatives directly affecting Iran would have lasting and ever-widening repercussions.

In July of 1979, the Organization of Petroleum Exporting Countries (OPEC) announced yet another oil price increase, and gasoline prices in the US went through the roof. That was followed by purported shortages nation-wide. The result was long lines and short tempers at the gas pumps. Gasoline that had sold for $14 per barrel rose to the then-unheard-of $40 per barrel on the spot market. Prior to that time, the price of OPEC oil had fluctuated between $2.50/barrel and $14/barrel.

I asked Dr. Mina, director, National Iranian Oil Company, if it was cor-rect to blame the Shah for the rise in oil prices. "The whole OPEC was looking for that possibility of increasing the…price of oil," said Dr. Mina. "One day OPEC should be able to control prices and not leave it entirely in the hands of the international companies to decide what the price of [oil] should be…naturally Iran was in favor of one day being able to control the prices. Because nowhere in the world was a commodity produced by a country and the price determined by someone else. It was natural for OPEC countries to say that we are producers of crude oil…we have to have a say in the price of the commodity like any other commodity."[56]

US Energy Secretary James R. Schlesinger lit a match to an already volatile situation when he reported to Congress that the energy crisis and the lack of Iranian oil imports were "prospectively more serious" than the oil embargo enforced by the Arabs in 1973.[57] Although covertly maintaining a diplomatic understanding with Israel, Iran had aided Egypt during the 1973 Yom Kippur War by providing crude. The Shah had also furnished transport planes and pilots to Saudi Arabia and evacuated wounded soldiers to Iran for medical care. (Perhaps it was this, as much as anything, that led Sadat to welcome the Shah to Egypt following the Islamic revolution in Iran.)

Pahlavi refused permission to the Soviets to overfly Iran with military transports, but he did permit civilian airliners to deliver parts and supplies to the Arabs. While not engaged in actual warfare, the Shah allowed Iranian transport planes to ferry a Saudi battalion into battle and to evacuate wounded Syrians to Tehran for treatment.

Covertly and at a crucial time during the Yom Kippur War, Pahlavi returned a shipment of artillery shells and electronic equipment sold to him by the Israelis. The Shah, however, was averse to joining the 1973 oil stoppage and refused to use Iran's black gold as a bargaining chip against the US or Israel. Following the 1973 conflict the Shah offered a multi-million dollar loan to Anwar El Sadat that would enable the Egyptian leader to expand the Suez Canal, reconstruct Port Said, and erect a pipeline between Suez and Alexandria. This action negated the need for the Israeli line from Eilat to Ashkelon and would have allowed the Shah to halt or severely restrict the flow of oil. The Israeli government was able to compel the Shah to honor their past agreement and continue the flow of oil as usual.

It was becoming more obvious to political observers that the underlying turmoil in Iran was at the point of near-eruption. Few had any reason to suppose that US policies would ultimately result in plunging Iran into the grasp of the Grand Ayatollah Ruhollah Khomeini.

Mixed signals had been sent to the Shah regarding the action Pahlavi was to take to preserve his leadership in Iran. He had no idea whether or not the US would continue to support him if he took resolute measures to quell the rising tide of revolution. The Shah was left wondering just what actions he should take.

In May 1977 US Secretary of State Cyrus Vance was sent to Iran for a Central Treaty Organization (CENTO) meeting. Vance embarked with a twenty-page classified memo, which did not mention possible opposition led by religious figures. It erroneously concluded, "We expect this stability [in Iran] to persist for the next several years." [58] The briefing paper also mentioned human rights initiatives and gave Vance specific directions for its inclusion in discussions with the Shah. After meeting with Vance, Pahlavi's opinion of the secretary of state was that he was "more a bureaucrat than a politician."[59]

A CIA report delivered in August of 1977 seemed to support the State Department's evaluation of the situation in Iran. This intelligence organization opined: "The Shah will be an active participant in Iranian life well into the 1980s. There will be no radical change in Iranian political behavior in the near future." The CIA was convinced it was "looking at evolution not revolution" in Iran.[60]

A January 7, 1978, article in *Etela'at*, an Iranian newspaper under the editorial control of Minister of Information Dariush Homayoun, sparked riots in the religious center of Qom. The article openly denigrated Khomeini: He [Khomeini] "was not truly Iranian; he had British connections; he led a dissolute life; and he wrote Sufic [mystical Persian love] poetry." The purpose of this article was unclear, but its effect was crystal clear: the seminary and bazaar in Qom closed, and four thousand theology students and other Muslims demonstrated, calling for a public apology...the next day a communiqué from Khomeini began orchestrating the opposition's response."[61]

A meeting of what Ambassador Sullivan described as "An Eclectic Group of [Iranian] Oppositionists…Blaming the USG [United States Government] via the Shah for Iran's Ills," drew this comment:

> "Except for the problem of fighting for the turn to speak, the group had a grand time. They were polite but pitiless in assailing USG policy and our puppet Shah… [We] delivered our semi-official Embassy message that troops will be ready when the Shah leaves. Therefore, crowds should do nothing to provoke them. And meanwhile, we will use whatever influence we have to restrain [the Iranian] army. Moderate religious leaders had previously accepted this message graciously, as did several leading bazaaris. This group, however, reacted sharply."[62]

Homayoun later told a press conference in Tehran that the troubles in Qom were "extremely well planned." Rioters were being moved from city to city by private transport. He said there was evidence that Palestinian extremists were involved. Demands were being made for the rigid enforcement of Islamic law with the closure of cinemas, bars, and nightclubs. The agitators opposed television and the emancipation of women.[63]

Unlike those who attributed the Shah's downfall to his desire to modernize Iran, Eric Rouleau, a Middle East journalist for the French newspaper *Le Monde*, was of a different opinion. Rouleau wrote in an article on the revolt against the Shah:

> The first signs of revolt passed unnoticed. The explosions of rage in the spring of 1978, first in Tabriz and then in Qom, were attributed to "obscurantist mullahs" hostile to the Shah's agrarian reform. The immense demonstrations by millions of Iranians, as well as the strikes in the administrations, factories, schools, universities, and oil fields, which paralyzed the state and in the last analysis caused the

monarch's inglorious departure, were attributed to the fanaticism of the Iranian people.

Rare were those who suggested that modernity is not necessarily synonymous with progress or well-being, or that the concepts of economic development current in the West, where quick material gain is often the only valid criterion, do not necessarily correspond to the true needs and interests of developing nations.[64]

In April Ambassador Sullivan fired off a then-secret telegram to Secretary Vance. It was marked "NODIS" (No Distribution). He wrote:

"I am becoming increasingly concerned by the evidence that Iranian authorities have decided to resort to heavy-handed means to discourage dissident political action."[65] Undersecretary Warren Christopher responded to Sullivan's disquiet: "We share your concern about recent violence in Iran, including evidence of strong-arm tactics by the GOI (Government of Iran.) We believe GOI should itself be concerned over widespread reporting in US media of these indications of unrest in Iran." Christopher's memo advised Sullivan to discuss his fears with the Iranian prime minister.[66]

A telegram from Sullivan to Vance on June 19, 1978, indicated:

"Lawyers have been at the forefront of the opposition movement in Tehran, and we can expect a renewed determination of this group to keep pressing for further change. They have told us privately that they will be monitoring court cases closely for evidence of improper procedure on the part of government officials, including prosecutors and judges."[67]

Where were these same lawyers when Khomeini's revolutionaries began to execute their fellow countrymen after the Shah's departure and why were they not present to represent those charged and condemned before kangaroo courts?

Late in 1978 the Shah presented a lengthy shopping list for arms and communications devices to the administration. Sullivan was concerned about the effects such a massive arms build-up would have on the general Iranian population and on the economy. The other side of the coin was the amount of money such sales poured into US coffers. Iran topped the list of buyers at over $4 billion annually.

In my conversation with Her Majesty Farah Pahlavi, I asked about the quantity of arms purchased by the Shah. She replied:

> "In those days when my husband was making a strong army much of the equipment was bought from America. We were buying also from Europe…Then all the opposition people said, "The Shah loves these; it's like toys, a game, buying arms. He doesn't need it." But then, the Iraq/Iran War happened.
>
> "If it were not for that army and for the trained military, especially pilots, we would have lost to Saddam Hussein in the first two days…The Islamic Republic had assassinated many of our generals and military; many flew away from Iran, and some were in jail. They took the pilots out of jail; their families were held hostage so that they wouldn't fly away, but rather would fight against the invaders. Those who were against us must remember that."[68]

The Shah's arms list included F-14 and F-16 fighters, 707 tankers, P-3Cs, and other military supplies. Pahlavi was particularly interested in the purchase of the F-18, but his request was denied. Also on the list were crowd-control devices such as tear gas, ammunition, and riot gear. Ambassador Sullivan strongly opposed the sale of riot gear to the Shah. It was his opinion that such an infusion of equipment would only serve to encourage the Iranian military to consider a coup should the Shah be ousted. Both Sullivan and Cyrus Vance further pointed out that the British had already provided the necessary paraphernalia and instruction needed for crowd-control. Some State Department heads, including Patricia Derian (assistant secretary of state for human rights and humanitarian affairs), Anthony Lake (policy planning), and Leslie Gelb (political-military bureau), were fiercely opposed to the request. According to Sullivan, there were some who "were so strongly opposed to the Shah because of the human rights abuses of his regime that they wished to see him collapse no matter what the consequences for the United States or its allies."[69]

National Security Advisor Zbigniew Brzezinski was dispatched to Tehran for talks with the Shah. The Shah was confident in presenting his shopping list; after all, Brzezinski had assured the king of continuing support:

> "The US supports you without any reservation whatsoever, completely and fully in this present crisis. You have our complete support...Secondly, we will support whatever decisions you take regarding either the form or composition of the government that you decide upon. And thirdly, we are not, and I repeat, not encouraging any particular solution... it seems to me [you] have a problem of combining some gestures, which would be appealing in a general sense with a need for some specific actions which would demonstrate effective authority."[70]

Now, *that* was certainly a clear-cut solution to the Shah's growing predicament! Pahlavi telephoned Sullivan for clarification of Brzezinski's vague advice. Sullivan also sidestepped the Shah with promises to contact Washington. When no answer was forthcoming either from Washington or Sullivan, the Shah concluded, "The fact that no one contacted me during the crisis in an official way explains about the American attitude...the Americans wanted me out."[71] The Shah's former son-in-law and ambassador to the United States, Ardeshir Zahedi, told me of the Shah's frustrations with Sullivan. Pahlavi felt he was a victim of US hypocrisy. He was getting mixed signals from Sullivan and felt the American ambassador was not heeding Brzezinski's instructions.[72]

It was also in 1978 that Moscow issued a warning to the US regarding support of the Shah. Leonid Brezhnev, the Soviet Premier, cautioned:

> "It must be clear that any interference, especially military interference in the affairs of Iran—a state which directly borders on the Soviet Union—would be regarded as a matter affecting security interests...The events taking place in that country constitute purely internal affairs, and the questions involved in them should be decided by the Iranians—the Shah has ruled with an iron will."[73]

Although Iran was vitally important in maintaining security in the Persian Gulf area, President Carter, Brzezinski, and Vance were like-minded in their determination to push the human rights agenda and to halt the sale of arms to the Shah. Vance wrote in *Hard Choices* that, "Neither the president nor I wished to use human rights as an ideological weapon but rather as a basic element of our foreign policy. We applauded and supported the measures the Shah was beginning to take to improve human rights; he had already begun to curb SAVAK...in its use of extralegal measures to control subversion."[74]

When the Shah was finally overthrown in 1979, the debacle that followed his departure wreaked havoc in the oil-rich Persian Gulf. It opened the door not only to the meteoric rise of Islamic fundamentalism but also for the Soviet invasion of Afghanistan. Almost overnight Afghanistan was converted from a neutral nation to a springboard for the Russians to move closer to the Indian Ocean.

Zahedi had also warned of the Soviet Union's intentions to subdue Afghanistan. By failing to sufficiently back the Shah in Iran and abdicating its position of strength in the region, the US was unable to take overt steps to halt the forward progress of the USSR. Attempts to enlist needed allies in

Egypt, Pakistan, and Saudi Arabia would still find the US unprepared for the Soviet invasion of Afghanistan.

As Brzezinski wrote in his memoir, *Power and Principle*, "The longer-range strategic and political implications of the Iranian crisis came to be appreciated in Washington only gradually...until [the seizure of the hostages]...the US public was not overly aroused by a shift in power from a relatively unpopular Shah to a group of 'reformers.'"[75]

It is incomprehensible to think that the Ayatollah Ruhollah Khomeini could so mesmerize the majority of an entire nation with his persuasive rhetoric that the populace would blindly follow him. Khomeini had promised them what would be in US political terms "a car in every garage, and a chicken in every pot," and they believed him. Khomeini promised nothing in the way of programs to achieve his ends. Even though he emphasized "change," Khomeini offered no plan for its implementation.

In 1977 Iranian Islamic leader Ali Shari'ati died, thus removing a huge potential rival to Ayatollah Ruhollah Khomeini and solidifying his support against the Shah in Iran. Shari'ati was a French-trained sociologist of the same period as Khomeini.

Two other events also took place; both linked to the Shah and both spurring Khomeini and his followers to revenge. These two events essentially sealed the fate of the monarch. First, Ayatollah Hossein Ghaffari, a vocal critic of the Shah's regime, was allegedly tortured to death by Pahlavi's security forces. The cleric and Khomeini had corresponded during Khomeini's exile in Najaf; his death only added fuel to the Islamic revolutionary fires already burning in the Grand Ayatollah's chest.

Second, in October 1977 Khomeini's son Mustafa died of bulimia with heart complications, but antigovernment forces pointed the finger at the Shah's secret police, SAVAK, and Mustafa was proclaimed a martyr. This only served to further incite Khomeini's followers against the Shah. While there were various groups opposing the Shah's regime, i.e., leftists, the People's *Mujahedin* of Iran (MEK), communists, and other groups, Khomeini had suddenly become the most popular opponent to Pahlavi's rule.

The Shah was being pressured by Washington to ease his control and allow more political freedom. This prompted the release of more than three hundred political prisoners, relaxed censorship, and the overhaul of the court system, which had the unforeseen side-effect of allowing greater freedom for opposition groups to meet and organize.

Pahlavi was confident about the US commitment to Iran during an interview with *Kayhan International* in September 1977:

> "Relations between Iran and the United States are good and I do not think they could be otherwise…When a new administration takes over, there are those who imagine everything will be changed. But it is only individuals who change; the long-term interests of a nation cannot change… We will not accept anything less than a first-class position for Iran…Iran must have a first class status."[76]

When Secretary of State Cyrus Vance visited Iran for the CENTO meeting, he was accompanied by an "unidentified spokesperson" from the State Department who leaked the information that the United States was pleased with the Shah's human rights efforts and was therefore willing to sell the Shah AWACS aircraft.[77] In July, Congressional members were informed that the objective was to sell seven AWACS planes to Iran.

After months of congressional wrangling and intense debate, the sale was approved. The final package included an additional $1.1 billion in spare parts and technical instruction. The Shah, however, sorely missed the Nixon administration's willingness to provide an almost unlimited entrée to military equipment.

While the Shah's internal changes in his country were making an impression in the US, young men and women in Iran were swarming to radical Islam. Iran had never seen anything like this in the nation's history. University students gathered at Islamic study centers to debate the imams of Shi'a Islam. Young women clothed themselves in the *chadors* (long black veils) that had been outlawed by the Shah. This new, radical Islam exploded on the campus of Tehran University in October 1977. A group of students calling for the isolation of women on campus rioted, leaving behind a trail of burned-out buses and broken windows.

Pahlavi's desire to see Iran dragged, sometimes kicking and screaming, into the twentieth century, to see the Iranian people with the advantages offered by westernization, hastened his downfall. He wanted to create a modern, industrialized nation that was productive, strong militarily and economically, and diverse culturally. Visionaries require a retinue of detail-oriented people around them to implement the vision and reach the goal.

In an article published in *New Yorker*, an unnamed Iranian official in Isfahan summed up the situation very succinctly; the summation was appropriate for any city in Iran:

> "Students have grown up under the Shah, and they don't know what things were like before development started. All they know is that the Shah promised that Iran was going to be like France or Germany. That isn't happening. The huge surge in population means that services are spread too thin and are constantly breaking down. There aren't enough telephones. It's impossible to buy a car. The schools are jammed. Housing is scarce. During the past three years there has been a recession, especially in building, and many laborers are out of work. So the students are in a mood to reject everything that has happened. They are turning back to the old days and pursuing an idealized version of what things were like then. They are pushing the mullahs to go back and re-create the wonderful past. The mullahs see a chance to regain their prestige and power. The students provide them with a power base for putting pressure on the government to give them the consideration and importance they have been seeking for years. So the mullahs go along. That's the dynamic of trouble in Isfahan."[78]

Unfortunately for the Shah, many of those with whom he surrounded himself were not averse to using any means to justify the end result. The outcome, of course, was unrestrained human rights violations. The poorer Iranian classes, seeking wealth, flocked into the cities where they encountered abysmal living conditions. Corruption proliferated and inflation skyrocketed. Violence ran rampant, and the SAVAK did not hesitate to implement any method to control it.

— 7 —

END OF AN ERA

"Men and women in Iran broke old chains only to forge new ones. They demolished the rule of one man and then submitted to the tyranny of another."
—FOUAD AJAMI[79]

In an attempt to solidify his position in the region, Mohammad Reza Shah Pahlavi had sought to align himself with his neighbors as early as 1974. The Shah, who was able to move Iran into a leadership role in OPEC during the Nixon-Ford administration, felt the time had come to move his country into a more central position in the region. (In a 1976 display of largess, Pahlavi gave away nearly two billion dollars to countries such as Egypt, Jordan, and Syria in order to achieve his goal.) Pahlavi sent his trusted emissary, General Gholam-Reza Afkhami, to Cairo to research the possibility of greater cooperation between Egypt and Iran. As a result of Afkhami's hard work, Egypt garnered a state-of-the-art radar system and an opportunity for Egyptian pilots to view the flight of Iran's Phantom jets. It also paved the way for the first visit of an Iranian monarch to Egypt in twenty-three years. During that visit Sadat asked Pahlavi to intervene with Israeli Prime Minister Yitzhak Rabin over the Sinai oil fields.

The Shah's visit in Cairo led the monarch to inform Rabin that the Eilat-Ashkelon pipeline was in danger of being shut down in early 1975. Rabin sent his Foreign Minister Yigal Allon to Tehran for meetings with the Shah. The two men were able to reach an agreement that allowed the flow of oil to continue, albeit with a higher rate for transfer fees but with a lower price for the oil.

In May of that year, however, the Shah surprised Israel by siding with Sadat over Israeli withdrawal from the territories captured during the Six-Day War. This placed an inordinate amount of stress on Israel-Iran relations. Israeli Ambassador Uri Lubrani was informed that relations between the two countries would be deferred until Israel decided to acquiesce to calls for withdrawal at least from the Abu-Rudeis oilfields. Secretary of State Henry Kissinger was finally able to exact a commitment from Pahlavi that he would not stop the flow of oil to Israel. Even with this agreement, Rabin felt it necessary to return to Tehran for another secret visit with the Shah. Unfortunately, Rabin was unable to maintain his anonymity among the Jews in the region. Pahlavi, however, was able to assure Rabin that Israel's oil needs would be met.

While the Shah was also reaching out to Egypt and other Arab countries, he was determined to allow neither the Soviets nor Americans to establish bases in his area of the Persian Gulf. The fact that the Soviets defied an agreement to withdraw from Iran in a timely manner following World War II and created two republics within the territory occupied—Azerbaijan and Iranian Kurdistan—was very distressing to Pahlavi. It was not until UN intervention in 1946 that the Russians abandoned their territory in Iran. Perhaps that is why the Shah considered the USSR to be the most important threat to Iran; after all, the two nations shared a 1,240–mile border. For centuries the Russian agenda included securing a warm-water port facility and subverting any nation considered to be pro-Western. Pahlavi felt the Russians had the most to gain should Iran plunge into internal unrest. An April 1974 document from the State Department outlines the Shah's fears regarding Soviet aggression:

> The Shah believes Soviet activity in the Middle East indi-
> cates a continuing use of proxies such as Iraq and South
> Yemen to accomplish Soviet foreign policy goals. The Shah
> remains concerned by the potential for instability—and
> Soviet exploitation of it—in neighboring countries. He is
> concerned about radical movements in the Persian Gulf;
> Iraq's hostility towards Iran...He recognized the need for,
> and has been seeking, improved relations and cooperation
> with the more moderate Arab governments...Establishing
> this cooperation is not easy because of long-standing Arab
> wariness toward Iran.[80]

It was thought by some to have been the signing of a peace treaty with
the Kurds in Northern Iraq that may well have signaled the beginning of
the end for the monarch. In allowing some ten thousand religious pilgrims
the right to freely travel from Iran to Iraq, the Shah opened the door for
the smuggling of Ayatollah Khomeini's fanatical and mutinous views across
the border. It was through this pipeline that Khomeini's cassette tapes were
transported into the hands of the opposition in Iran.

While the Shah was seen to be the principal patron of the Iraqi Kurds'
struggle for independence and had supported the Kurds with arms and training, Iran's assistance came to a halt with the signing of the Algiers Accords
between Iran and Iraq. During an OPEC meeting the two sides met and ham-
mered out an agreement to end an ongoing dispute over borders, water, and
navigation rights. The Shatt-El-Arab waterway was designated the defining
border. On June 13, 1975, the two nations signed the treaty. Unfortunately
for the Kurds, the Accords also meant the end of the Shah's support of the
Kurdish rebels. Without that support the Kurds were powerless to provide
any deterrent to Saddam Hussein's invasion of Iran.

Earlier in 1975 Secretary of State Henry Kissinger and Iran's Finance
Minister Hushang Ansary had inked an agreement totaling $15 billion for
purchases by Iran from the US, "the largest agreement of its kind ever signed
by the two countries."[81] Such a massive sum of money was unfathomable to

the vast majority of Iranians. This served to further distance the Shah from his people.

It was also in 1975 that the Shah established principals regarding private ownership of mining and industrial operations. Pahlavi gave the owners a period of three years to offer to the public 49 percent of the industries. This edict created a chaotic situation for the Shah. Wealthy industrialists were furious. They felt they were being forcibly stripped of their assets. Private citizens were equally disturbed at the thought of having to incur unwanted debt in order to purchase shares in the various companies. In his zeal to better the lot of the Iranian people, the Shah played right into the hands of human rights activists by placing what appeared to be an unnecessary burden on the Iranian people.

With an agreement in place between Iran and Iraq, the Shah ordered a sequence of liberalization policies. He permitted the reorganization of the National Front, an on-again-off-again, loosely organized political faction committed to "establish Iran's unequivocal sovereignty within and without; in other words...rule of law within, and political independence...without."[82]

The National Front had been inactive for a number of years. In its absence a generation of students had arisen who were devoted to radicalism and Islamic fanaticism. As an island of stability of what was increasingly becoming a turbulent sea of discontent in Iran, the National Front seemed content to protect the monarchy with the understanding that the "monarch reigned, but did not rule."[83] This seemed to be supported by the protest marches that crippled Tehran on December 10 and 11, 1978. A CIA assessment of Iran indicated:

> The protest marches in Tehran...which brought out as many as a million demonstrators into the streets, were masterfully organized and controlled. The evidence suggests that local community leaders called *dastehoardan*, whose traditional functions include organizing religious processions, mobilized small crowds around local mosques and then moved these groups to join others from around the

city...The ability of these local community leaders to bring out large numbers of people in response to directives from members of the Islamic clergy gives the religious opposition in Iran an organizational strength which distinguishes it from any other group within the opposition...The Ayatollah Ruhollah Khomeini has served as the focal point for the loyalty of the religious opposition...There is no evidence to substantiate the claim...that behind the pattern of events lies the guiding hand of "foreign elements," "leftists," or... the Tudeh party...demonstrations in Tehran on the high holy days of Moharram...were the most impressive display of organizational ability thus far seen in the recent incidents of civil unrest in Iran.[84]

The report went on to indicate that Khomeini had a strong following, particularly within the lower classes, urban centers, bazaar merchants and shopkeepers, and students who often chanted his name during rallies.

In a manifesto apparently drafted specifically for the December 10-11 marches, the Khomeini-inspired revolutionaries laid out their position. The document stated:

✧ Ayatollah Khomeini is our leader. Whatever he asks we will carry out. This march is a vote of confidence in Khomeini.

✧ The apparatus of the governmental dictatorship must be overthrown and power transferred to the people.

✧ The rule of Islamic social and individual justice must be established on the basis of the votes of the people.

✧ This is Human Rights Day. We ask for the human rights, which our struggle has sought.

✧ The imperialism of East and West must be
removed. The Iranian people will continue and
extend their relations with other nations.

✧ People should not make money from money.
The exploitation of human beings by others
should be stopped. The collection of wealth
in the hands of some people and the property of others should be redistributed.

✧ We salute the martyrs of the Iranian struggle.

✧ We demand release of all political prisoners and return of all who have left the
country because of lack of freedom.[85]

The Embassy also asked the questions: Will the Shah call for martial
law, and if so, how heavy-handed will the government be? And perhaps most
importantly, would the opposition be able to unite sufficiently to be able to
approach the Shah convincingly?

The State Department telegram concluded:

Situation...offers both danger and hope. Danger in that
radicals will instigate violent incidents which will draw
moderates' attention away from rather pleasant feeling of
success and provoke severe military reaction. Hope is that
opposition can get unified proposal ready to move forward
to coalition government reasonably soon.[86]

Also in December the Shah approached National Front leaders Shapour
Bakhtiar and Gholam Hossein Sadiqi (the Shah's first choice as prime minister) to pursue the idea of instituting a civilian government or a constitutional monarchy. The men also explored the possibility of military rule.
Unfortunately, the National Front, unlike the exiled Khomeini, had no acces-
sibility to a network by which to propagate its message across Iran.

Dr. Parviz Mina told me of his last visit to Tehran and his certainty that the Shah's monarchy would not survive:

> "When the plane took off it circled over Tehran. And I was looking down...on the northwestern side of the city... there was this famous avenue running from east to west... this street right from the beginning to the end was packed with people who were demonstrating against the Shah. I said, 'By God, that's the end of it.' That was the day I thought that he was...not going to survive."[87]

Waiting in the wings was the Ayatollah Ruhollah Khomeini, whose vendetta against the Shah of Iran began in 1963 when Pahlavi's forces successfully thwarted a religious movement headed by Khomeini and deported the fanatical cleric first to Turkey and then to Iraq. From that time on, Khomeini became obsessed with the overthrow of the Pahlavi monarchy.

It was Khomeini's ability to turn local mosques into cauldrons of revolutionary turmoil that was absolutely remarkable given the territorial nature of the mullahs and ayatollahs. Former Israeli Ambassador Uri Lubrani summarized his feeling about Khomeini's rise:

> "The religious establishment was the only organized body in Iran...in each village. If you ask about Khomeini having a network, he had the best possible network in Iran. I tried to touch base with the religious establishment in 1973; they wouldn't talk to me. The Shah didn't have an agent in each village, neither a policeman. Nobody was allowed [by the Shah's government] to organize...only the religious establishment...add to that what Khomeini was disseminating from his exile first in Iraq and then in France, you'll see that this big network was being fed with dissent and sedition... By the beginning of 1978 I began to have forebodings...to feel uneasy...to look for more urgent signs...of something brewing. I went to see my foreign minister, Moshe Dayan,

and told him of my concerns. I said, 'I have my forebod-
ings…we ought to begin to phase out.' I knew at the end of
the day…Israel will have no place in Iran…the new regime
will be an unfriendly regime to Israel."[88]

In a move that in hindsight was likely one of his most imprudent decisions, Pahlavi freed a number of pro-Khomeini mullahs from Iran's prisons
in 1978. These disgruntled clerics bent on revenge gladly joined Khomeini's
underground and were among the many whose mosques were made available to the radicals.

The network of mosques proved to be much more effective than the
efforts of the National Front. Khomeini, however, was slow, methodical, and
determined to seek revenge against his adversary, the Shah, no matter the
time or cost in money or lives. The Grand Ayatollah recruited from the ranks
of mid-level mullahs who whipped their followers into rabid, pro-Khomeini
militants.

The Shah, of course, had charted his own path simply because he
wanted the favor of his subjects, the Iranian people. He professed to be
a pious Muslim; he made the required trips to pay homage at the various
shrines. The Shah craved the favor of the clerics and submersed himself in
prayer. How could he openly declare war on the mullahs whose support he
so actively sought?

Khomeini's charisma was especially appealing to the lower classes, the
mostazafin…the dispossessed. They saw him as their savior, the one who
would rescue them from their lives of toil. Ahmad Ashraf wrote of the
Ayatollah: "Khomeini gave the masses a sense of personal integrity, of collective identity, of historical rootedness, and feelings of pride and superiority."[89]
In their hysterical longing for the coming of the *Mahdi*, the risen one that
would free the masses from privation, discrimination, and tyranny, some
claimed to have seen the Ayatollah's face in the moon.[90] This would certainly
be consistent with the Persian penchant for superstition, numerology, and
dependence on "omens, symbols, prophecies, and revelations."[91]

It would be in the name of this *Mahdi* that a rogue Muslim fanatic and his faction in Saudi Arabia would seize the Grand Mosque in Mecca, seal the doors, and hold hostage the pilgrims inside the holiest of Muslim sites. The two-week siege would end only when French mercenaries and Saudi National Guard troops stormed the mosque. Hundreds were killed in the crossfire. This attack, though unsuccessful, was to be only a foretaste of the tactics Islamic fanatics were willing to use to achieve their goal...world domination through the return of the revered *Mahdi*. Khomeini, himself, was reputed by some to be the long-awaited redeemer of Islam.

Author Jahangir Amuzegar wrote of the mesmerizing Khomeini's appeal:

> He [Khomeini] spoke of such misty but universally pop-
> ular goals as political and religious freedom, independence
> from pernicious foreign influences, social justice...the obli-
> gation to help the poor...the villainy of corruption, a need to
> conserve precious natural resources...and other goals.[92]

With his smooth rhetoric Khomeini managed to ensnare leaders of *The People's Mujahedeen-e-Khalq* and the Marxist-inspired *Fedayeen-e-Khalq* ("freedom fighters" with strong ties to the PLO) and entice them to join his brand of Islamic revolution. It was the *Mujahedeen* with its thin veneer of Islam that endowed Khomeini with the venerable title of "Imam." The group joined hands with Khomeini, deeming the Shah to be too secular. The *Fedayeen* was more interested in launching a Marxist revolution akin to that of Fidel Castro in Cuba or Che Guevara in Latin America.[93] Both organizations had ties to the PLO. The Ayatollah had asserted he would be a "guide to the people."[94] Few realized that he would, instead, grip the reins of power in Iran and rule with an iron fist, squashing all opposition in his path. Khomeini managed to pull the wool over the eyes of the likes of intellectual James Bill, who described the tyrannical ruler as a man of "impeccable integrity and honesty, who has denied again and again that he will hold office."[95]

To fund his campaign to depose the Shah, Khomeini relied in part on both the PLO and Syria's Hafez Assad. The Soviet defector, former General

Ion Pacepa, also revealed that another source of funds to support this direct onslaught against the Shah came from the Soviet Union. Khomeini's fanatical influence on the mullahs in Iran was to be driven home to Pahlavi with powerful potency on October 9, 1977: twenty-plus students with covered faces rampaged through the University of Tehran, vandalizing classrooms, torching buses, and demanding that women be totally segregated from the male student population.

It was, however, during *Ramadan* (the Muslim month set aside for fasting and reflection) in August 1978 that large protest rallies erupted all across Iran. Curfew was imposed in some cities following days of mass rioting. The city of Abadan was the site of a mass murder said to have been staged by Islamic radicals. The doors of the *Rex Cinema*, hosting an Iranian film, were barred while the building was torched; 477 people died in the conflagration, including a number of children and their mothers. The clergy that directly supported Khomeini avowed that the fire was set by SAVAK, the Shah's secret police. Iranian police determined that followers of the Ayatollah were responsible for the murders of so many innocent people. In retrospect, this reeks of the tactics used later by radical Islamic terrorists in countries such as Egypt, Algeria, and ultimately in the United States.

In Qom, the center of Islamic education in Iran, police fired into a group of rioters who were protesting a denouncement of Khomeini in the newspaper. Several clerics were killed in the melee. The Shah's attempts to suppress the rioting were rejected by enemies and supporters alike. His enemies saw it as a weak attempt at appeasement, and his supporters just saw it as weakness, period. Khomeini saw it as the beginning of a tsunami that would sweep the Shah out of power. It was becoming more obvious that the threat to Iran was not from the communist Soviet Union, but from socio-economic, religious, and political sources.

Under the tutelage of his former son-in-law, Ardeshir Zahedi, the Shah was encouraged to offer up a scapegoat to appease the mobs of demonstrators. Zahedi, who had been appointed ambassador to the United States, suggested such substitutes as Amir Hoveyda, and SAVAK heads Hasan Pakravan and Nematollah Nassiri. Zahedi assured Brzezinski, back in Washington, that he had the situation in Iran firmly in hand; obviously he was badly mistaken. Not even a counter demonstration organized by the ambassador could quell the unrest in his homeland.

— 8 —

MEDDLING MEDIA

"Jihad means the conquest of all non-Muslim territories. Such a war may well be declared after the formation of an Islamic government worthy of that name, at the direction of the Imam or under his orders. It will then be the duty of every able-bodied adult male to volunteer for this war of conquest, the final aim of which is to put Qur'anic law in power from one end of the earth to the other."
CLIVE IRVING[96]

IN THE LATE 1970s THE WORLDWIDE MEDIA WAS CONTROLLED BY ITS COUNTERPARTS in three very powerful countries. In the United States *The New York Times* was the media power of record. In Great Britain the British Broadcasting Corporation (BBC) led the way; and then there were the newspapers and media sources in France.

It's difficult to imagine life as it was then—no Internet, CNN, CNBC, Fox Network, no iPhones, digital cameras, or text messaging. News was delivered principally via ABC, NBC, or CBS. At that time, what we now refer to as "mainstream" media was extremely powerful. In the 1960s this newly dominant media outlet introduced America to its first "television war." Night after night Americans ate their evening meals to the horrifying scenes of bloody and battered combat troops, body bags, and atrocities in Vietnam.

According to the Museum of Broadcast Communications, the Saigon Bureau was the third largest after New York and Washington. It kept five camera crews busy a majority of the time. The result of the nightly bombardment of horror was revulsion and exhaustion. Eventually, Americans began clamoring for the troops to be brought home.[97]

Just as the Ayatollah Khomeini became the darling of the media, so the Shah became the pariah. He and his monarchy bore the full brunt of media revulsion during those years. *The New York Times* influenced decision makers, especially during the crucial months of 1978 and 1979. In France, Khomeini's country of choice during his exile, the press and television created a soft, fuzzy image of the Ayatollah. But perhaps the most damaging entity of all was the *British Broadcasting Corporation* (BBC). Through its Persian language *BBC Persian Service* network, it became a primary voice for the Islamic Revolution. Pahlavi didn't stand a chance in the battle for public opinion with each of these powerful outlets as his foe. It is said that Mehdi Bazargan, Iranian scholar and activist, expressed his appreciation for both the BBC and the French *Le Monde* following Khomeini's seizure of power.[98]

Iranian military leaders were very concerned with BBC broadcasts being aired from the island of Masirah, just off the Omani coast. The Shah had met with British Ambassador Anthony Parsons in an attempt to stop the broadcasts announcing to the Iranian people when planned demonstrations against the Shah had been scheduled. The ambassador reminded the Shah's chief of protocol, Amir-Khosrow Afshar, that the BBC was an independently owned and operated entity and not controlled by the British government.

The most curious and mysterious relationship between the media and the Shah was with the BBC. It was the only Western broadcaster to have a service that aired in the Persian language. The BBC Persian Service had been established during WWII to counterbalance the Nazi influence in Iran. In the 1950's it was opposed to the nationalization of Iranian oil, which at the time had been held by the Anglo Iranian Oil Company (AIOC).[99]

At the beginning of the Shah's reign in 1953 the BBC Persian Service appeared to be a friend of his. In fact, early in the Iranian revolution the opposition forces still viewed the BBC Persian Service with distrust. It took

Abullhassan Bani Sadr, later president of the republic and the same person who connected Paul Balta of *Le Monde* with Khomeini, to get the Ayatollah to trust the BBC. Bani Sadr said later:

> "I suggested to Khomeini to give an interview to BBC, assuring him that they will broadcast exactly what he says. Khomeini rejected saying, 'BBC belongs to the British and it will not benefit us to give them an interview.' I convinced him when I said all the other media you give interviews to are also all foreign, so what is the difference? Khomeini then accepted."[100]

Soon the BBC Persian Service was broadcasting the rantings of the Ayatollah and other leaders of the revolution directly into Iran. It was well known that the BBC World Service, under which the BBC Persian Service fell, was funded by the British Foreign Office. The Foreign Office by the 1970's was claiming to have no control over the journalists. Friends of the Shah appealed a number of times to the Foreign Office and the BBC but to no avail.[101] In the meantime, the BBC Persian Service Broadcast had become a national event.

In Ehsan Naraghi's book, *From Palace to Prison, Inside the Iranian Revolution,* he reconstructs a dialogue between himself and the Shah regarding the BBC:

> Shah: "We've stressed...that while respecting the BBC's right to freedom of expression, we considered that it was taking things too far...The information that it was broadcasting about the situation in Iran was tantamount to instructions to the opposition on how they should behave from one day to the next."
>
> Naraghi: "It's true, Your Majesty, that the BBC has a very large audience in Iran. During the time when it broadcasts its evening program, from 7:45 to 8:30, I've noticed that the

city looks completely different because so many people go home to listen."[102]

Perhaps understandably, the British Foreign Office has yet to open its files regarding this time period and the BBC Persian Service.[103]

The conversations regarding the BBC Persian Service led to another charge of bugging by Lt. General Azarbarzin. He was called into the Shah's suite following the meeting with Parsons and told:

> "Destroying this station will create a political scandal... You go ahead and make all preparations, and I'll give you confirmation in the morning at 9:00 a.m." When I went to see the Shah, Ambassador Sullivan was ahead of me...he had requested an emergency audience with the Shah at 8:30 a.m....After Sullivan had left, the Shah told me, "Don't take any action on what we discussed yesterday...By the way, did you discuss yesterday's subject with anyone?" I answered, "I do not discuss my missions with anybody." The Shah said, "I am surprised, because Ambassador Sullivan mentioned the words *political scandal* exactly as I told you yesterday."[104]

General Robert Huyser, deputy commander in chief of the US European Command, recorded that his Iranian counterparts were asking, "Why can't the big United States silence Khomeini? Cannot the US silence the British Broadcasting's Farsi broadcasts?" Huyser said that "young and old alike carried transistor radios...The BBC Persian Service was set up during World War II in order to help destabilize the regime of the Shah's father...and the Shah himself probably had this in mind when they protested against the role of the BBC during this crucial period in the late 1970s."[105]

The New York Times in the 1970's was considered the "Gray Lady" of US print media. It claimed to provide, "All the news that's fit to print." With extensive Foreign Affairs coverage that was only rivaled by the *Washington Post*, *The New York Times* was mandatory reading for foreign policy analysts, professionals, and diplomats in the US and abroad. It was also one of the morning papers on the desks of the television news producers at the three major networks of that day.

Many of the news stories on the national nightly news broadcasts came directly from the pages of the *Washington Post, The New York Times* and, occasionally, the *Wall Street Journal.* (It was, after all, Woodward and Bernstein who broke the Watergate scandal in the prestigious *Post.*) These three newspapers had nationwide circulation—making them the only "national" daily newspapers. When it came to an overseas story, no paper had more clout than *The New York Times.*

The Shah and his diplomats were not ignorant, uninformed individuals. They were aware of the sway held by the *Times.* Pahlavi's press office in Iran communicated frequently with news reporters stationed in Tehran, including the famous *Times* correspondent, R. W. Apple. Unfortunately for the Shah, his attempts to generate goodwill yielded strange results.

Over the next few months articles and the editorial page of *The New York Times* repeatedly pursued the Shah and the proposed US sale of military aircraft.[106] Seemingly, *The New York Times* seized every opportunity to castigate the Shah, even in something as innocuous as the newspaper's June 1977 tribute to *The Crowned Cannibals: Writings on Repression in Iran,* penned by Reza Baraheni. Reviewer John Leonard engaged in the "moral equivalence" doctrine so popular at the time. He drew such a comparison between events in the Soviet Union, Nazi Germany, and among America's allies. Leonard wrote:

> First of all, the writer as witness of the Holocaust, of Stalinism, of the Shah and his thuggish SAVAK, is one of the few honorable callings in a bestial century.[107]

This review might have been attributed to a seasoned publicist with a penchant for seizing the moment and linking his client's book to the president's human rights campaign; however, the New York Times piece was not the end. Another article entitled, "Publishing: Human Rights," also featured Reza Baraheni and his Crowned Cannibals book. The article tied the publishing of the book to a meeting in Belgrade to examine the effects of the Helsinki

Accords: "Including the human rights section calling for freer exchange of people and ideas, several books are published here that cast light in the dark corners of literary freedom."[108] None of the other books were mentioned. It was simply another opportunity for the New York Times to denigrate the Shah.

During the crucial months of late 1978 and early 1979 leading up to the departure of the Shah, the Times ran a series of editorials along with its news stories. On November 6, 1977, the editorial read, "Suddenly, Iran No Longer Stable." It opened with the question, "How much more time for the Shah of Iran?" Previously, it had been only the anti-Shah protestors who demanded the Shah must go. Certainly no one in the US government had been so crass as to utter those words aloud. Yet, here was the most influential foreign policy daily in the US raising the question. The editorial ended by planting the idea: "Pressure on the Shah has mounted and many of his opponents have raised their sights from reducing his power to driving him from the throne."[109] Apparently that included *The New York Times* editorial board.

On November 8, 1978, and for reasons known only to the editorial staff, *The New York Times* took a step back. It noted that the Shah promised "that newly installed military rule will be brief and will be followed by free elections." It questioned, "Has it come in time?" but concluded, "so far, at least, they warrant continued Western support."[110]

Had the *Times* staff had a change of heart? Were they now proposing the monarch remain in power? By December 14th, however, the editorial headline read: "On the Ropes in Iran." They gave the Shah a conciliatory nod by observing he "may yet weather the crisis. He has been a good ally; and as long as his rule remains plausible he is entitled to the respect and support that [has been] extended. But the Shah has gotten as he has given over the years, and the United States cannot be expected to leave all its stakes piled on one throne...All the avenues require American contacts with the opposition."[111] It obviously did not explain how the US could extend "respect and support" to Pahlavi and at the same time meet with the opposition. Iranians knew the Shah had returned to power with the help of the CIA in 1953. The U.S opening contacts with the opposition would have again been interpreted in Iran as a vote of no confidence in the Shah.

By December 29, 1978, while the Shah was trying to work out a government of national reconciliation, the *Times* published an editorial entitled, "The Ideal and the Real in Iran." While it praised the idea of the Shah staying in a figurehead role, it determined that: "The policy, however, has a serious flaw; it appears to be increasingly unrealistic." Oddly, the editorial concluded, "The United States should not, probably could not, encourage the Shah's departure." The paper appeared to be free to urge Pahlavi's ouster. It opined, "Every day, there seems to be more reason to doubt that present policy can prevent such an outcome."[112]

In September 1978, before fleeing to Paris from Iraq, Khomeini had been placed under house arrest. At that time, the Liberation Movement of Iran (a group which will play a prominent role later in this book) contacted the US Embassy in Tehran and asked for its help in freeing Khomeini. The missive implied that Khomeini wished to leave Iraq. The group's leaders also asked for a high-level meeting with US officials and indicated they would unveil their strong religious connections at the meeting. The Embassy staff declined the request.[113]

In an aborted attempt to flee Iraq, Khomeini and his entourage became stranded at the Kuwait border when that country would not grant him entry, and he was then refused reentry into Iraq. Finally, the Ayatollah received permission to return to Baghdad where, on October 6, he was allowed, at the Shah's urging, to fly to France. The DST, the French secret service, urged French President Giscard d'Estaing to turn Khomeini away. In my personal interview with d'Estaing, he seemed not to have realized just who Khomeini was when the cleric arrived in France:

> "No one knew in France exactly the name...and I heard he was here in Paris after the Interior Minister M. Christian Bonair delivered me a note, the day after his arrival. He [Khomeini] received a number of favors. He [Bonair] had a personality who disembarked yesterday at the airport and all his documents were in order saying he was coming from Iraq...Yes, Najaf...He was fleeing Iraq...and he was

welcomed by a member of a small group who owns a house in Western Paris. He was driven there by his supporters. And then we realized he was active in politics…and that he was very important in the post-Shah regime. Then we appointed a man from (French Intelligence) to check on him…We considered him…a sort of political refugee. And you know in France, we accept political refugees."[114]

Giscard then seemed to jump on the "downfall of the Shah" bandwagon and agreed to provide asylum for the Ayatollah. Far from halting his interference in Iran, Khomeini's exile only fired the passions of the Islamic radicals in that country. His freedom to plan and execute a revolution while under French protection would prove to be the final straw for the Shah's regime.

A telegram from Ambassador Sullivan to the State Department revealed religious leaders close to Khomeini were urging him to exercise caution and restraint because the civil unrest in Iran was becoming unmanageable. The clerics were also alarmed at surfacing rumors indicating that Khomeini was cooperating with the Tudeh Party, the communist opposition, and some Iranians were beginning to believe the gossip.[115]

It was thought by some individuals that, as stated by Barry Rubin in his book, *Paved with Good Intention*, the French allowed Khomeini into the country because he was perceived as the future leader of Iran.[116] Rubin also writes, "The CIA rented a villa near his [Khomeini's] home. American Embassy political officers began to meet occasionally with one of his advisors, Ebrahim Yazdi [leader in 1968 of the US branch of Muslim Students' Association of America]."[117] Others in France went so far as to try to predict when the Shah's end would come.

— 9 —

FRANCE HARBORS
KHOMEINI

*"Khomeini…insisted that, since his version of Islam was the only
true version, all Muslims should follow it… Khomeini blithely
allied himself with anyone who could advance his cause…
[His] version of Islam was unquestionably bloodthirsty."*
—MICHAEL A. LEDEEN[118]

PRIOR TO KHOMEINI'S ARRIVAL IN FRANCE, President Giscard d'Estaing had dispatched
his personal representative, Michel Poniatowski, to Iran to meet with the
Shah. Poniatowski reported back to Giscard that, "[The Shah] understands
nothing of what's going on; he thinks Khomeini is without importance and
he asks us to welcome him…I don't want to; he should not be welcomed."[119]

Giscard then sent his chief of secret services, Alexandre de Marenches,
to interview the Shah and to confirm Poniatowski's impression. Marenches
reported back to Giscard that the Shah appeared almost beaten and that
the best thing to do would be to prepare in France for the aftermath of
Khomeini's revolution.[120] According to Marenches, the Shah declined to use
armed force against his people. Marenches replied, "Sir, in that case you are
lost."[121] Uri Lubrani is of the opinion that France courted Khomeini as a way

of "buying political influence…resting on their reputation of being a liberal country [that gave] political asylum to all sorts of renegades…'France is a whore,'" said Lubrani.[122]

On January 7, 1979, a New York Times editorial labeled the Shah as, "The Friend That Failed," an interesting title given that reading the previous two years of the Times would have made Pahlavi seem more a burden to the US than a close friend and ally. The editorial condemned the US penchant for sticking with its friends abroad as a "suicidal devotion" and that "such theories blind their devotees to all objective diplomatic reckonings."[123] The New York Times' strange reversal of standing up for human rights was considered noble, but at the same time the "real politick" of the Kissinger years was denounced. While devotion to principle was considered a weakness, the Times did not need to worry about such contradictions. In the end, "It was the Shah who failed in Iran, not the United States."[124]

One vastly important decision was reached on January 14, two days prior to the Shah's departure from Tehran. A meeting between Warren Zimmerman, the US Embassy political advisor in Paris, and Ebrahim Yazdi, Khomeini's US mouthpiece, was approved by the president. Meanwhile, Huyser was equally busy trying to persuade the military heads in Iran to open a line of communication with the Ayatollah. On that same evening Khomeini stunned many by telling a CBS reporter that a large number of the Iranian armed forces were loyal to his cause, and he would be the "strongman" in Iran.[125]

After the Shah's departure from Tehran on January, 17, 1979, a New York Times editorial sighed theatrically, "The Shah Departs, Finally." The question was posed: "Is there something to regret in this turn of events?" The editorialist felt compelled to answer the question for the readers: "Chiefly, that the Shah dallied too long before going."[126]

Zimmerman and Yazdi reportedly held several secret meetings in Paris during which they discussed topics related to possible Iranian military interference with Khomeini's plan to return to Tehran. Yazdi outlined three basic questions to which the revolutionaries wanted an answer. They reportedly were:

- ✦ Would Khomeini's return trigger a military reaction or create such uproar among the Iranian people that the military was forced to respond to the chaos?

- ✦ Would the upper echelon of the military insist on backing the Shah or would it acquiesce to Khomeini's leadership and transfer allegiance to the cleric?

- ✦ Did Americans working in Iran have the right to destroy what was described as "sophisticated military equipment" before departing the country? It was Khomeini's contention that the equipment fell under the auspices of the Iranian military.

On a bitterly cold day, January 16, 1979, the Shah, who had ruled Iran for thirty-seven years, and his empress, Farah Pahlavi, boarded one of two planes destined for Egypt. Ironically, the two passenger jets were parked in front of the lavish and luxurious Imperial Pavilion where the Shah had often greeted kings and politicians who visited Tehran. The *Gulf News* reported his departure:

> Two officers of the Shah's royal guard fell to their knees and tried to kiss the monarch's feet at Tehran's airport, but he motioned for them to rise, court sources said. Two other officers, standing face to face, held aloft a copy of Holy Quran and the royal couple passed beneath the impromptu arch to board the "Shah's Falcon," a royal Boeing 727...
>
> With tears in his eyes, Shah Mohammad Reza Pahlavi and Empress Farah Diba left Iran for Egypt and the United States, piloting his own jet on a journey many believe will end in permanent exile. His departure touched off jubilant celebrations throughout Tehran.

"The Shah is gone forever," people chanted as millions poured into the streets of Tehran, showering each other with sweets and rose water, cheering and shouting with joy at what they saw as victory in a year-long, bloody uprising to topple the 59-year-old Shah.[127]

Following January 1979 meetings it was reported that the Shah was ready to relinquish the reins of government to his hand-picked successor. As a result, it was announced that the Shah and his family were welcome to visit the United States home of Walter Annenberg in California or travel to Egypt at the invitation of Anwar Sadat. (Sadat had no regard for the fanatical Khomeini and felt he would only drastically harm Islam.) The Shah chose to spend a week in Cairo with Sadat and then travel on to Morocco for a two-week visit with King Hassan. It was in Marrakesh on February 11, 1979, that the Pahlavi family heard of the collapse of Bakhtiar's government. The next day, news of the slaughter of military officials reached the king.

Unfortunately, the Shah's stay in Morocco as a guest of King Hassan soon came to an end. Alexandre de Marenches contacted the Shah to inform him that King Hassan was in danger due to the presence of the Pahlavi family in Morocco. Khomeini's far-reaching hand was stirring the pot of unrest among students on the university campuses in that country, and the Shah was asked to leave.

The Shah requested that he be allowed to stay in Morocco, where he was able to maintain constant contact with his most loyal military contingent, the Royal Guard. He felt he could be called upon at any moment to return to Iran and resume the throne. King Hassan was forced to respond negatively to Pahlavi, and the Shah and his royal entourage departed Morocco. He was denied entry into France, which had clasped Khomeini to its bosom. Both Monaco and Switzerland, bastions of neutrality, also rejected a request to host the deposed monarch. Even the "Iron Lady" of Great Britain, Margaret Thatcher, declined to welcome the Shah and his family to England.

In abandoning the Shah and Iran to the Grand Ayatollah Ruhollah Khomeini, the US State Department had completely overlooked Khomeini's tendency to refer to the United States as the "Great Satan"—a superpower to be brought to its knees. Under Khomeini's regime, blood would flow again through the streets of Tehran and repression would reach new heights in the coming years simply because multiplied tens of thousands of Iranians viewed the Shah as a tool of the "Great Satan."

Predictions of what would follow the embrace of Khomeini, while proving to be true, didn't begin to paint the picture of the bloodshed that occurred in the ranks of the military in Iran. Stunned by the loss of the generals and hierarchy under the Shah, the rank and file of the Iranian security forces was cast adrift. The army was in total disarray. Khomeini was swift to deactivate the Shah's military and substitute his own, drawn from the revolutionaries that now surrounded him.

Khomeini instructed his followers in the ways of martyrdom as a means to disengage the Shah's troops:

> "You must appeal to the soldiers' hearts even if they fire on you and kill you. Let them kill five thousand, ten thousand, twenty thousand—they are our brothers and we will welcome them. We will prove that blood is more powerful than the sword."[128]

General Alexander Haig, Supreme Allied Commander of NATO during the Carter administration, said of the ouster of the Shah:

> "It didn't take long for the world to realize that the Shah was an enlightened liberal next to the bloody reactionary regime that followed, and which executed more people in three months than the Shah had done in thirty years."[129]

Mohammad Reza Shah Pahlavi's jet was hardly airborne on January 16, 1979, before Iranian newspapers screamed, *"Shah Raft!"* or "The Shah is Gone." He had ruled over Iran from the age of twenty-one; now, he was leaving in ignominious defeat, not knowing he would never return. Former Iranian Ambassador Dr. Ahmed Tehrani summed up the

Shah's feelings, perhaps better than anyone, when he said, "The Shah never, ever believed the United States would let him down. He believed Russia would do it, he believed the British would do it, but not the United States or France."[130]

In an interview with Houchang Nahavandi during a trip to Poland and Czechoslovakia in early 1978, the Shah was certain he was "irremovable." When asked what would happen to him should the US change its policy and forsake the monarch, Pahlavi answered, "The Americans will never abandon me."[131] That assumption would prove to be unalterably false.

Perhaps it was as Ardeshir Zahedi suggested: The Shah didn't think the radical cleric Khomeini could command change in Iran. He was certainly not the most influential ayatollah at the time; that honor belonged to the leader of the Shi'ite world, Ayatollah Shairatmadari. Though not altogether pleased with the Shah, Shariatmadari was not clamoring for a regime change. Neither he nor the leading cleric in Najaf, Ayatollah Kho'ei, was pushing for the Shah's ouster.[132]

This was not the case with the ultra-radical Khomeini. A declassified document from the secretary of state to the US Embassy in Iran detailed the situation:

> There are...all strains of religious leadership...Those religious elements presently dominating the Iranian scene both organizationally and ideologically are committed to violence and obstruction as tools for attaining power. Ayatollah Khomeini has specifically called for the Shah's violent removal, and some of his followers in Isfahan and Shiraz have openly called for the death of the Shah...Moderates such as Ayatollah Shariatmadari do not at this time feel capable of opposing Khomeini openly, though they reportedly still work for moderation within the religious movement... Whatever the Shah wishes to do next, he must meet head-on the violent challenges to both his government and Iran's

social fabric...Many Iranians believe the Shah is not acting forcefully enough...Some believe the Americans forced him to be restrained.[133]

Khomeini, as the world would soon see, boasted an underground network of fanatical mullahs, i.e., Ayatollah Mahmoud Taleghani and Mohammad Behesti, who favored regime change. Khomeini's calls for an end to the Shah's reign were taken up by bands of radical hooligans who were only too happy to carry out the Ayatollah's wishes. One wonders if Khomeini and his followers felt they had the backing of the US in their determination to destroy the monarchy.

Shapour Bakhtiar, who was at the helm of the provisional government left by the Shah, pled with Ayatollah Ruhollah Khomeini to delay his arrival in Tehran for several months so that civil order might be restored. The determined Ayatollah adamantly refused. Gary Sick's description of the Ayatollah fit him perfectly:

> Khomeini was the arch-type of the medieval prophet emerging from the desert with a fiery vision...His God was a harsh and vengeful deity...demanding an eye and tooth of retribution... Khomeini's philosophy had great tolerance for pain, human suffering, and political chaos, but no tolerance for opposition. His opponents were satanic, and the remedy was to "cut off their arms."[134]

Given its association with Israel, it would not have been beyond the realm of possibility for Iran to seek the help of the Mossad in stopping Khomeini. However, Uri Lubrani, who was stationed in Iran in the 1970s, has suggested that Israel might have considered backing a military takeover in Iran, but the US was slow to support such a move. Perhaps, like the United States, Israel had chosen to take a "wait and see" attitude regarding the situation in Tehran.

With the Shah's departure Khomeini's Paris entourage made hurried preparations to get the Imam back to Tehran. Having decided against the use of an Iranian airliner for fear of being attacked by the Shah's air force, a jumbo jet was chartered from Air France for a mere pittance of $3 million dollars plus an undisclosed sum to cover the insurance premium for the aircraft. The crew that manned the jumbo jet was comprised totally of volunteers.[135]

One of Khomeini's closest advisors, and coincidentally a naturalized US citizen, Ebrahim Yazdi, was aboard the jet that carried the triumphant Khomeini back to Iran. According to Yazdi:

> "The civil airline in Iran arranged independently a flight from Tehran to Paris to bring Khomeini back. They called it the Revolutionary Flight. But we didn't trust them, because we knew that there was a possibility that the army might attack, or the army might force the aeroplane to land in some remote area. So, we didn't accept that. Instead, we chartered an Air France plane. In addition to that, we took with us more than a hundred and twenty journalists—reporters from all over the world. I have to confess that we took them as a human shield, so to speak. We knew that nobody would dare to shoot at such a plane, with so many reporters from so many nationalities."[136]

Fear of an attack on the Air France jet prompted Khomeini to leave behind his wife, daughter, and grandchildren, as well as the wives and children of those in his inner circle. Before departing Paris the Ayatollah thanked the French government for allowing him to remain in France. Perhaps subtly, he was thanking the French for allowing him to wage an unhindered war against the Shah of Iran and to topple his government. Were the truth known, it is more likely that the government of France was happy to see the backside of his turban.

On the plane with Khomeini was Peter Jennings, a young ABC reporter. During the flight Jennings is said to have asked the Imam, "What do you feel [about returning to Iran]?" Khomeini replied, "Nothing." That was a strange answer from a man whose life had been consumed in recent years with the overthrow of the Shah and a triumphant return to Iran.

The Air France jet that bore the Grand Ayatollah Ruhollah Khomeini touched down in Tehran at precisely 9:33 AM on February 1, 1979, following a brief discussion on whether or not the airport should be reopened. It had been closed for five days due to demonstrations and riots. Lt. General Azarbarzin received a phone call from the air force chief instructing him to open the facility. Azarbarzin asked on whose authority he was to proceed, and was told it was at the direction of Prime Minister Bakhtiar. When the lieutenant general questioned the order, Bakhtiar personally ordered him to reopen the airport.[137]

The Imam, who had slept for much of the five-and-a-half-hour flight, was ending an exile that had lasted more than fourteen years. There exists a photograph of Khomeini while on that historic Air France flight. While traveling through the night, Khomeini sat off by himself in a comfortable, first-class seat. The surviving photograph shows the Imam in a moment of self-satisfied meditation. A deep inner joy appears to emanate from his face. At this moment, Ayatollah Khomeini was probably savoring the approaching moment when his life-long aspirations were finally to be realized.

In the photograph his eyes have a distant look, as if he is peering into the past or maybe into the future. He is 78-years-old. He appears venerable, but by no means vulnerable. His trademark black turban sits atop his head, his visage is distinguished by a flowing white beard, and his dark eyes highlighted by thick eyebrows are fierce and piercing. The Imam's lips are pursed in a private smile, and his hands lie quietly in his lap, gracing the folds of his long robe. Perhaps he realized that, at last, his deal with the devil was about to produce his date with destiny.

The photographer captured a moment of calm for the imam before the storm of frenzied public adulation broke upon him. Khomeini was now ready to receive his triumphant welcome and lead an Islamic revolution that would shake the entire world. He stepped off the plane surrounded by his entourage and knelt to kiss the soil of Iran. Some say that his welcoming committee boasted several US officials.

There is a certain irony in the fact that Khomeini, despiser of all things American, the man who had referred to President Jimmy Carter as "the vilest man on earth,"[138] was hustled into a Chevrolet Blazer for the trip to his first destination—the Behesht-e-Zahra Cemetery, the burial place of ten to twelve thousand who died during the revolution. According to a BBC report,[139] some five million Iranians lined the streets from the airport to the cemetery. Not even fifty thousand Iranian police could control the massive crowd. They were so overjoyed at the sight of their returning Imam that, again, Khomeini had to be rescued by a US-made air force helicopter in order to complete his pilgrimage to the cemetery. Occupying the helicopter with Khomeini was the Shah's Commander-in-Chief of the Air Force General Amir Hussein Rabii.

In the days that followed, Khomeini's progress was hampered by the disarray in the Iranian military following the Shah's departure. General David Ivry explained the confusion in the ranks:

> "Some of them were not secure and they sent their families abroad…with money…deep inside they were afraid… [After Khomeini's arrival.] They were called to a meeting and told, "You are fine. Stay in your positions." Everyone went home calmly, and then they were caught in their homes."[140]

The first act of the Ayatollah was to declare in no uncertain terms that the caretaker government of Bakhtiar was illegal. "If they continue," said Khomeini, "we will arrest them. I will shut their mouths. And I will appoint a government with the support of the Iranian people."[141]

Ambassador William Sullivan, on the front line in Tehran, could see signs of increasing instability. He felt the State Department was not heeding his information until long after it was presented. Sullivan was not surprised, therefore, when Khomeini seized control of the government on February 11, 1979. When Sullivan received a call from the White House on February 12, giving him the go-ahead to encourage the Iranian military to keep the revolution in check with the use of deadly force, if necessary, it is said, "Sullivan declined, using colorful language."[142]

Ayatollah Khomeini had returned to bring his radical Islamic rebellion to Iran. He believed this was the first step of his revolution sweeping across the world. Khomeini's one, fervent desire was to see the West, led by the United States, submit to the grip of radical Islam. Soon, he felt the "illegitimate" state of Israel would be decimated. He was certain all other religions would yield to his version of Islam. Then a Muslim theocracy would be established in every corner of the world. This was the Grand Ayatollah Khomeini's vision of destiny. He informed the Iranian people, "This is not the final victory, but only a prelude to victory." He called upon the army to destroy its new, sophisticated US weapons, and for the people to strike and demonstrate against the Bakhtiar regime.

The day following Khomeini's arrival in Tehran, the Israeli Embassy was ransacked and set afire. Several dozen Palestinians were among the rioters, who breached the walls of the building, tore the Israeli flag from its mooring on the top floor, and burned it. Cries of "Death to Israel! Israel get out!" could be heard from the mob. The Palestinian standard was then raised from the roof of the mission.[143] Israel's friends in the Shah's government turned a blind eye. General Yitzak Segev, military attaché in Iran, called on a friend in the Iranian air force to afford them a military cargo plane to fly to safety. The contact, General Rabii, responded:

> "The Revolutionary Guards control the airport and I cannot help you. But if you find a plane, please evacuate me as well."[144]

What influence Rabii may have had with Khomeini was short-lived. He was tried for "corruption on earth; war on God and the people of God; actions designed to weaken the country's independence and security; shaking the foundations of the country's system of government; defiling all that is sacred, whether religious or national, to the Muslim people of Iran and the world." Rabii was executed by firing squad on April 8, 1979. During the first year under Khomeini's rule, the Iranian armed forces saw their ranks dwindle by one hundred thousand troops. Even as Iran's military might faded,

Saddam Hussein was building his Iraqi army and stockpiling military supplies at an alarming rate.

It was left up to Mossad in Tehran to try to protect those Israeli attachés who remained in the city. Eliezer Tsafrir, a Mossad agent stationed in Iran recalled: "Israel was now the infidel enemy ("the Little Satan") and [I] had to evacuate thirteen hundred Israeli engineers, agronomists, and businessmen from Iran before they fell into the hands of the mullahs...[The Iranians] intended to shoot first and ask questions later."[145]

Samuel Segev wrote of the harrowing escape from Iran of the thirty-three last remaining Israelis, including General Yitzhak Segev, Ambassador Harmelin, former Knesset member Mordechai Ben-Porat, and El Al employees:

> The Israelis left the Hilton Hotel for the airport in a bus plastered with pictures of Khomeini. Two sixteen-year-olds, armed with Kalashnikov rifles and trained in Palestinian camps in Syria, served as bodyguards. Other armed youngsters...members of "the Imam Khomeini's Guards," subjected the Israeli passports to minute examination. They arrested the El Al and Kour Corporation representatives and one Israeli security man, charging that they were ...Iranian Jews who were forbidden to leave the country. Harmelin... would not leave Tehran without the three men. After five hours...and at the personal intervention of...a leading member of the religious establishment, the three prisoners were freed and allowed to leave Iran. The Israelis took off on a Pan Am Flight to Frankfurt, arriving in Israel in a special El Al plane...bringing an end to twenty-five years of Israeli cooperation with the [Shah].[146]

— 10 —

AYATOLLAH ARRIVES — CHAOTIC CONSEQUENCES

"We do not worship Iran, we worship Allah. For patriotism is another name for paganism. I say let this land [Iran] burn. I say let this land go up in smoke, provided Islam emerges triumphant in the rest of the world."
—AYATOLLAH RUHOLLAH KHOMEINI

SOON AFTER HIS ARRIVAL IN TEHRAN and contrary to his in-exile rhetoric about retiring to Qom, Khomeini commandeered the Refah girls' school as his nerve center and appointed Mehdi Bazargan to head a new "Provisional Government." Bazargan, who had been incarcerated several times by the Shah, had met in late 1978 with a contingent from the US Human Rights Committee. The Iranian proffered five points that both he and the Ayatollah felt essential to the future of Iran:

✧ The Shah must leave the country.

✧ The Shah must be replaced by a Regency Council.

❖ A liberal government acceptable to all must be established.

❖ Iran's current parliament must be disbanded.

❖ Iran must be allowed to have national elections.

The US committee agreed to Bazargan's stipulations but balked when mention was made of removing all references to the Shah from the country's constitution. In a later meeting the group also insisted upon the restoration of law and order within Iran. What no one was willing to admit was that only Khomeini could stop the run-away train of Islamic revolutionary fervor that gripped the country. In the end, the Ayatollah flatly rejected the proposals by the US, calling them a "joke, a compromise destined to abort the revolution."[147]

What would later come to light was that Bazargan and members of his government, including Ebrahim Yazdi and Amir-Entezam, had met secretly on two occasions with US officials Robert Clayton Ames and George Cave (CIA), Bruce Laingen (Chargé d'Affaires), and Ron Smith (an energy specialist). Minutes of meetings taken from the US Embassy would be used to damage the reputation of Bazargan, Yazdi, and Amir-Entezam, and would ultimately end in their being targeted by Khomeini's extremists.

Clark Clifford, former Secretary of State under Lyndon Johnson, had somehow managed to establish communications with Khomeini insiders and confirmed that initially Khomeini planned to leave the determination of Iran's future up to the people. Bazargan's appointment was a shrewd political move by Khomeini, as it gave a false sense of security to the moderates in Iran whose vision of an "Islamic republic" may not have quite meshed with those of the Imam. (Lt. General Shapur Azarbarzin, former vice-chief of the Iranian air force during the early days of the revolution, related to me that the United States was committed to supporting Bazargan rather than Shapour Baktiar, the Shah's choice for prime minister.)[148]

The moderate Bazargan's government would be used to quietly pacify the military and create a rapport with Khomeini. Meanwhile, defections from the military were occurring at an alarming rate, and ultimately Chief of Staff General Gharabaghi declared that the armed forces had become a neutral factor. Bazargan's Provisional Government was ecstatic with the general's announcement.

As might have been expected, one of Bazargan's early moves as the new leader was to sever all ties with Israel, although the Israeli government attempted to establish a working relationship with Khomeini's regime. Though both countries espoused different ideologies and outlooks, it was a move designed to sooth the leftist revolutionaries, who felt Israel was a protégé of "The Great Satan," and the mullahs, who felt that Israel's very existence was offensive to Islam.

Khomeini was shrewd enough to couch his aversion to Israel in religious terms. He simply declared Israel a "cancer" that had to be removed, a usurper in the Middle East that despised the Koran and would destroy the Muslim holy book.[149] The fanatical new regime occupying Tehran saw Israel as "an illegitimate state and a usurper of Muslim land,"[150] and was "by its very nature against Islam and the Koran."[151] Khomeini's ultra-fanatical mullahs and clerics lectured that it was the responsibility of every Muslim to challenge Israel. By August of 1980 Iran's foreign ministry office demanded an end to the export of oil to nations that supported the Jewish state.

The truth is, both Israel and Iran are countries with vastly differing ideologies that will never mesh. For Jews and Christians, there is only one answer: the long-awaited coming of the Messianic Age. For Muslims too there is only one solution to this age-old problem: a worldwide caliphate with all inhabitants bowing a knee to Allah. Because these Islamic extremists believe their caliph will return due to a cataclysmic war, it is critical, therefore, for Israel to call attention to the probability that as soon as Iran's mad mullahs have full access to nuclear weapons, not only Israel but the world as a whole will face an imminent attack.

In spite of the Ayatollah's rabid pronouncements against Israel, just months later the Israelis returned a number of tanks the Shah had sent to be repaired. Soon thereafter Ahmed Kashani visited Israel. Kashani, whose father, the Grand Ayatollah Abol Qassem Kashani, had a vital part to play in the nationalization of the Iranian oil industry in 1951, flew to Tel Aviv to discuss arms purchases and possible military teamwork between Iran and Israel. It seems that clandestine meetings between Israel and her Arab neighbors in the Middle East were acceptable, as long as it was kept under the radar. At one point Khomeini accepted a large shipment of arms from Israel. (Being supposedly unaware of the origin of the weapons, the Ayatollah could adopt a "laissez-faire" attitude.)

Khomeini felt it was his divine duty to advance the cause of Islam. "Islam," he said, "is not peculiar to a country...Islam has come for humanity."[152] His calling was to secure Iran for Islam and then spread the revolution. His ideology was one of world dominance, and his fanaticism strained ties with his Arab neighbors.

Even as Khomeini reassured the Shah's military leaders that they had nothing to fear from his newly-established regime, the slaughter began. US General Dutch Huyser had already departed Iran at this point, but he would tell me later that he was grief-stricken because he felt he had betrayed the Iranian generals. According to one observer:

> "Of the eighty top generals, more than seventy were tortured and executed, along with hundreds of lower-ranking officers. By one estimate almost 75 percent of the Shah's senior officers were killed by the end of summer. The Bakhtiar government protested these often-grisly executions...The executions, coupled with the appointment of mullahs as military prosecutors, totally demoralized the military and sent a signal that the real power lay with Khomeini and his Revolutionary Guards. The PG was equally powerless to stop the purge and arrest of some 15,000 to 30,000 civilian members of the Shah's regime."[153]

General Yitzhak Segev sadly recalled the mass executions of army generals following Khomeini's arrival in Tehran:

"Some succeeded in running away and reaching America...most of them were executed...The executions were merciless. They were brutal, not only for revenge purposes, but because...they were preventing the option of revolution against themselves [Khomeini's regime.] The first four were executed while I was still there...[the executions] were broadcast live on television. Then, one at a time they killed hundreds of generals...each general had a carpet placed beneath him...before he was shot in the head...They executed the generals because they were connected to the old regime, and because they were a threat to the new regime... There was total purification."[154]

One of those executed by Khomeini's kangaroo court was former Prime Minister Amir-Abbas Hoveyda. Under Hoveyda's leadership in the mid-1960s Iran had filled the vacuum left by departing British troops from Persian Gulf bases by establishing two armored divisions that were outfitted with US-made Patton M-60 tanks. He was also responsible for major expansions of the Iranian air force and navy. Hoveyda, who had been placed under house arrest by Pahlavi, was a sitting target for Khomeini's revolutionary forces. Having been the Shah's prime minister for thirteen years, Hoveyda was a senior official in the monarch's government and, therefore, a prized catch. He was dragged out, tried, and executed in short order.

In his book detailing his tenure as president of France, Giscard d'Estaing wrote of his attempt to persuade Khomeini not to execute Hoveyda:

"I decided to intervene personally with the Ayatollah Khomeini...I asked someone to bring him a message. Some Iranian sources told me that after he received my letter... Khomeini wrote a letter to the prime minister. In his note he says: 'His Excellency the President V. Giscard d'Estaing... has asked me to prevent the execution of Mr. Hoveyda. To the request of the French president, I would ask you to delay any action in this way.' Unfortunately, the revolutionary court prepared its work very quickly, and Mr. Hoveyda was executed three days later, on April 7,…after he was interviewed by a journalist from the French television…Two days later the Tehran revolutionary court met during the night and allowed the execution of eleven persons from the old regime only half an hour after the verdict."[155]

Senators Jacob Javits and Henry Jackson, staunch supporters of Pahlavi, endorsed a resolution criticizing Khomeini's new government for its violent executions of those associated with the Shah's rule.

One can only wonder why a nation of radical Islamists with no thought of "human rights" was preferable to the regime of the insecure and ailing Shah. Although the leaders of the Islamic revolution boasted that between 60,000 and 100,000 had perished as martyrs for their cause, the more realistic number of deaths in Iran, as reported by Said Arjomand in *The Turban for the Crown: The Islamic Revolution in Iran*, was "approximately three thousand in the whole of Iran." Arjomand calculated the number from September 1978 until the fall of the monarchy in February 1979.[156]

Shortly after assuming the role of leader in Iran, Khomeini approved the erection of a training center on the site of what was to have been Empress Farah University for Girls. Manzarieh Park would become the training ground for Iran's elite Revolutionary Guards and for Shi'ite Muslim fundamentalist terrorists. Although Khomeini later banned the training of Yasser Arafat's terrorists in Iranian facilities, he apparently had no such qualms about using North Koreans and Syrians as trainers. The camp was also the site where the fifteen- to eighteen-year-olds that would become the first line of attack against Saddam Hussein's troops were instructed. Especially singled out were those students who had flooded back into Iran from the US to serve as volunteers under the revered Ayatollah Khomeini. They were often required to recount the decadence found in America, the decadence that it was thought would bring about its downfall by the sword of Islam.

The Ayatollah espoused and quoted the tenet of Islam that declared, "Islam says: Whatever good there is exists thanks to the sword and in the shadow of the sword! People cannot be made obedient except with the sword! The sword is the key to Paradise, which can be opened only for the Holy Warriors! There are hundreds of other [Qur'anic] psalms and Hadiths [sayings of the Prophet] urging Muslims to value war and to fight. Does all this mean that Islam is a religion that prevents men from waging war? I spit upon those foolish souls who make such a claim."[157] In Khomeini's Iran, training "with the sword" began at an early age.

By 1985 Khomeini had overseen the establishment of fifteen terrorist training facilities in the country, including commandeering the ritzy resort hotel near Qom. The Afghans, Arabs, Southeast Asians, Irish, Americans, and Lebanese, as well as women terrorists trained in these facilities were slated to become "the spearhead of the Islamic conquest of the world."[158]

Meanwhile, back in Washington and just after Khomeini's return to Iran, President Carter's straddle-the-fence diplomacy had permeated the administration. Secretary of State Cyrus Vance urged the president to reach out to the Ayatollah. This suggestion was supported by Ambassador William Sullivan and by Vice President Walter Mondale.

Egyptian journalist Mohamed Heikal wrote of Vance's attempts to contact Khomeini's Revolutionary Government to reassure them of four critical directives:

✧ The Shah's reign was at an end.

✧ The US and Iran must remain
   allied against the Soviets.

✧ The Iranian Revolution and Khomeini's seizure of
   power were recognized by the American people.

✧ The US wished to open a door
   of dialogue with Iran.

Upon hearing Vance's proposal, Khomeini, with Hafiz's communiqués regarding the Shah's arrival in the US in hand, asked: "You mean he didn't talk about the Shah's arrival in the United States?"[159]

Vance would later write that the administration was erroneously charged with the downfall of the Shah because of the president's human rights agenda.[160]

Dr. Majidi talked to me of his disappointment in the administration's stance on Iran:

> "Even if someone would have told me that Americans are willing to help Khomeini and his group, I would have said, 'Certainly, it's impossible.' American long-term and short-term interests both require that America stand behind the Shah, behind Iran...That was my idea, my philosophy, and my thinking; and I think was the same as the Shah's...You never forget the [New Year's] speech of Carter...he talked of stability in the area of turmoil of the region. I think he was believing that; but he didn't have the guts to implement it and present it...It's only how brave and how courageous to make the hard decision. Carter to my mind was not that person, and he didn't have the confidence in what he's doing and what he must do."[161]

Italian journalist Oriana Fallaci interviewed Khomeini shortly after the end of the Islamic revolution in Iran. It was she who wrote: "[The] art of invading and conquering and subjugating [is] the only art at which the sons of Allah have always excelled... Islamism is the new Nazi-Fascism. With Nazi-Fascism, *no compromise* is possible. No hypocritical tolerance. And those who do not understand this simple reality are feeding the suicide of the West."[162] Excerpts from her interview with Khomeini ran in the *New York Times* in October 1979. Fallaci, who came to believe "the Western world is in danger of being engulfed by radical Islam," wrote of her encounter with the Imam:

It did not take long to realize that in spite of his quiet appearance he represented the Robespierre or the Lenin of something which would go very far and would poison the world. People loved him too much. They saw in him another Prophet. Worse: a God...Do believe me: everything started with Khomeini. Without Khomeini, we would not be where we are. What a pity that when pregnant with him, his mother did not choose to have an abortion.[163]

—11—

A CHESS GAME
PLAYED WITH LIVES

*"Man is a strange animal. He generally cannot read the
handwriting on the wall until his back is up against it."*
—ADLAI E. STEVENSON

SLOWLY BUT SURELY KHOMEINI BEGAN TO MOVE his hand-picked mullahs into place in
the moderate transition government. Fundamentalists began to seize power
more openly. Dr. Parviz Mina related to me how shocked the National Front,
the Tudeh (Communist) Party, and the Marxists were in Iran when they realized the mullahs had used them as a way to achieve their aims. They were
even more shocked to realize they had been bested by a cleric. Khomeini's
radical revolutionary forces exiled or murdered many of the members of
these groups and completely seized the reins of the country.[164]

Had the Tudeh Party leaders had access to a declassified US State
Department document, it would have shown what Khomeini's intentions
were. The Ayatollah "expressed his conviction that the young malcontents
who today claim communism will tomorrow rally to the Islamic government. Even supposing those who demonstrate with communist slogans are

Marxists, they do not constitute a force in the face of thirty million Persians who are in revolt in the name of Islam."[165]

A March 1979 referendum gave the Iranian people only two basic choices for which to vote: Yes, they wished an Islamic Republic; or no, they did not wish an Islamic Republic. Overwhelmingly, the people voted yes, although few Iranians knew what Khomeini meant by "Islamic Republic." According to the Shah's later assessment of the referendum:

> "It was a grotesque farce. People over the age of fifteen voted. A green ballot meant one vote for the 'Islamic Republic' and a red indicated a no-vote. Since this public election was held under the surveillance of the Guards of the Revolution, is it surprising that 98 percent of the voters cast green ballots? The Iranian media announced that the 'Islamic Republic' had been voted on by approximately 23 million Iranians...nearly 18 million people were less than fifteen years of age...that would make at least five million votes too many...and Iran...returned to the Middle Ages."[166]

Many political organizations inside Iran protested the election on the grounds that "it did not provide any opportunity for the people to express their ideas about the government's reform."[167] The new constitution drawn up by Khomeini's emerging Islamic Republican Party was vastly different from that proposed by the moderates. The core of the resulting document endowed Khomeini as the ruler of Iran for life, or *velayat-e faqih* (guardianship of the jurisprudent.) The rule of law, of course, was Islam. Everything was permitted except when it was contrary to Islamic law; and almost everything, presumably, was contrary.

In a confidential memo from Chargé d'Affaires Bruce Laingen in Tehran to the State Department, he reported a meeting with Tehran lawyer, A. E. Lahidji. Laingen related some interesting observations regarding Khomeini:

> Khomeini currently controls the masses in Iran, and there is little moderate intellectuals...can do to check Khomeini's

creation of a totally Islamic state. Khomeini...is becoming increasingly isolated and surrounded by "yes" men. Most of his advisors are weak...or opportunists...Khomeini has changed since [Lahidji] visited him in Paris. At that time Khomeini told the moderates that the clergy should stay out of politics. Lahidji said he and several other lawyers...had written the original draft constitution along Western lines... the religious leaders [in Qom] objected to the secular draft... and when Khomeini returned the draft to the lawyers several weeks later, it had been changed to give it a more Islamic flavor...Lahidji felt that Khomeini was behind the much more Islamic constitution...and, in particular, behind the idea of *velayat-e-faqih*. Absolute power corrupts absolutely, and Khomeini has apparently decided he must run the country himself...Khomeini has alienated all the moderate groups... Few clergymen are willing to make an open break with Khomeini and face charges of weakening revolutionary unity.[168]

By summer's end in 1979 Khomeini's true vision began to be revealed. Far from establishing the enlightened, democratic government anticipated by some US State Department employees, Khomeini, now the supreme leader of Iran, created a medieval Islamic totalitarian state controlled by the mullahs and ayatollahs. It was defined by intolerance, censorship, revenge, tyranny, vile torture, and executions. Khomeini's murderous attacks against the Shah's former officials had spread to include ethnic and religious cleansing. Compared to Khomeini's regime, the Shah had been a benevolent ruler!

Her Majesty Farah Pahlavi talked with me about the human rights issue:

"What happened to those who cared so much for human rights? How come when the Shah left, the Iranian people didn't have any rights anymore? What happened to the women?...Flogging, stoning, amputations, insults, all the killing of not only women, children, workers, intellectuals,

and whoever even comes outside to demonstrate peacefully
for their salaries…the head of the bus drivers, they took him
and they cut his palms…They took his family to jail, his wife
and his children of three or four in the jail. There is oppression, which exists in the name of religion in Iran. What happened to those who cared?"[169]

The horror for which no one seemed to be prepared engulfed Iran. The
Shah was not the only Iranian to flee the country; he was joined by multitudes of his fellow countrymen. Europe and the United States were the
recipients of many of these well-educated and technically skilled émigrés.
They fled from what would become a massacre of vicious proportions and a
reign of terror the likes of which the Iranian people had never seen nor imagined under the Shah. Not only was Iran gripped by the iron fist of murder
and mayhem, it was stripped of an entire generation of highly trained and
competent young men and women—all at the whim of a fanatical old man
bent on revenge.

Rule by "scapegoat" seemed to be the order of the day under Khomeini.
When his government or authority was challenged, he looked for a scapegoat. His first were the Kurds in Northern Iran. They were avowed enemies
of the Ayatollah and his Islamic Republic, and open season was declared
against the Kurdish population.

Khomeini, though outwardly advocating a coalition with other Arab
countries in the vicinity, in reality wanted only to dominate through his
own brand of radicalism. In order to begin his march beyond the boundaries of Iran, however, Khomeini had to first subdue the Persian influence and
replace it with a maniacal devotion to fundamentalist Islam. The Ayatollah
knew too that he would have to expunge all traces of Western influence in
Iran.

Although Khomeini was initially ambivalent about ties with the US, the
fear of US intervention and the return of the Shah plagued the Iranian people. That fear was, of course, fueled by the clerics. It was within the context
of this domestic chaos that the death knell for the administration sounded.

Empowered by his assault on the Shah and the success of his Islamic Revolution, Khomeini had set forth to spread his particular brand of Arab nationalism throughout the Middle East. Next on his list was Saddam Hussein's Ba'athist regime. His tactic of engaging the people had worked in Iran; why would it not work again in Iraq? The Ayatollah had begun to exhort the Iraqi people to rebel against Hussein's government. Iranian terrorists had attacked principal Iraqi leaders. Then Hussein invaded Iran.

Khomeini saw the Iraq invasion as the perfect vehicle to bring the Ba'athist regime to its knees. He was forced to repair relations with other Persian Gulf states, reach out to the Europeans, and even contemplate talks with the dreaded "Great Satan." It was a setback to his hopes of uniting the Arab world under the banner of his Islamic revolution. His only real success was the export of Hezbollah to Lebanon, and even that was tied more to the destruction of Israel than to a globe-encircling Arab state. Khomeini firmly believed Israel was simply a diversion instituted by the West to keep Muslims from uniting as one.

Lured by the turmoil in Iran, seduced by visions of power, and backed by other Persian Gulf regimes, Hussein was determined to conquer his equally oil-rich neighbor. Like so many others, Hussein may have thought the chaotic take-over in Iran, the execution of so many of the military hierarchy, and Khomeini's lack of experience in conducting warfare, would open the door to a swift and decisive victory for the Iraqis. He was as wrong as those who thought Khomeini was only interested in spiritual matters. Khomeini rallied the troops in Iran and somehow produced an effective war machine to repel the Iraqis.

It seemed that nearly the entire world sided with Saddam Hussein against Iran. In Iraq's corner were Saudi Arabia and Kuwait, which infused Iraq's coffers with billions in loans and grants. Support came primarily from the Gulf States that viewed Iran as the greater danger. Also involved in furnishing arms and other war materiel to Hussein were Egypt, Jordan, the United States, France, the USSR, and the PLO. Iran's backing came from Syria, North Korea, Libya, and China…mostly in the form of missiles.

It took two long years of death and destruction before the UN Security Council felt it incumbent to seek troop withdrawals. It would be another five years before questions of chemical warfare used by Hussein against Iran's troops and civilian population would arise.

Khomeini's newly-instituted "Government of God" failed to draw the majority of the Arab world to his side; in reality, the opposite was true: Iran became abhorrent and friendless, especially in the Gulf region, and squandered its most productive resource—oil revenues—by slowing oil production. At the same time, Saddam Hussein was taking advantage of the chaotic situation in Iran to bolster his relationship with the US. There are those who believe the US may have subtly encouraged the Iran-Iraq conflict because of what it surmised to be the benefits of such an encounter. Khomeini, who had outwardly shunned both Washington and Tel Aviv, was suddenly faced with the dilemma of how to hold off an invasion by Saddam Hussein without much-needed spare parts and arms from both the US and Israel.

After eight long and bloody years, on August 20, 1988, an embittered Khomeini agreed to the UN Security Council Resolution for an immediate ceasefire. In the aftermath, nothing was resolved between the two nations. Besides the horrific loss of human life, the toll to achieve this impasse was a cost of hundreds of billions of dollars and the disruption and wreckage of the oil fields in both countries. One major outcome of the war, however, was to produce a growing alliance between Iran and Syria and a slackening of the relationship between Khomeini and Arafat's PLO.

During those eight years of warfare between Iran and Iraq, statisticians place the death toll on both sides at seven hundred thousand to one million people, most of them Iranians. Baghdad resorted to the use of chemical weapons against the Kurds and Iranian troops, while Tehran conscripted children to act as human minesweepers in advance of Iranian troops.

Not having learned his lesson from the disastrous war with Iran, it took only two years for Saddam Hussein to again accost a neighbor—Kuwait. On August 2, 1990, Hussein's army invaded its neighbor and quickly seized Kuwait's rich oilfields. Tehran took advantage of Iraq's invasion of Kuwait to remind Washington and the Arab world that Iraq, not Iran, was the enemy in the region.

From the moment Ayatollah Ruhollah Khomeini stepped from the plane onto Iranian soil in 1978 and on April 1, 1979, (April Fools day) declared his Islamic Republic he had given little thought to Israel. Instead, he was emboldened and determined to begin the spread of fanatical Islam using a network of terrorist organizations. According to the Council for Foreign Relations, today Iran supports such proxy groups as Hamas and Palestinian Islamic Jihad[170]; and Brookings Institution reports that another sub-contractor, Hezbollah in Lebanon, has been responsible for killing more Americans than any other single global terrorist group.[171] These fanatical Muslims are, thanks in large part to Iran, parked on the borders of Israel—Hamas in Gaza, Hezbollah in southern Lebanon, and the Muslim Brotherhood in Egypt.

Iranian officials deny, of course, that they support terrorist groups; but that is a matter of semantics. What the Western world calls "terrorists," such as Hamas and Hezbollah, the Iranian hierarchy simply calls liberation movements. Iranian political analyst Hassan Abbasi addressed Iran's ties with Hezbollah. Referring to the group's agenda as "sacred," he said:

> If something can be done to terrorize and scare the camp of infidelity and the enemies of God and the people, such terror is sacred. This terrorism is sacred. Lebanon's Hezbollah was trained by these very hands. Pay attention! Do you see these hands? Hezbollah, Hamas, and Islamic Jihad were trained by these very hands.[172]

It seems that Mr. Abbasi was readily boasting of training the very terrorists who continue to threaten the security of Israel and the United States. He obviously does not comprehend Israel's patience and/or reluctance to further endanger its citizenry.

Hamas terrorists are akin to pesky hornets—they dive in, fire off a load of venom, pull back and declare it was all the fault of the person who got in the way of their stingers. Obviously Hamas has taken lessons from the insect in order to reach its major objective: Muslim control of a Palestine free of Jewish inhabitants. To achieve this goal, Hamas is intent on firing Iranian-supplied rockets deeper and deeper into Israeli territory.

Israel patiently swats at the invading rockets and desists from taking substantial military action against Iran's proxy, but eventually she must act before greater harm comes to her populace.

In June 2008, Israel and Hamas in Gaza agreed to a truce brokered under the leadership of then-President Hosni Mubarak. The ink wasn't even dry on the document before Hamas terrorists sent rockets flying into southern Israel.

Showing great restraint, the Israelis withheld retaliation for months. During the period that Israel's leaders honored the agreement Hamas fired 329 rockets and mortars into the beleaguered nation. Conversely, the Israelis boosted the quantity of goods distributed to Gaza. While the cease-fire was supposedly in effect, Israeli negotiators were working feverishly to secure the release of Gilad Shalit, an IDF soldier kidnapped by Hamas in 2006. The negotiations were foiled at every juncture by the demands from Hamas to increase the number of prisoners wanted in exchange for one Israeli captive. Gilad was released on October 18, 2011, after five years in captivity.

In December 2008 at the end of the so-called cease fire, Hamas began to launch hundreds of rockets and mortars into Israel. Louis Michel, European Commissioner for Development and Humanitarian Aid, said in an interview of the terrorist provocation:

> "At this time we have to also recall the overwhelming responsibility of Hamas. I intentionally say this here—Hamas is a terrorist movement and it has to be denounced as such."[173]

It didn't take long to determine that during the six-month cease-fire, Hamas was busy making upgrades to its tunnel system and smuggling Qassam and Grad rockets in readiness for the next round of attacks on Israel. The rocket launchers were secreted in populated areas in an attempt to prevent attacks by the much more humane Israeli military.

While the Israelis work diligently to prevent the deaths of civilians in the Gaza Strip, the leaders of Hamas seem not only unconcerned about the sufferings of the Gazans, they appear to take great delight in parading casualties before the media in blatant attempts to exploit them.

The general concensus among those who support Israel is that the country must be allowed to defend itself. Apparently Hamas has not learned its lesson—not now, and presumably not ever. In November 2012, after months of dodging Iranian rockets placed in the hands of Hamas terrorists, months of running for bomb shelters at the first wail of a siren, and living under constant danger, Israel again began a series of airstrikes aimed at rocket-launch sites. The world media immediately condemned the Israelis and took up the lament for the endangered Gazans. Little mention was made of the death and destruction on Israel's side of the border.

When another cease-fire brokered by Egypt and the US and agreed to by the Israeli and Gazan leaders went into affect on November 21, Hamas fired three additional rockets into Sderot, Israel, before celebrating its "victory" against Israel. Now that the smoke and dust has settled, the Gazans are again busily restoring and rebuilding the tunnel system between the Gaza Strip and Egypt. (It is likely that this latest cease-fire will have been broken by the time this book comes off the presses.)

Often thought to be a shaky and unstable system of moving goods between the two countries, the tunnel system is in actuality a sophisticated network with "high quality engineering and construction...some include electricity, ventilation, intercoms, and a rail system."[174] It is little wonder that arms and rockets are easily transported from Iran to Gaza via the underground system under the cover of darkness. Little has changed since Khomeini's death; Iran's leaders still want to wipe Israel from the map.

Once Khomeini seized the reins of power in Iran, Pandora's Box was flung open and the demon of terrorism was allowed to escape. As the biblical prophet Hosea predicted, the whirlwind had been unleashed. Islamic fanaticism has inarguably become one of the most important issues with which the West has to contend—topped only by Iran's nuclear ambitions. While once democracy had been sought by the multitudes in the Middle East as the panacea for all ills; now Islam appeals to the masses with its seemingly unlimited resources due to oil money, its global spread, and its message of world domination through intimidation. Khomeini's success against the Shah and the resulting Islamic revolution became a model for other terrorists worldwide.

In 1982 Iran scored a logistical victory when Revolutionary Guard troops were moved into Lebanon. When Israeli and US troops were forced to withdraw, as were the Italians and French, Lebanon was destined to become a hotbed of terrorist activities. Israel and America became the main targets of Syrian-backed and Iranian-funded Hezbollah. The plan: to wage war against Israel, America's staunchest ally in the Middle East. Iranian Major General Ataollah Saleh, declared, "The Americans will run away, leaving their illegitimate child [Israel] behind, and then Muslims will know what to do."[175] Riding the wave of Khomeini and his predecessors, the current president of Iran, Mahmoud Ahmadinejad, is utilizing every opportunity to snub the Western world and apparently edge closer to the chasm of nuclear conflagration.

—12—

THE DERRICK
VERSUS DEMOCRACY

"Islam is politics or it is nothing."
—AYATOLLAH RUHOLLAH KHOMEINI

ON JANUARY 20, 1981, RONALD WILSON REAGAN was sworn in as the fortieth president of the United States. As the newly-elected commander in chief completed his twenty-minute address to the crowd gathered in Washington, DC, the remaining fifty-two US hostages detained during the Carter administration were released after having spent 444 days in Iranian captivity.

As president, Reagan did not entirely sit out the 1980s Iran-Iraq war. A key calculation in the Iran-Contra scandal was the administration's willingness to provide arms to Iran that would be useful in waging the war against Iraq. There was also the calculation by the Reagan Administration that the price of oil could be manipulated so as to cause the fall of the Soviet Union. Manipulating the price of oil would also harm both Iraq and Iran who were heavily dependent upon oil revenues to continue financing the war against one other.

In his 1994 book, *Victory*, author Peter Schweizer documented a strategy that President Reagan and a few key advisers put in place in 1982. The strategy was designed "to attack the fundamental economic weaknesses of the Soviet system."[176] Schweizer based his argument on a review of national security decision directives of the time and on interviews he conducted with top Reagan administration aides, including Secretary of Defense Caspar Weinberger, Secretary of State George Schultz, and National Security Advisor John Poindexter.

In 1983, the Soviet Union's most important export was oil; it accounted for more than half of the Soviet hard currency.[177] Reagan's advisors, with the assistance of a secret Treasury Department report, calculated that if oil could be driven down from the 1983 price of $34 a barrel to approximately $20 a barrel, the US would benefit and the Soviet Union would lose. US energy costs would be lowered by approximately $71.5 billion, a transfer of income to US consumers amounting to 1 percent of the gross national product. Oil prices that much lower would act basically like a tax cut, with the resultant positive stimulation of the US economy.

Part of the plan was to convince Saudi Arabia and other Middle Eastern oil producing countries to increase output by about 2.7 million barrels a day, to a total of 5.4 million a day. The result would be a 40 percent drop in the world oil price. Every $1 change in the price of oil resulted in a $500 million to $1 billion impact on hard currency holdings for the Kremlin. These calculations formed the basis for a deal which Reagan's aides hammered out with the Saudis. Thrown into the formula was America's willingness to extend national security guarantees to the Saudis.[178]

Early in 1985, the oil deal was finalized in meetings between President Reagan and Saudi King Faud in the White House. In 1985, the Saudis increased their oil production from 2 million barrels a day to almost 9 million barrels a day. As Schweizer told the story, the results were apparent:

> In November 1985, crude oil sold at $30 per barrel; barely five months later, oil stood at $12. For Moscow, over $10 billion in valuable hard currency evaporated overnight, almost half its earnings. And the Soviet economy began breathing even more heavily.[179]

Reagan dealt a mortal economic blow to the Soviets. The move also made clear the oil mismanagement of the Carter Administration. Carter had been hamstrung by his inability to reverse high oil prices. The price of oil had been a drag on the US economy since the 1973 OPEC oil embargo and the painfully long gasoline lines of the Ford Administration. The Saudis, able to produce oil at a $1.50 cost per barrel, still made a handsome profit even at the lower price. Both Iran and Iraq protested the Saudi decision to increase oil production, to no avail. As a result, the two countries came to understand and appreciate how oil economics could be used as a political weapon, and as an exchange medium to bolster Iran's nuclear objectives.

Since 1992, Russia had been building Iran's nuclear reactor at Bushehr. With the decision at the end of 2005 to sell Iran $1 billion in TOR-1 anti-missile systems, Russia moved to strengthen its alliance with Iran. When Iran defied the EU-3 by resuming uranium processing at Isfahan in August 2005, the negotiations broke off. Russia surfaced to offer a solution that Iran could enrich uranium at a nuclear facility within Russia. This solution went counter to the desire of the Iranian regime to control "the full fuel cycle" within Iranian territory, but the offer showed Russia's desire to support Iran.

US diplomacy pushed the EU-3 and the IAEA to declare Iran "non-compliant" for its repeated refusal to run a nuclear program "transparent" to international inspection. At the end of November 2005, the IAEA once again postponed referring Iran to the United Nations Security Council, this time choosing to give the country more time to consider the Russian proposal and resume negotiations. Iran told the world that Russia's proposal was unacceptable, unless the Russians were willing to help them enrich uranium at nuclear facilities located in Iran. Still, as 2005 came to a close, few diplomats had any doubt that Russia was aligned with Iran, even as President Ahmadinejad stepped up his openly belligerent charges against Israel.

The game of chess was now well into middle game: Israel was becoming increasingly isolated. Would she have no choice but to launch a preemptive military attack on Iran, much as Israel had taken out Iraq's Osirak nuclear reactor in 1981? Given the distances involved and the degree to which Iran had decentralized and hardened its nuclear facilities, there was no assurance that a conventional attack by Israel's war planes would succeed this time. With Russia at Iran's side, how would these calculations change?

In 2005, Vladimir Putin saw an opportunity to do to America what had been done to the Soviet Union – using the same weapon, oil. Prices had spiked at over $55 a barrel, providing both Russia and Iran with windfall profits amounting to several hundred millions of dollars a day. The US had conveniently removed Saddam Hussein from power in 2003, effectively winning for Iran its 1980s war with Iraq. Now it was America's turn to fight a costly war on terrorism, this time in Iraq. Money to fight the Iraq war poured from the US Treasury. Iran could easily have rejected Russia as a foreign intruder, just as Iran rejected Great Britain and the United States after the fall of the Shah. Yet, that did not happen. Iran shared the Russian ambition to weaken the United States in the Middle East. That was enough for the Iranians to realize that an historic opportunity to embrace Russia, despite the past differences that lay at their feet.

With the United States fighting in Iraq, public opinion slipped at home and around the world. Moreover, this time US troops in Iraq would be cast in the uncomfortable role of Christian "crusaders": occupying a Muslim land. Vladimir Putin demonstrated that he had not lost the cunning he gained as a KGB officer. By turning the tables on America in Iraq, Putin behaved true to form: as a former communist who was still not happy that the Soviet Union lost the Cold War.

A close relationship with Iran gave Russia a substantial lock on world oil. Again, this was similar to the power and influence wielded by President Reagan in his close 1980s relationship with the Saudis. Moreover, the Iranian regime had never lost its nationalistic desire to increase influence in Iraq. Iran may have lost the 1980s war with Iraq, but many Iranians still savored the idea of seizing political control of Iraq, along with economic control over the huge oil and natural gas resources. Having seen the radical regime take hold in Iran and knowing that the religious clerics at the head of the regime saw the destruction of Israel as their destiny, the Russians knew they had a partner with whom they could undo the damage that had been done to them, starting with Afghanistan.

What was in the deal for Iran? Russia had all the nuclear know-how Iran would ever need. The Russians were more than happy to provide assistance, on terms Iran found acceptable. Moreover, the Russians and Iran had common enemies—Israel and America.

Russia never developed a strategic alliance with Israel which had just been a convenient dumping-ground for unwanted Russian Jews. At most, it could see some strategic value to playing Israel, almost as a pawn, in a game where Russia's real aim was to win favor with the Arabs and other Islamic nations of the Middle East. For both Iran and Russia, a world without Israel and without America would be a better place. What more was needed for a strategic alliance formed in Hell?

By the end of 2005, Russia and the United States had changed places: the United States was potentially overextended in Iraq, both politically and economically, as the Soviets had been in Afghanistan in the 1980s. Now, the Russians were positioned to exert a more firm influence in the Middle East, just as President Reagan had done in the 1980s. Russia planned to accomplish that with its influence through Iran, a radical Muslim ally with regional and worldwide ambitions of its own. Russia could help the radical Islamic Republic spread its fundamentalist revolution, so long as Russia remained in control.

Russia's goal was to wage against America the type of economic war that Reagan had waged against the Soviet Union. Overstretching economics had caused the Soviet Union to fall; now the United States would be drawn into a long and costly war against terrorism. Ultimately, America would have to be drawn in, if only to save Israel.

The world had watched as 19 hijackers cost America over 3,000 lives[180] and $1 trillion in damages after the 9/11 attack on the World Trade Center and the Pentagon. The recession which followed nearly cost George Bush his re-election, despite spectacular military victories in Afghanistan and Iraq. Watching this drama unfold, Russia saw strategic advantages to supporting Iran, the next likely enemy America would choose in the Middle East.

Reagan had defeated the Soviet Union by waging an oil war in which prices were lowered; Putin would defeat the US by waging an oil war in which prices were raised. Before Russia moved for final and complete victory against the United States, the Russian leadership had to calculate a strategy that would turn the oil tables completely on the United States. To advance this strategy, a political and economic partnership with Iran made all the sense in the world to Russia. The Russians calculated that if the price of oil were to go from $55 a barrel to a sustainable level of near $70 a barrel, the cost to the US would be approximately $65.7 billion a year. At this writing, the price of a barrel of light crude oil was fluctuating around the $100.00/ barrel price.

— 13 —

A TABLE SET WITH CHINA

"The oil can is mightier than the sword."
—SENATOR EVERETT DIRKSON

CHINA IS THE SLEEPING GIANT OF THE WORLD'S FUTURE ECONOMY. The country continues to emerge from a predominately rural population. While great pains are being taken to ease the restrictions imposed by the nation's Communist Central Planning, the country has been plagued by the inefficiencies and resource mismanagement typical of all government bureaucracies trying to control economic growth and development. Still, with over 1.3 billion people and a staggering 2004 increase of 9.5 percent growth in real gross domestic product (GDP) and a slide backward to a 7.6 percent GDP in 2012, China remains an economic powerhouse.

It is responsible for 40 percent of the growth in demand for oil worldwide since 2000. In 2011, China consumed 8.2 million barrels of oil per day[181], a number the Energy Information Administration of the US Department of Energy expects to hit 14.2 million barrels of oil per day by 2025.[182] These numbers are certain to increase.

By US standards, China's need for oil is still relatively small. Worldwide, approximately 85 million barrels of oil are consumed daily. The United States uses some 20 million barrels a day, roughly 25 percent of the total world consumption. Yet, in 2003, China surpassed Japan for the first time, becoming the world's second largest consumer of oil.

Like the United States, China imports most of its crude oil. In the United States, we today import approximately 60 percent of the oil we consume. This reflects our growing oil dependence on foreign countries. America's oil fortune has suffered a dramatic reversal from World War II, when US domestic production was depended upon to fuel the war machine of the Allied nations.

China is expected to continue importing 75 percent of its oil at least through year 2025. So, like the United States, it must establish trade relations with other countries to get the oil it needs for continued economic growth at home. Iran is the top choice on China's list as a potential partner from which to import oil. Moreover, the partnership works for Iran as well. China is willing to invest generously in the development of the Iranian oil fields. This is an important concession, given Iran's lack of capital to invest in developing its ample reserves of oil and natural gas.

Iran's oil industry has suffered under the mullah's regime. Under the Shah, Iran's daily oil production reached 6 million barrels of crude oil in 1974. Since the 1979 revolution, crude oil production in Iran has never exceeded 3.9 million barrels a day on an annual basis.

Iran's oil fields are hampered by an aging infrastructure, plagued by dilapidated equipment and inadequate investment. Moreover, during the 1980s war with Iraq, Iran is believed to have syphoned crude from its oil fields. Trying to get every possible dollar out of oil to purchase weapons in the war against Iraq, Iran itself may have permanently damaged its oil fields.

Iran's economy remains heavily dependent upon oil export revenues. Fully 80-90 percent of Iran's total export earnings come from oil. Oil export revenue makes up 40-50 percent of the government's annual budget.[183]

With oil at $55 a barrel on world markets, Iran realized over $200 million a day in oil revenue. As the crisis with Iran developed in 2006, oil began to spike on world markets at prices in excess of $70 a barrel, and prices have increased exponentially. Oil windfall profits flow largely into the government budget, since even today Iran's government-controlled oil companies pay oil workers poorly. Oil revenue is diverted to keep the Iranian mullahs and their cronies wealthy, as well as to support terrorism and develop the Iranian nuclear program. Meanwhile, millions of people in Iran continue to live on what is estimated by some to be approximately $1.00 a day.

It appears that sanctions imposed by world leaders are having an effect, and especially on the populace—although Ahmadinejad denies the squeeze. According to various sources, the impact of the sanctions is supposed to bring Iran's oil industry to its knees. Not so! Countries such as Sri Lanka, China, Japan, Italy, South Korea, Spain, Greece, Turkey, and South Africa have remained aloof and refused to join the United States and the European Union in banning the import of Iranian crude. These countries represent a petroleum importation ratio of anywhere from 10 percent to 100 percent.

The pinch, however, is being felt in the area of foreign currency sales. According to the IRNA news agency in Tehran, Ahmadinejad has increased interest rates on bank deposits "up to 21 percent." Iranians have been instructed to buy dollars only when traveling.

Hoarding of US currency had become *de rigueur* in aristocratic circles in the country. It was once the currency to covet, but no longer. Now it will be at a premium, and will require government permission to purchase dollars. Ahmadinejad has acknowledged—albeit subtly—that the sanctions have seriously worsened the value of the Iranian rial. One anonymous Iranian politician depicted the current economy as the worst since the Iran/Iraq war.

In October 2004, Iran and China announced that China's second largest oil firm, Sinopac Group, had agreed to invest $70 billion in Iran. This investment would buy a 50 percent share to develop the oil and natural gas resources of the newly discovered Yadavaran field in southwestern Iran.[184] Iran currently supplies about 15 percent of China's oil, a percentage expected to rise dramatically once production in the Yadavaran field begins.[185]

Sinopac is a Chinese state-owned oil company. In October 2000, Sinopac sold a minority 15 percent interest in an international $3.5 billion Initial

Public Offering on the New York and Hong Kong stock exchanges. About $2 billion of the Sinopac IPO was purchased by ExxonMobil, BP, and Shell. The US oil companies made their investment in Sinopac before the Iran-China oil deals were proposed. The Iran Libya Sanctions Act of 1996, passed under the Clinton Administration, placed Iran under sanctions and threatened penalties for any large international oil companies making deals with Iran. Still, when the Sinopac deal was made with Iran for the Yadavaran oil fields, the Bush Administration brought no penalties against Sinopac, or their minority US owner, ExxonMobil.

The complexity of ExxonMobil owning a minority interest in Sinopac reveals how intertwined the international oil business is. Through ExxonMobil's ownership interest in Sinopac, America will be indirectly involved in developing Iran's oil economy, despite US sanctions currently in place against that nation. The unwillingness of the Bush Administration to impose penalties on ExxonMobil raises questions of whether our economic oil self-interest complicates our policy on Iran.

The hardline theocrats controlling Iran see this as typical US capitalist hypocrisy. The mullahs believe that oil economics are at the core of Washington's opposition to the regime, as well as the reason America invaded Iraq. Nor was Washington able to exert pressure on Beijing not to do the oil deal with Iran, despite the US being China's leading trade partner and primary export market. How can we impose strong sanctions on Iran over its nuclear policy when we keep hands-off the Iranian oil deal with China?

When the Yadavaran field was discovered, Iranian Petroleum Minister Namdar Zanganeh announced that the discovery held an estimated 328.3 billion cubic yards of recoverable natural gas, plus an estimated 442 million barrels of liquid natural gas, in addition to 17 billion barrels of crude oil.[186] These estimates immediately shot the Yadavaran field to the top of the list; it instantly became Iran's largest oil and natural gas field.

Petroleum Minister Zanganeh claimed that this new discovery put Iran in the "Number 2" world position in global crude oil reserves. That statement, however, might be disputed by Saudi Arabia and Russia. Still, the ongoing discoveries of enormous energy resources in Iran, such as the

Yadavaran field, leaves no doubt that Iran continues to hold strategically valuable reserves of oil and natural gas, despite the possible depletion of older oilfields. Any new discovery in Iran is of enormous tactical and economic value to the ruling mullahs.

Without its abundant energy resources, Iran would have no economic strength from which to advance its radical revolution regionally or worldwide. Iran's oil revenue is the ultimate source of the funding which finds its way to Hezbollah, and other terrorist organizations, such as the Islamic Jihad and Hamas, which Iran directs as surrogates in its war against Israel.

This Sinopac deal also shows Iran's awareness that any newly discovered energy resources can be capitalized for immediate revenue. Hungry for cash as usual, the mullahs wasted no time turning the newly found oil field into ready cash for themselves, in total disregard for the indigenous, ethnic owners of the land in Iran. The Yadavaran oil fields in the Khuzestan region of southwest Iran are on the ancestral land of the Ahwazi Arabs. Some 4 to 5 million Ahwazi-Arabs live there, in a region they have traditionally called al-Ahwaz, or Arabistan. *Arabistan* is a term that roughly translates into the "State of the Ahwazi-Arabs."

When the Iranian regime realized that the Iranian Oil Engineering and Development Company had found some 17 billion barrels of oil there, the leaders in Tehran quickly expropriated the land and gave the oil field a Persian name. Yadavaran, the renamed oilfield, was assigned to the government-owned and operated Iranian Oil Engineering and Development Company, a part of the National Iranian Oil Company, operated under the Ministry of Petroleum.[187]

The regime typically took the land from the local Arabs without compensation. Moreover, the government planned to pay the tribal owners of the field for oil and natural gas production from it.[188]

Almost immediately, the regime in Tehran began negotiating with major international oil companies from France, Russia, Norway, and China, to see who would invest the most capital to develop the field. The memorandum of understanding signed with China at the end of 2004 proved China had paid the top amount. The "rightful tribal owners" of the oil field including the Kaab, Adris, Albo-Nassar, Zergan, Bawi, and Bani-toroof—all of whom are Arabs—were left high and dry.

In January 2005, the National Iranian Oil Company sold a minority 20 percent share of the Yadavaran oilfield to India's ONGC Videsh Ltd (OVL) in a deal valued at $40 billion. The deal also involved a fixed-price formula that set a ceiling on what India would be charged for the oil developed.[189]

Ownership in the Yadvaran oil field ended up being 50 percent China, 20 percent India, and 30 percent Iran. The Iranian deal with India resembles its deal with China; in both cases, Iran received much-needed capital, while China and India made long-term commitments. In the deal, China and India received reliable future access to a large quantity of energy at moderately fixed prices.

All this should greatly trouble the US. India and China are increasingly looking to Iran and Russia for strategic alliances. Iran and Russia have oil, India and China need oil. The deals being made are expected to tie the countries together over the next 25 years.

When the Indian deal to invest in the Yadavaran oil field was announced, Russia also let out word that China's Sinopec and India's ONGC had each been offered the opportunity to invest $2 billion for a stake in Yuganskneftegaz, the main production unit of Yukos. Yukos is Russia's second-largest oil company and one of the largest non-state oil companies in the world, having been privatized by Russia in the late 1990s.[190] Yukos holds the largest proven reserves of oil and natural gas in Western Siberia, responsible for nearly 20 percent of Russia's total oil production in 2003.[191]

In 2004-2005, a series of top-level meetings was held by government leaders and energy ministers between Russia, China, India, Pakistan, and Iran. A framework of economic cooperation agreements was signed whose purpose was for Russia and Iran to provide oil to India and China. Pakistan was willing to see oil pipelines built across Pakistani territory to transport Iranian oil to India and China.

When Indian Petroleum Minister Mani Shankar Aiyar met in Moscow in 2004 for energy discussions with Russian government officials, he proposed Indo-Russian cooperation in the security field. "In the first half-century of

Indian independence, Russia has guaranteed our territorial integrity," Aiyar noted in Moscow. "In the second half it may be to guarantee our energy security. What I am talking about is the strategic alliance with Russia in energy security, which is becoming for India as important as national security."[192]

Subsequently, when Russian President Vladimir Putin visited India, the two countries signed a memorandum of understanding for joint exploration and development of Iranian oil and natural gas from the Caspian basin. Included in the agreement was a proposal for building underground natural gas storage facilities in India and transferring Russian energy technology to India.

In 2005, India and Pakistan agreed to start work by 2007 on a 1,750 mile $4 billion pipeline to transport oil from Iran to India via Pakistan by 2010.[193] The agreement, reached over the objections of the United States, was viewed as a breakthrough. Suddenly the nuclear states of Pakistan and India, that have traditionally been enemies, were cooperating. The pipeline was proposed originally in 1996, but never got off the ground because of Indian concerns over the security of the pipeline in Pakistan.

In 2004, China's Premier Wen Jiabao and Russia's President Putin exchanged visits. The joint statement issued at the conclusion of Putin's state visit to China repudiated the Bush Administration's policy of pursuing a unilateral War on Terrorism in defense of US national security interests.

In a reference that easily applies to Iran, China and Russia declared together that "it is urgently needed to compose international disputes under the chairing of the UN and resolve crisis on the basis of universally recognized principles of international law. Any coercive action should only be taken with the approval of the UN Security Council and enforced under its supervision."[194] With China and Russia both members of the Security Council, the joint statement reinforced the conclusion that any US-initiated resolution to place further sanctions on Iran for non-compliance with IAEA nuclear inspections would be blocked.

A Tehran-Moscow-Beijing axis looked like it might be forming to protect Iran from US or Israeli preemptive military actions. Today, Iran is working closely with Russia, China, India, and Pakistan on energy issues. Surprisingly,

even India and Pakistan resolved their differences and moved closer to building a pipeline to funnel Iranian oil across Pakistan to India. With careful
maneuvering, Iran has used its ample oil and natural gas resources to leverage a working alliance with four of the world's small club of nuclear armed
nations.

According to David Francis of *The Fiscal Times*:

> If Russia and Iran were to collude to fix prices or cut
> supply, the impact on the global energy market would be
> immediate and severe. The two could cause an acute short-
> age of natural gas that would be felt the world over. And as
> the endgame between Iran and the West quickly approaches,
> creation of such a shortage might be Tehran's only hand to
> play. And, it would give Putin yet another opportunity to
> play spoiler to the West.[195]

Iran's leaders are asking the world why the country should not be
allowed to pursue nuclear technology unimpeded, on an equal basis with its
energy partners Russia, China, India, and Pakistan.

On December 26, 2005, Iran's Foreign Minister Manouchehr Mottaki
said during a visit to the Afghan capital of Kabul that Iran did not need
anyone's permission to pursue nuclear technology. "We do not accept global
nuclear 'apartheid' and 'scientific apartheid,'" Mottaki told the news conference. "We are not waiting for any country's permission for the right of the
Iranian nation and the Islamic republic to enjoy nuclear technology."[196]

Here, the argument is that America is invoking a double standard.
Evidently, the United States has no problem that Israel possesses nuclear
weapons, but Iran is considered unworthy to have the same nuclear privi-
leges. Iran charges that the United States and Israel are the true aggressor
nations. Iran claims that America's real goal is to establish US hegemony in
the Middle East so she can hold on to cheap access to Middle Eastern oil.

Iran resolves to continue terrorism, as long as the US continues to occupy
Middle Eastern countries and so long as Israel continues to exist. Ultimately,

Russia, China, and Iran fear US hegemony. Iran predicts America will be defeated as other imperialist nations have been when they over-reached in colonialist ambitions.[197]

Moscow and Beijing continue to pursue their own nationalistic objectives as well. Russia and China see advantages in leveraging for their benefit Tehran's radical revolutionary zeal. Russia and China both want to counterbalance the military and economic power of Washington.

Iran dismisses Washington's argument that the US invaded Iraq and Afghanistan to establish democratic reform as "a thinly disguised method for the US to militarily dispose of unfriendly regimes in order to ensure the country's primacy as the world's sole superpower."[198] In other words, Iran charges that President George W. Bush launched a war of choice against Iraq, not to combat terrorism, but to transform the Middle East. Israel is then seen as a client state of the United States. Iran believes Israel is another threat to impose the Western principle of democracy on the Middle East, a region where Iran wants to establish rigid Islamic theocracies.

With Tehran taking the lead against the US on the question of Israel, Russia and China can remain in the shadows, prepared to defend Iran if that nation should be attacked. Moreover, Russia and China derive the additional advantage of seeing Iran assume the surrogate role of pressuring the US on the question of Israel, so that Russia and China can achieve their geopolitical goals while staying in the background.

— 14 —

SITTING AT THE
FEET OF THE
AYATOLLAH

*"Anybody who recognizes Israel will burn in the
fire of the Islamic nation's fury."*[199]
—PRESIDENT MAHMOUD AHMADINEJAD

RADICAL STATEMENTS BY IRAN'S MAHMOUD AHMADINEJAD against Israel and the United States serve to bolster attempts by Russia and China to restrain any expansion of US powers. Iran fears democracy in Iraq and Afghanistan. The more democracies that flourish in the Middle East, the more Iran feels it is losing an edge. So, as the argument goes, fair is fair. If the United States can have a surrogate in the state of Israel, then Russia and China can have a surrogate in the state of Iran.

In 2005, Russia and China conducted their first-ever joint military exercise. Involving as many as 10,000 soldiers plus naval ships, submarines, missiles and Russian strategic bombers, the war games began in the Russian port city of Vladivostok and ended in China's Shandong Peninsula in the Yellow Sea. China remains Russia's largest customer for arms sales. According to the

Moscow-based Center for the Analysis of Strategies and Technologies, China has been buying an average of $2 billion worth of weapons from Russia each year since 2000. Between 2001 and 2004, China led the list of weapons purchases "buying $10.4 billion worth of weaponry, most of it from Russia."[200] One clear reason for conducting the joint exercise was to show America combined power of Russia and China working together. A tightening Russian-Chinese alliance could counter the growing US influence in the Middle East.[201]

In late 2005, Russia successfully tested a Bulava missile, a submarine-based version of the Topol-M. The tests were loudly touted by Moscow in order to make certain the world appreciated the Kremlin's continuing concerns about US military involvement in Iraq. Apparently Russia feared that Iran might be attacked for defiantly enriching uranium on its own soil. Too, Russia was determined to protect the abundant oil resources of the Caspian basin from being seized by the United States.[202] The Topol-M missile series launched a new round in the nuclear weapons arms race, as the US military, nuclear scientists, and engineers would be forced to adapt the US anti-missile defense system to combat this more sophisticated Russian ICBM.

On Christmas Eve 2005, Col. Gen. Nikolai Solovtsov, the head of the Russian Strategic Rocket Forces, participated in a ceremony at a missile base in Tatishchev in the Volga River's Saratov region, where the Russians deployed a new class of ballistic missiles. The Topol-M missiles are said to be able to hit targets at distances of 10,000 kilometers (6,000 miles) and are designed to penetrate any anti-missile defense system the United States has, including those that use electromagnetic blasts to incapacitate in-coming missile attacks. In this test, the Russians only deployed the single warhead version of the Topol-M in fixed silo structures, but announced that a mobile version would be ready soon, as would a multiple independent re-entry vehicle (MIRV) version.

On November 29, 2005, the United Nations hosted a conference at its New York Headquarters to commemorate an "International Day of Solidarity with the Palestinian People." Typically, the UN is one-sided in describing Israel as the "occupier" of "Palestinian land." Still, this ceremony went one step further, displaying prominently a Palestinian map without the state of Israel. On one side of the map was the UN flag, and on the other side was the Palestinian flag. Israel, a UN member state for 56 years, was not displayed anywhere on the map.

With the "map of Palestine" prominently hanging in the room, UN Secretary General Kofi Annan spoke before the presidents of the Security Council Andrey Denisov and the General Assembly Jan Eliasson. During the ceremony, those assembled rose to observe a moment of silence "in memory of all those who have given their lives for the cause of the Palestinian people and the return of peace between Israel and Palestine." This was widely interpreted as a commemoration to suicide bombers. The unspoken message served to affirm Ahmadinejad's contention that peace between the Israelis and the Palestinians would come only when Israel had been wiped off the map.[203]

Clearly, the United Nations was siding with Iran in not giving respect to Israel as a legitimate state. When Ahmadinejad attacked Israel, saying the tiny state should be wiped from the map, the United Nations did almost nothing about it. The UN Security Council did issue a statement pointing out that members of the UN should refrain from the threat to use force against any member state. Yet, no action other than the issuing of a letter of reprimand was planned by the Security Council.

In the years that have passed since the conference, the UN has continued to turn a blind eye to threats against Israel's peace and safety. Ahmadinejad strides to the podium at every UN meeting and points his bloody finger at Israel. If any response at all is offered, Palestinian assaults are met with the mildest of reprimands—a mere slap on the wrist.

On September 20, 2011, the Palestinians attempted to sidestep further negotiations with Israel's leaders in a plan to be admitted to the UN as an independent state—returning the region to pre-1967 borders, and with East Jerusalem in PA hands. The ploy failed, and President Mahmoud Abbas vowed to continue the fight to gain statehood by any means other than admitting the existence of the State of Israel and her right to exist.

On November 29, 2012, Abbas achieved his devious end: The UN General Assembly approved the resolution giving recognition to the PA as a non-member state. One hundred thirty-eight nations voted in favor, nine voted against the move, and forty-one abstained. The nine dissenters joining the US and Israel were the Czech Republic, Canada, Panama, the Marshall Islands, Micronesia, Nauru, and Palau.

Days later, the PA president proclaimed, "One day…the Palestinian flag [will fly] over Jerusalem, the eternal capital of the state of Palestine!" The UN vote was on the sixty-fifth anniversary of the partition of Palestine between the Jews and Palestinians. Just three short years following the devastation of the Holocaust, the Jewish people were back in their God-given land, but without access to Jerusalem or the Western Wall. Before the ink was dry on the declaration proclaiming Israel a state, five members of the Arab League encircled the tiny Jewish nation and launched an all-out attack.

In direct violation of the UN partition treaty, and after five months of fighting, the Israelis were successful in defending their territory. The Israelis have protected their homeland time after time, in war after war. They have been assaulted, accused, attacked, censured, and critized, but few have supported their rights to the land God bequeathed to Abraham. To add insult to injury, the United Nations has ignored its own resolution to uphold the rights of the Jewish people.

The isolation of Israel continues in the second decade of the twenty-first century. She struggles to win even weak support from a diminishing audience in the court of world diplomacy.

At the end of December 2005, CIA Director Porter Goss visited Ankara, Turkey, following a visit there by FBI Director Robert Mueller. Reports circulated that Goss warned Turkish officials to anticipate US air strikes against Iran and Syria. Immediately, Iranian Foreign Ministry spokesperson Hamid Reza Asif warned Ankara, "We ask our Turkish friends to be careful."[204]

Turkey is a member of NATO, with yet many complicated ties to Iran. Since the 1979 revolution in Iran, scores of Iranian dissidents have escaped that regime by walking out of the country's largely rural northwestern section into Turkey. Many of these dissidents fled after being imprisoned and tortured by the Iranian regime. Many required medical treatment for their injuries; many others died in the attempt to reach freedom. Turkey also has had excellent relations with Israel; for many Israelis, Turkey is a vacation destination where they do not experience the anti-Semitism typically found in the Middle East.

According to newspaper reports, CIA Director Goss took with him to Turkey two important portfolios: one was aimed at showing Turkish officials US intelligence reports that Iran was pursuing a clandestine nuclear weapons program. The second was aimed at proving to Ankara that Tehran was continuing to support the terrorist PKK group in Turkey, promoting from Tehran the *Partiya Karkeren Kurdistan* (PPK) relationship with al-Qaeda.[205]

PKK is the Kurdistan Worker's Party, whose goal is to establish an independent Kurdistan embracing the Kurdish minorities across the region, including those in Turkey, northern Iran, and northern Iraq. The Kurds, some 30 million in number, are the largest ethnic minority without a state in the Middle East, despite claims of the Palestinians to the contrary.

The PKK was formed in 1978 as a Marxist-Leninist insurgent group, composed primarily of Turkish Kurds.[206] In the 1980s and 1990s, violence between the PKK and the Turkish army reached the point of there being virtually a war, with some 35,000 deaths estimated to have occurred on both sides together. Today, the PKK is estimated to number around 4,000 to 5,000 active members. Its ranks swelled significantly following the invasion of Iraq. The group continues to attack Turkish security forces and target tourist destinations in an attempt to press their cause.

In December 2005, a Turkish court explained the convictions the previous July of nine Turkish Islamist militants in a long-running case involving the 1990s murders of four prominent pro-secular Turkish intellectuals. Turkey had accused Iran's "Qod Force" of training and funding these militants.

The "Qods" (or "Jerusalem Force") is a major terrorist agency active in Tehran. Qods combines an intelligence agency and foreign operatives, estimated to number some 21,000 personnel, into an operation that is headquartered in the former site of the US embassy in Tehran. The Qods was designed to train and fund terrorist operations in Muslim states that are considered too secular, such as Turkey. Apparently Iran considers Turkey not sufficiently radical according to the Iranian revolutionary model.

Qods has trained operatives in a wide range of countries, including Iran, Afghanistan, Pakistan, India, Turkey, Morocco, and Lebanon. Its operations have reportedly branched from the Persian Gulf to reach as far as Central Asia, North Africa, Europe, and North America.[207] Rumors such as these reinforce the impression that Iran wants to destabilize any Islamic states it believes not to be on the right course.

On the diplomatic front, Iran has been openly courting favor with the Turks, and wants to quiet that nation's concerns that the real agenda is to expand the revolution into Turkey. Also in 2005, Iran's former president Hashemi Rafsanjani, in his new capacity as Chairman of the Iranian Expedience Council, met with Turkish Ambassador to Tehran Halit Bozkurk Aran. The meeting was prompted by Aran's retirement after a 23-year career as Turkey's ambassador in Tehran. At the meeting, Rafsanjani promoted the theme of positive bilateral relations and urged the two nations to form stable and peaceful ties in the region.

Despite funding terrorism in the region, Iran still maintains that its goal is to end terrorism and establish stability. Rafsanjani urged trilateral cooperation between Iran, Turkey, and Syria, Iran's closest ally in the region.[208]

Cutting through the diplomatic niceties of the meeting, Iran's underlying agenda is to solidify its diplomatic position in the region. Iran would like to be seen as a responsible international player. Still, the regime will not renounce Ahmadinejad's extremist statements attacking Israel, nor will Tehran abandon its support of terrorism, or its direct funding of terrorist groups such as Hezbollah. Iran comfortably maintains a public face proclaiming its theocratic aims for stability and economic growth. Meanwhile, its leaders quietly advance the dark underside of terrorism and secretly pursue the manufacture of nuclear weapons.

On a visit to Egypt when the reports about CIA Director Goss's visit to Turkey broke on international wire services, Turkish Deputy Premier and Foreign Minister Abdullah Gul was asked at a press conference if his country had agreed to support alleged American-planned air strikes against Iran and Syria. Gul responded that any reports the US had pressed Turkey to back military action against Iran and Syria were not true. Examined closely, Gul's statement did not constitute a denial that Goss had visited Ankara to brief Turkish officials about a planned military strike; his statement only denied that the US had pressed Turkey to support such a move. In the same press conference, reporters questioned Gul about Turkey's continued close relations to Israel. Again, Gul spoke carefully, noting only that Israel enjoys good relations with many countries, in addition to Turkey.[209]

Turkey has continued to rely on NATO and the US nuclear guarantee to protect itself against a nuclear Russia to the north. The Turks have been wary of Russian geopolitical objectives since the end of World War II.

Turkey's relationship with its Islamic neighbors in the Middle East has been influenced by history. Since the collapse of the Ottoman Empire, which was closely associated with the Turkish Republic, the Turks have sought to maintain stable relations in the region, and especially with Iran who has no ties to either the old empire or the republic.

Israel has played a major role in modernizing the Turkish military, including supplying both military equipment and training. This relationship is an ever-present undercurrent creating tensions in any discussions Turkey has with either Iran or Syria. As long as Turkey continues to enjoy a strong relationship with the United States and NATO, the threat from revolutionary Iran remains ever-present.

Iran's leaders, however, are not content to allow Turkey's close ties to the US and Israel to remain intact. They have begun an all-out pursuit of the only Muslim country to afford Israel any status in the Middle East. On August 14, 2008, President Ahmadinejad flew to Turkey for the first time at the invitation of its President Abdullah Gul. The two men reportedly considered both regional and mutual concerns and talked at length about boosting an energy partnership between their countries.

In May 2010, Turkish Prime Minister Recep Tayyip Erdogan flew to Tehran to sign an agreement in union with Brazilian President Lula da Silva for outsourcing the enrichment of Iranian uranium in order to circumvent additional sanctions on Iran. As an excuse for joining forces with the fanatical Muslim state, Erdogan fawned: "In fact, there is no nuclear weapon in Iran now, but Israel, which is also located in our region, possesses nuclear arms. Turkey is the same distance from both of them. What has the international community said against Israel so far? Is this the superiority of law or the law of superiors?"[210] His comments followed on the heels of increasing force from the US and Great Britain for Turkey to support sanctions on Iran.

The bloom on the rose faded a bit when in September 2011, Turkey, a NATO member, agreed to accommodate a radar system that would track missiles fired from Iran. Ahmadinejad was not pleased with the arrangement. The Iranian leaders were certain the defense shield system was designed solely to protect Israel should she target Iran's nuclear sites. An aide to Ayatollah Ali Khamenei, Major-General Yahya Rahim-Safavi warned:

> "If Turkey does not distance itself from this unconventional political behaviour it will have both the Turkish people turning away from it domestically and the neighbouring countries of Syria, Iraq and Iran reassessing their political ties."[211]

Following the Iranian admonition, US Secretary of State Hillary Clinton cautioned that "Iran would be badly miscalculating if they did not look at the entire NATO allies, like Turkey."[212]

The exchange of verbal volleys did not seem to slow the economic relations between the two countries. Iran and turkey are members of the Economic Cooperation Organization (ECO). In 2005, mutual trade rose from $1 billion at the beginning of the decade to $4 billion. The figure reached $10 billion in 2010, and is expected to increase exponentially over the next few years. Incidentally, over one million Iranians travel to Turkey yearly.

When Iran develops nuclear weapons, it seems certain that Turkey's security concerns will intensify. Ian Lesser, a Senior Scholar at the Woodrow Wilson International Center writes of the danger:

Could Turkey act more radically, outside multilateral arrangements, to meet risks posed by a nuclear-ready Iran? The short answer is yes, but it is not very likely. Could Turkey "go nuclear"? Again, the answer is yes, but it is not very likely. The key in both cases would be a sharp deterioration in the quality of Turkish defense cooperation with the West, and a sense that Turkey was being left to go it alone in a dangerous geo-strategic setting. Overall, the existence of a nuclear-ready Iran poses some direct risks to Turkish security—and many indirect but highly consequential ones. Implications for US and Western policy abound.[213]

Clearly, the continued involvement of the United States in the Middle East will be a factor determining whether an atomic Iran will lead to a regional nuclear arms race. Should US presence further weaken in the Middle East, a nuclear arms race becomes a likely possibility as countries such as Turkey take steps to protect themselves from Russia and Iran.

— 15 —

THE DIMINUTIVE DICTATOR'S DECREES

*"We do not humble ourselves in the poisoned atmosphere created
by foreign sources. We will remain strong and vigilant and work to
overcome the obstacles in our way to achieve our goals and objectives."*
—MAHMOUD AHMADINEJAD[214]

PRESIDENT AHMADINEJAD'S UNASSUMING, ALMOST HUMBLE PRESENTATION of himself should not deceive those who look below the surface. Underneath a self-effacing exterior, Ahmadinejad is hard, serious, and calculating. His rants against Israel are carefully premeditated and fully coordinated with the wishes of Ayatollah Khamenei. His goal is to unite the anti-Israel world, just as Egypt's President Nasser did some fifty years ago.

Ahmadinejad has moved some top henchmen into his cabinet, many of whom are former intelligence officers. This group, dominated by dark figures that have played key roles in the suppression of human rights and free expression, has characterized the Islamic Republic of Iran since the 1979 revolution.

Iran is a closed society, governed by the strict rules of orthodox Islam. Like other ideologically-driven states, free expression as we know it in the West simply does not exist. Under Ahmadinejad, the Iranian government has gone through a conservative crack-down, its own form of Islamic Cultural Revolution, with the goal of imposing the firm grip of the regime even more tightly. Suppression of free speech and repression of political dissent that has swept through Iran in past decades both pale in comparison to what Ahmadinejad and Ayatollah Khamenei crave for Iran.

This new wave of internal repression is fundamental to the vision of the two men on how Iran's revolution must be expanded. Attempting to fulfill the predictions of Ayatollah Ruhollah Khomeini that Israel and the United States are both doomed to fall, Iran's leadership is determined to maintain tighter control at home as a precondition for attempts to expand the revolution abroad.

The reform movement inside Iran has been forced deeper underground, fearful of arguing too loudly for liberalization in the regime's ultra-conservative social, economic, and political policies. With Ahmadinejad's fist holding Iran in an iron grip, the conditions for a democratic movement to succeed in changing the government peacefully are extremely unlikely to happen.

The Ministry of Information in Iran is the agency generally responsible for intelligence activities. As Minister of Information, Ahmadinejad appointed Gholamhossein Mohseni Ezhei, another crony with a long history of human rights violations.

Ezhei has held several judicial positions, including serving as a representative of the Judiciary in the Ministry of Information from 1986-1988 and again from 1991-1994. Human Rights Watch points out that in his various roles as a judge Ezhei presided over past purges of reformist clerics:

> A prosecutor-general of the Special Court for the Clergy, Gholamhossein Mohseni Ezhei led the prosecution of several reformist clerics. In addition, he presided over the politically-motivated trial of former Tehran mayor Gholamhussein Karbaschi, who had played a pivotal role in campaigning for

Khatami's election to the presidency. Mohseni Ezhei is also suspected of ordering the murder of Pirouz Davani, an Iranian dissident and activist whom agents of the Ministry of Information allegedly kidnapped and killed in 1998.[215]

In 1999, Ezhei led the judiciary's offensive against the press that resulted in the closing of more than 100 newspapers in Iran. He is considered a leading judicial hard-liner against clerics who stray from the orthodox interpretation of Islam. Ezhei remains a prominent opponent of free-speech.

Under President Khatami, the Culture Ministry defended the media organizations against attacks by the hard-line judiciary; under Ezhei, the Culture Ministry resumed contacting suspect media to rescend permission to publish, in accordance with the directives and wishes of the judiciary.[216] In 2009, Ezhei was abruptly and without explanation removed from office. Ahmadinejad stopped just short of blaming Ezhei for the bloody riots that followed the election.

Another hard-line appointment was Manouchehr Mottaki, who Ahmadinejad named as the new Foreign Minister. Mottaki was a radical Islamist when he was a student at Bangalore University in India. He returned to Iran soon after the fall of the Shah in 1979. Once back in Iran, he became a fervent follower of Ayatollah Khomeini and a member of the Revolutionary Guards.

In 1985, Mottaki was Iran's ambassador to Turkey. During his tenure in Ankara Mottaki became involved in a series of terror incidents where some 50 Iranian dissidents were kidnapped or assassinated in Turkey by Iranian secret agents who were working closely with diplomats from Iran's embassy. With Mottaki as ambassador, the Iranian embassy in Ankara was reportedly turned into safe houses for Iranian agents that were hunting down and killing expatriate political dissidents.

In October 1989, Turkish authorities ordered Mottaki to leave the country because of his alleged role in these kidnappings and assassinations. Turkey's request was made according to the protocol of diplomatic courtesy, and to avoid a crisis Turkey agreed to allow Iran to withdraw Mottaki as ambassador to avoid public embarrassment.[217]

With a hard-line cabinet in place, Ahmadinejad countenances no internal grumbling about the regime's determined push for nuclear technology. Nor does he expect any backlash against even his most outrageous statements attacking Israel.

On January 4, 2006, Ahmadinejad held a three-hour closed-door meeting with cabinet members and the Foreign Policy and National Security Committee of Iran's Majlis (parliament). There, he made a series of statements openly criticizing the foreign policy of his immediate predecessors, presidents Mohammad Khatami and Hashemi Rafsanjani. According to the the Iranian leader:

> "In the past 16 years we implemented a policy of détente and tried to get closer to Europe and to trust them," Ahmadinejad noted, "but this policy has achieved nothing." He noted that by the end of Khatami's second term in 2004, "we were distanced from the goals of the 1979 Islamic revolution and our activity in the Islamic world had been somewhat diminished."[218]

In the same meeting, Ahmadinejad insisted that his remarks calling for Israel to be "wiped off the map" and describing the Holocaust as a "myth" were a calculated policy to produce a "shock" designed "to waken Muslims who are living in a state of lethargy." He argued that his chain of statements contained a logic that was designed to unify the Islamic world, preparing for what he fully anticipates will be the final elimination of Israel.

Ahmadinejad spoke clearly: "Some in Iran and abroad thought we were making these statements without a specific plan and policy, but we have been pursuing a specific strategy in this regard. The wave that these speeches have caused has a lot of supporters among young people in the Muslim world and it will continue to move forward."[219] This logic was consistent with the teachings of Ayatollah Khomeini since before the fall of the Shah.

Ahmadinejad also made clear how the policy to attack Israel fit in with the strategy of causing the United States to fall. "Those who defend today the crimes of the Zionists," he told the combined meeting of his cabinet with the Majlis committee, "must be held accountable and sentenced. Of course, they claim that they are very strong, but this is one of their big lies."

In direct reference to the United States, Ahmadinejad said: "The revival of Islam is whipping the frail body of the Global Hegemon. This Global Hegemon will soon be toppled."

He rejected the authority of the UN mandate that created the state of Israel, emphasizing yet again, "You who claim that there was a Holocaust are today repeating such a thing in Palestine." He defied the international condemnation his remarks had drawn: "We do not fear their screams. The more they shout, the more they show their own weaknesses."[220]

These are not the ravings of a madman. They are the calculated statements of a zealous religious bigot who is also a head of state. For us in the West who are accustomed to the separation of church and state, we must combine the two spheres to comprehend Ahmadinejad. As Ayatollah Khomeini taught, in Shi'ite Islam, politics and religion are one.

Khomeini predicted that the Shah would fall, that the Soviet Union would fall, and that Saddam Hussein would fall. All three events happened. Now Ahmadinejad was telling his government the time had come for Israel to fall; and that by defending Israel, the US would create its own downfall. All this fits together as seen through the lens of Ayatollah Khomeini's predictions.

Ahmadinejad was attacking Israel verbally because he was setting the stage for Israel to be attacked in reality. Iran would never divert from pursuing nuclear technology, because that too was seen as within Iran's sovereign rights.

In the extreme religious views held by Ahmadinejad, all this was fated by God, such that no human intervention could change Iran's destiny, not as long as Iran remained true to Khomeini's 1979 revolution. Ultimately, Khomeini had prophesied that Shi'ite Islam would conquer the apostate Sunni version of Islam, all a prelude to Shi'ite Islam sweeping across the

world. The final destiny of Islam would be realized under the personal direction of the Twelfth Imam, the Mahdi.

Thus, Ahmadinejad's mystical vision is that he is destined to be the
agent who does what is necessary to instigate the Mahdi's second coming.
Before the Mahdi returns, Muslims believe there must be chaos, a world
apocalypse. For all this to happen, Iran will have to possess nuclear weapons
in order to force the removal of Israel and the return of Palestine to Islamic
control.

Again, we should remember that Ahmadinejad's chief spiritual advisor is
Ayatollah Mohammad Taqi Mesbah Yazdi, known as "the Crocodile" for his
rugged facial features and his hard-line orthodox religious views.

Ayatollah Yazdi has proclaimed Ahmadinejad as the "chosen" of Imam
Mahdi, the person designated to prepare the way for the Mahdi's second
coming.[221] Yazdi heads the Imam Khomeini Research and Learning Center
in Qom, site of the Jamkaran well, down which the Twelfth Imam supposedly disappeared as a child centuries ago. The Center also functions as a
seminary, to which the members of the Basij militia are sent for training. The
Basij volunteers act as street thugs, virtually an unofficial "morality police,"
under the regime.[222]

Yazdi is also a member of the Assembly of Experts, the select group of
clerics responsible for electing the Supreme Leader from within their ranks.
With his acknowledged years of learning, Ayatollah Yazdi qualifies to be
ranked an Imam, a distinction Ayatollah Khamenei does not share. Without
Yazdi's support, Khamenei would never have been selected Supreme Leader.

Among the members of the Assembly of Experts, Yazdi would have to
be considered a possible future Supreme Leader himself, something both
Ayatollah Khamenei and President Ahmadinejad undoubtedly keep in mind.
The mysticism surrounding the Mahdi, Ayatollah Yazdi, and President
Ahmadinejad becomes politically important as we further understand that
the Iranian regime is a theocracy in which politics and religion are completely intertwined.

A strong belief in the Mahdi runs through the radical version of Shi'ite
Islam to which Ahmadinejad adheres. Ayatollah Khomeini insisted that the

Prophet Mohammed did not complete the job of bringing Islam to its rightful place. He insists that his fate is to carry forward the divine plan. Ayatollah Khomeini claimed he was born to complete the work of Allah, to advance Islam to be the world's only religion, with all non-believers destroyed.

Ayatollah Yazdi heads an even more radical sect, the Hojatieh, a group which maintains a belief that the second coming of the Mahdi is instrumental to realizing its goal. Ayatollah Khomeini's disapproval of the Hojatieh sect drove it underground in 1983. The Hojatieh still maintains a covert presence, such that only fully initiated believers, such as Ahmadinejad, are truly allowed on the inside.

The Hojatieh believe a suffering world stricken by poverty must reach a crisis point before the Mahdi returns. The Hojatieh are comfortable with allowing evil to spread, believing that tyranny and misery only hasten the Mahdi's return and the final triumph of Islam.[223]

Traditional, reformist mullahs undoubtedly consider the Hojatieh the lunatic fringe, having become comfortable in their ability to move freely in the Western world as they acquired international business investments and personal wealth. Extremist religious zealots, such as Ahmadinejad, at the height of their cultural revolutions can easily sour on "corrupt" leaders they feel have gotten too comfortable with worldly ways. Since becoming president in August 2005, Ahmadinejad reportedly has placed Hojatieh devotees in key government positions.[224]

There is another shadowy presence in Ahmadinejad's life. When he was Mayor of Tehran, Ahmadinejad was constantly accompanied by Mojtaba Somreh Hashemi, a close confident who had no official government position. Hashemi was there again when President Ahmadinejad appointed his cabinet. Hashemi accompanied Ahmadinejad to New York, to address the United Nations General Assembly. Ahmadinejad rarely introduces Hashemi or explains his presence.

Hashemi's relationship with Ahmadinejad goes back to the Iran-Iraq war in the 1980s, when he was Ahmadinejad's military commander.[225] His influence is derived from being a close friend of Ayatollah Yazdi. Hashemi's constant presence, despite his unofficial status, reinforces a conclusion that

Ahmadinejad sees himself on a divine mission from Allah to prepare the way for the return of the Mahdi. This degree of religious zeal is consistent with Ahmadinejad's belief that former Revolutionary Guard associates and cabinet ministers associated with violent repression of dissent make appropriate top officials in his revolutionary government. As of June 2012, Hashemi still holds the office of senior advisor to Ahmadinejad as his deputy interior minister for political affairs.

Likely about to be long-gone are the freedoms introduced under "reform" presidents such as Rafsanjani and Khatami, as limited as those freedoms were. "Reform" is not a word likely ever to be associated with Ahmadinejad's terms in office.

The idea that Ahmadinejad may be moving world events toward some religious vision of an Islamic apocalypse, as preposterous as that idea appears to secular Western minds, needs to be taken seriously given the abundant evidence of his apocalyptic beliefs. Is it possible that the key "Minister of Death" in this radical Islamic regime may be Ahmadinejad himself, despite his humble exterior? If death is required to bring back the Mahdi, Ahmadinejad could well consider that part of his divine mission is to confront the evil of the "Little Satan" Israel and the "Great Satan" the United States, regardless of the consequences.

War, chaos, and massive death—even if all that and more came—Ahmadinejad and other true believers would only interpret the calamity as a sign from Allah that the return of the Mahdi was imminent. Restoring the Iranian people to rigid Islamic orthodoxy is also part of the mission. When asked by the people of Iran what they can do to bring about the Mahdi's return, Ahmadinejad's simple admonition is "be pure and devout."

Ahmadinejad ran for president in 2005 on what in United States politics would be considered a populist theme. Born in 1956 in Garmsar, a small town outside Tehran, he was the fourth of seven children. When he was one year old, his family moved to Tehran where his father, an ironworker (who is sometimes described as a "blacksmith") had better chances of gainful employment. In 1975, Mahmoud entered the University of Science and

Technology where he studied civil engineering; in 1987, he received a doctorate, with his specialty being traffic management.

Following the 1979 revolution, Ahmadinejad became a member of the ultra-conservative faction of the Office of Strengthening Unity Between University and Technology Seminaries. This group was founded by Ayatollah Mohammad Beheshti, a close associate of Ayatollah Khomeini. The purpose of this office was to organize radical Islamic students against the radical socialist Mojahedin-e Khalq (MEK) who at that time were growing in strength as a rival to Khomeini.

With the start of the Iran-Iraq war in 1980, Ahmadinejad joined the Revolutionary Guards Corps (IRGC) and was rushed to the front. He advanced to become a senior officer in the Special Brigade of the IRGC, stationed at Ramazan Garrison near Kermanshah in western Iran. This was the headquarters of the IRGC "Extra-territorial Operations" unit which was organized to launch attacks to kidnap or kill Iranian expatriate dissidents. Ahmadinejad participated in these covert operations, notably around the Iraqi city of Kirkuk. When the IRGC "Qods" (translated, "Jerusalem") Force was founded, Ahmadinejad became a senior commander, directing assassinations in the Middle East and Europe.[226]

Before becoming Mayor of Tehran in April 2003, Ahmadinejad had served as governor of Maku and Khoy, cities in the northwestern province of Kurdistan, for two years. In 1993, he was appointed as governor general of the newly established northwestern province of Ardebil, although he was removed by the newly-formed "reform" administration of President Khatami. In 1997 he became a member of the scientific board of the Civil Engineering College of the University of Science and Technology.

As mayor of Tehran, Ahmadinejad reversed many policies of the previous reform mayors. He placed emphasis on a fundamentalist adherence to Islam, going so far as to transform the city's cultural centers into prayer halls during the Islamic holy month of Ramadan. He closed fast-food restaurants and required city male employees to grow beards and wear long sleeves. He instituted a policy of separating men and women in municipal offices, and insisted that women in municipal work always adhere to strict Islamic codes regarding conservative dress and no cosmetics.

— 16 —

IRAN: A NATION OF HOSTAGES

"The problem is that we have this kind of regime represented by such individuals who have taken, first-and-foremost, the Iranian people hostage for the past 30 years and who are completely uninterested about the state of our own citizens. They are only interested to use Iran as a base from which to launch what was from the very beginning the exploitation of a theocracy and Islamic ideology across the planet as a challenge to the rest of the world...
I think you should take him very seriously. The last time the world was not quite sure about the final threat was at the time of Hitler in Nazi Germany and we know the rest of the story."[227]
—CROWN PRINCE REZA PAHLAVI

MAHMOUD AHMADINEJAD HAS ALWAYS PRESENTED HIMSELF AS A SIMPLE MAN of no worldly means. This is in sharp contrast to the wealth accumulated by many mullahs. He would consider the lives of many mullahs today elaborate international life-styles not consistent with strict adherence to his code of orthodox Islam.

Given Ahmadinejad's extensive background in education, civil engineering, and government, one would be mistaken to assume that he is inexperienced or naïve. On the contrary, Ahmadinejad is fully aware of his political appeal to Iran's vast lower middle class and urban poor, as well as the country's still-extensive rural communities. Ayatollah Khomeini came to power through this same economic and rural base, his way paved by many rural clerics who continue to struggle in relatively second-class and out-of-the-way mosques.

When Ahmadinejad appeared on the international scene after being elected president, rumors were widely circulated that he was one of the student revolutionaries who held US embassy personnel hostage in 1979. While no connection has ever been substantiated that Ahmadinejad was the face in a prominent hostage photograph circulated on the Internet, there is no doubt that he was a student radical who played a conspicuous role in the revolution.

His experience in the Revolutionary Guards gives Ahmadinejad credentials that need no further discussion to place him in the first rank of today's middle-aged Iranian revolutionary leaders. Ahmadinejad has turned back the clock, reversing years of work by Iranian reformists. In his first four months in office, he completely destroyed the years of work done by Khatami and Rafsanjani to convince the world that Iran was not ruled by fanatics.

In running for election, Ahmadinejad presented himself as one of the common people. His uniform consisted of suits that were not foreign-tailored; simple, open at the neck shirts with no adornment.

His message was that he came to bring justice for the poor who had suffered in Iran, and that he was cut from the same cloth as the average Iranian who struggled to work and feed a family. Ahmadinejad powerfully invoked the name of "Allah the Merciful" and he ended his speeches with a plea to prepare the way for the Mahdi's return.

He drew great support from the Basij, a loosely-organized and unevenly-trained volunteer militia serving under the direction of the Revolutionary Guards to be the street-level morality police throughout Iran. The paramilitary Basij is Ahmadinejad's power base, his enforcers assigned to demand a strict adherence to Islamic law throughout Iran, reaching even into small towns and rural communities.[228]

The Basij movement was founded by Ayatollah Khomeini in 1979; it was to be his insurmountable twenty-million-man militia. Its assignment was to help usher in Khomeini's infamous Islamic rebellion. The Basij, a supplementary arm of the Revolutionary Guard, was to defend the ideology of the revolution. Initially staffed with underage children and men too old to serve as members of the Revolutionary Guard, little was heard from this group until it was marshaled for "crowd control" following the 2009 presidential elections in Iran. Prior to that time the Basij's major claim to fame had been its service during the Iran-Iraq War.

It was the younger members of the group—the children—who were used as minesweepers for advancing Iranian troops. Michael Eisenstadt, senior fellow and director of The Washington Institute's Military and Security Studies Program, described the citizen army: "Basij members made up with zeal what they lacked in military professionalism......I think cannon fodder is a fair way to characterize them."[229]

Having been whipped into a suicidal frenzy by Khomeini's promise of the perks of martyrdom, these young Basij died by the tens of thousands. After the war ended, the citizen militia became the dreaded morality police. They enforce hijab, making certain women are covering their heads and dressing modestly; they arrest women who violate the dictated dress code. They arrest young men and women who dare to attend parties together or appear in public with someone of the opposite sex who is not a family member. The Basij is also charged with confiscating materials deemed "indecent." This includes satellite dish antennae that have been carefully hidden by a vast number of Iranians.

Under the reform presidencies of Khatami and Rafsanjani, the religious piety and simple devotion displayed by Ahmadinejad were treated disparagingly and considered quaint. Under Ahmadinejad, orthodox religion serves as a direct connection to the vast Iranian underclass. Millions in Iran have never enjoyed the material advantages or the abundant lifestyles of the wealthy mullahs or the government officials who rose to the top in the reform years since the Ayatollah Khomeini died.

R. Nicholas Burns, Under Secretary for Political Affairs for the State Department, gave a speech in 2005 in which he noted once again that "Iran remains the world's most active state sponsor of terrorism," commenting also that "Iran's human rights record remains abysmal."[230] In this speech, Mr. Burns noted that two-thirds of Iran's 70 million people are under the age of 35, and have "no personal memory of the (Iranian) revolution and its hijacking by extremists."

Having lived under the strictures of this regime, Iran's new generation has renewed its historic struggle for political participation, free speech, and openness to the world. Many young Iranians desire an improved relationship with the United States. Over the past decade, this new generation has tried to make its voice heard—despite the attempts of hard-liners to silence it.

By the late 1990s, Iran appeared to be shifting toward reform and popular aspirations for democratic government. Tragically for the people of Iran, the hard-line defenders of absolute clerical rule struck back to suppress reforms and, for the moment, appear to be prevailing. They have used their control of the security forces, the judiciary, and other levers of power to frustrate reform and suppress critics. There is a clear struggle underway between the reactionary Iranian government and the moderate majority.

The problem is that Ahmadinejad's radical orthodoxy has strong appeal among Iran's underclass. Today, even the most rebellious students hesitate to speak out against the government, worried that their protest risks prison or death. Student hunger strikes, sit-ins, and demonstrations routinely break out across Iran, only to be put down by the Basij paramilitary acting as common street thug enforcers for the regime.

Within Iran the rigid rule of the mullahs has been resisted since the death of Khomeini. Yet always, the regime's control of the apparatus of force and social control has suppressed potential rebellions while brutally pursuing outspoken dissidents, even if they flee Iran.

With the universities graduating some 300,000 students a year and with some 800,000 young adults entering the job market each year, Iran faces a huge problem of having as many as 50 percent of those under age 35 unemployed.[231] If we take into consideration underemployment, we are forced to realize that even some 10,000 doctors in Iran have no jobs. Each year more than 150,000 Iranians emigrate, and over 80 percent of Iranians studying in foreign universities never return home.

In Tehran, families crowd into apartments, with young adult children afraid to marry simply because low incomes make raising a family impossible, not just for feeding children but even for paying for a separate apartment in which to live. Lower level employees in Tehran's government bureaucracy miss meals or work such second jobs as taxi drivers to put food on the table for the family.

Ahmadinejad raised expectations among Iran's underclass, promising to distribute "petro-dollars" to the people. Yet even today oil-rich Iran ends up importing gasoline because the country's antiquated energy infrastructure cannot refine enough gasoline to meet domestic demand.[232]

Iranian families in poverty continue to make tragic decisions to sell a child into sex slavery or prostitution on the streets, simply to feed the other children. Youth drugs and street crime remain a risk in Tehran, despite the severity with which women in public are forced to wear the *hajib* and even holding hands between lovers can cause severe repercussions if seen by an offended adult. Teachers, medical professionals, even bus drivers have gone on strike to protest low wages and economic misery.[233]

Ahmadinejad has so far failed to deliver on his crowd-pleasing campaign promises to improve the economic lot of Iran's underclass under his administration.

Moreover, under Ahmadinejad, the Iranian stock market has dropped nearly 25 percent. Share prices have lost up to 60 percent of their value, reflecting a flight of capital and a concern that Ahmadinejad is leading the country toward war. In the last 3 months of 2005, approximately $100 billion of Iranian capital was invested in nearby Dubai. The United Arab Emirates has become a vacation spot and international business hub where many of the more wealthy mullahs maintain luxurious vacation apartments. Another $100 million of Iranian capital fled to investments in Iraq and Kurdistan. More capital has fled to Europe and Canada. During his campaign, Ahmadinejad described stock market investing as "a game of chance, contrary to Iranian principles."[234] With the stock market at an all-time low, the Iranian regime was considering closing down the market altogether.[235] Ahmadinejad predictably responded to Iran's economic crisis with fixes that were more religiously or politically motivated than economically wise.

Then, the Economic Ministry appointed Abdolhamid Ansari, a former Revolutionary Guards commander, to head the Melli Bank, Iran's central bank. To fix the stock exchange, Ahmadinejad selected Ali Salehabadi, a 27-year-old economics graduate who previously worked in the finance department of the Khomeini Foundation.[236]

A month earlier, Ahmadinejad was reported as saying that "if it had been possible to hang a couple of people, the Tehran stock exchange would already have been put in order." Salehabadi was hired not for his financial experience, but for his radical views and his aversion to a free market, not exactly the type of manager to give Western investors any feeling of confidence.

Minister of the Economy Davoud Danesh Jaafari can claim experience on the Economy and Finance Committee when he was a member of the Majlis, but his additional qualifications are that he belongs to *Abadgaran*, a hard-line Islamist faction, and was a former member of Command Central of *Jihad Sazandegi*, a branch of the Revolutionary Guards.[237] A collapsing financial infrastructure does not bode well for the type of economic gains Ahmadinejad's government will have to make to survive.

According to the Iranian constitution, his second, and final, term of office will end on August 3, 2013 (unless term limits are altered—and that is certainly possible.) He has precious little time to make good on many of his audacious campaign promises. Ahmadinejad has been widely criticized domestically for his economic failures which include stringent gas rationing in 2007, and the lowering of interest rates that can be charged by private and public banks. Given the widely disputed second election results, Ahmadinejad may not be able to secure another government posting.

To further exacerbate his problems, in March 2012, the Iranian president was the first leader to ever be summoned before the Islamic Consultative

Assembly, also called the Iranian Parliament or People's House, to answer questions regarding his governance of the country.

It is ironic that Iran has a failing economy. As one of the richest countries in the world in oil and natural gas resources, we would expect that Iran should have a booming economy. Under Ayatollah Khomeini, most of Iran's major businesses, including the energy businesses were nationalized, run by inefficient state bureaucracies.

Under the reform presidencies of Khatami and Rafsanjani, the mullahs got rich. Under Ahmadinejad, the mullahs may not get quite as rich, but Iran's underclass will probably continue to suffer. If the people have Islam, Ahmadinejad may well argue, why do they need more?

Reversing years of reforms and turning back the clock to the ultra-conservative repression of the 1979 revolution, Ahmadinejad issued a directive banning all Western and "indecent" music from state-run television and radio stations.[238] Whether Ahmadinejad can really block all Western music from Iran's youth is doubtful, though the ban on state-run television and radio shows the direction in which Ahmadinejad is headed.

Throughout Iran, the Basij are today ever-present and ready to suppress dissent. In towns throughout Iran, including the central cities of Shiraz and Isfahan where Iran's nuclear processing plant is located, hundreds of Basij militia were deployed under the pretext of fighting hooligans, or tracking down drug or alcohol smugglers.

In reality, the regime wanted to flex its muscle, in the process harassing women under the usual pretexts of "non-observance of Islamic tradition" or not wearing the mandatory *hajib* veil in public.[239] In the northeast city of Shahrood, two female students were reported injured by Basij who splashed acid in their faces, reacting against dress code violations, a further effort to re-impose the "Gender Apartheid Policy" initiated with the 1979 revolution.[240]

Twice, soccer riots broke out at Tehran's Azadi ("Freedom") Stadium. Youth attending the game began attacking the symbols of the regime—flags and posters. When the Basij militia moved in the violence spilled into the streets and surrounding residential neighborhoods. The anger escalated to the point that protesting youth began smashing windows of security patrol cars and collective buses. The clashes continued until late in the evening and resulted in a huge traffic jam; dozens of people were injured before the turmoil subsided.[241]

In another skirmish, hundreds of students gathered at Tehran's College of Technology and began shouting freedom slogans critical of the regime. Again, Basij militia moved in, paying special attention to attacking the female demonstrators; members of Herrasat (a regime intelligence organization) took photographs of the students for later identification purposes.[242]

Scores of these incident reports come out of Iran every month. Expatriate groups document the occurrences, trying to build the case that internal dissent continues in the face of brutal regime suppression of protest. Still, study after study shows that the Iranian censorship on Internet websites is the most sophisticated and severe in the world. The Iranian regime uses high-tech filtering systems, playing a cat and mouse game between those who would speak freely and those who would stop them."[243] Bloggers writing in Farsi are today more likely to be blocked than those writing in virtually any other language, including Chinese.

In contrast, the Bright Future Institute in Qom operates a telephone hotline and runs an Internet site dedicated to spreading the message of the imminent return of the Mahdi. The most common question asked? "How will we know when the Mahdi is ready to return?" One hundred sixty workers at the center answer dozens of questions daily, respond to e-mails and write letters. The institute has a growing reach in local schools, publishes children's and teen magazines, and produces books and films. The day when the Mahdi returns is seen as the beginning of a new age, where Islam is victorious worldwide and people live in peace and harmony.[244]

—17—

BEHIND THE WALLS
OF OPPRESSION

*Iran is a major threat to the well-being of Europe
and America just as much as it is for the state of Israel.*[245]
—FORMER PRIME MINISTER EHUD OLMERT

FOLLOWING THE DISPUTED REELECTION OF AHMADINEJAD IN 2008, the dissent in Iran grew strong enough that many took to the streets in protest against Khamenei and his strong-armed tactics. Of course, the protests were attributed to "The Great Satan"—America—to Israel and, surprisingly, to Great Britain. Such far-fetched accusations may have sounded a bit suspect to many Iranians, but sadly, not to all. Some continue to believe Ahmadinejad's vitriolic rhetoric. He has to have someone to blame for Iran's ills, and who better than America? If that ploy were removed from his bag of tricks, how would he explain the country's problems to the Iranian people?

With memories of how Khomeini fostered revolution and then benefited from it, Khamenei was compelled to recognize the need for a post-mortem on the election. He knows, of course, that his ham-fisted hold on power is more tenuous than ever before. Millions, perhaps the majority of Iranians, have seen the emperor's imperfections and heard his lies. He will never again be able to recapture the adulation in which he was once held. His rule is that of a dictator holding the strings of his hand-picked puppet. His regime has lost its validity—if indeed it ever possessed any.

A courageous young Iranian reporter who covered events in Iran for *The Jerusalem Post* wrote:

> I think people recognize that the anger and bitterness at the regime is acute among the young Iranians. I'm talking about youngsters who've been watching Western TV for years, on the little satellite dishes everybody hides in their air-conditioning units, and want those freedoms...well-educated youngsters, graduates, who can't find work....They're aware that the Revolutionary Guards, the military face of the regime, are becoming increasingly powerful—that Iran is tending toward military dictatorship...the slogans of thirty years ago [are] now being directed at those who were supposed to be the guardians of the revolution.[246]

The emperor stood naked before his subjects. All the silks, satins, and brocades hiding the ugliness of his rule stripped away; his hand-picked president no more than a court jester appointed to deceive the Iranian people with his smoke-and-mirrors act. His bravado still, unfortunately, cows many in the West, making some leaders too afraid to challenge the tyrant's edicts and threats.

Ahmadinejad has garnered followers of his Twelver sect, which now totals some 80 percent of the population, by promising the soon-return of the Mahdi. This is the twenty-first century, and modern-day Iranians are finding it difficult to live separately but peacefully with those Shi'a still stuck in centuries past. As columnist Roger Cohen wrote:

> Iran has squandered a huge opportunity to bridge the gulf between the regime and an increasingly sophisticated population thirsting for greater freedom. A vibrant election campaign opened a door. It has been slammed shut.... Over

the past week [Iran] has looked more like a flag-bearing police state.... Khamenei...has looked more like a ruthless infighter.[247]

Cracks have become chasms too great to bridge. Tyranny has become sweeping and vicious. The leadership has lost an entire new generation. Iran's global oratory has been uncovered for what it is—meaningless. Ahmadinejad and the emperor, Khamenei, have lost all credibility. They have prevailed—for the moment—but the cost has been enormous. The Iranian people have once again been driven back behind walls of oppression, too fearful to venture forth into the light of freedom; too bowed to fight against the despotism.

Events in Iran herald no mere skirmish between oppression and liberty. The government has not been toppled, yet the political scene has been altered, fidelity extinguished, and the supposed infallibility of Iran's supreme leader obliterated. Khamenei has had to resort to diatribes against non-existent interference from outside influences. He has been reduced to backing Ahmadinejad, the man whose two terms as president have been divisive at best. One Iranian politician who wished to remain anonymous for obvious reasons said, "This man, Ahmadinejad, is destroying the whole system of the Islamic Republic, which includes Mr. Khamenei. But Mr. Khamenei supports him because he sits like a mouse in front of him and kisses his feet."[248] In the past years, and contrary to the counsel of his peers, Khamenei tied his wagon to Ahmadinejad's star. Rather than the court jester basking in the glow of the emperor, the reverse seems to be true.

Perhaps sensing an opportunity to wrest power from the ruling ayatollah, other clerics seized the moment to take sides in the struggle. Yes, the mullahs were divided, some siding with Ahmadinejad and puppet-master Khamenei and others with Moussavi and cleric Seyed Mohammad Khatami, a liberal reformer. As a former president of Iran, Khatami's modifications were thwarted by the Guardian Council before he could achieve any real success. It was because of him the ruling clerics apparently determined all elections, while seemingly democratic in nature, had to be manipulated to insure the victory of the chosen and anointed candidate.

Since 2003 the Guardian Council—the entity charged with vetting politi-cal candidates——has enacted even more stringent guidelines as to who may or may not run for the office of president. As one editorialist pointed out, "What may seem more surprising is that so many prominent first-generation revolutionaries have sided with Mr. Moussavi.... Even among the clergy, the best minds...have distanced themselves from Ayatollah Khamenei."[249] Moussavi was supported by former presidents Ali Akbar Hashemi Rafsanjani and Mohammad Khatami.

Dr. David Menashri, director at the Center for Iranian Studies, decries the actual process of selecting candidates, which eliminates about 50 percent of the population—the women. In a telephone conference arranged by The Israel Project, Dr. Menashri said these shadow citizens of Iran "have been disqualified because they do not fit the criteria.... [Only] four candidates... [were] approved by the council of experts and deemed acceptable by the rul-ing elite...what the Iranians are electing is a president in a system in which the president in the best of times can be considered as like the vice-president of the United States." He went on to say, "The council of guardians...dis-qualified seven hundred candidates...but does not even need to explain why a person is being disqualified."[250]

Dr. Menashri believes Ahmadinejad accomplished two major objec-tives during his first term in office: He challenged the world regarding Iran's nuclear proliferation; and he "painted all other Iranian officials as moderate pragmatists...[and himself as] more extremist, radical, conservative."[251]

According to another observer, "The association's statement also shows how deeply the political establishment is divided, and the extent to which the supreme leader now derives his power from military might not moral authority. It makes it much harder for the regime to arrest Mr. Moussavi and other opposition leaders."[252]

The mullahs who are in power seized control by revolution in 1979; they have seen what a united Iranian people can do. This is what Khamenei fears and why he has vowed that a "street challenge is not acceptable."

These mullahs have perfected the art of enmity over the past three decades. In spite of the hatred for all things Western spewing from the mouths of these supposed leaders, Iranian youth are as passionate about freedom as the mullahs are about repression. The upheaval that will surely come if they wage a successful revolution would change the complexion of the Middle East—just how dramatically, no one really knows. The challenge is great.

The uprising of angry and frustrated Iranians following each of the last two elections should have been enough to cause despotic Islamic regimes worldwide to listen for the unmistakable sounds of discontent and displeasure among the populace. Iran is outdistanced only by Saudi Arabia when it comes to funding Islamic schools, organizations, Muslim ideology, and military training. It must send a shiver down the backs of those who rely on Iran to sponsor their terrorist organizations and train the next wave of jihadists. After all, "From Somalia to Lebanon's Hezbollah, from Hamas to the Egyptian Shi'ite movement, Iranian support—whether through direct funding or military and training—will be jeopardized if the theocrats are unseated."[253]

For that matter, who is really in charge in Iran? Is it Khamenei, the supreme leader? Is it the Revolutionary Guard? Is it Ahmadinejad and his Basij militia? These are questions political analysts have bandied about for some time. Some believe the Shi'ite clergy has a stranglehold on the country. Others believe control may lie within the army, the guardian of the arms and ammunition necessary to repress uprisings. Just who holds the authority and how much has yet to be determined...possibly by the Iranians themselves.

Bernard Hourcade, a French expert on Iran, confirmed the situation:

> I don't know who has the power, and that is the problem
> in Iran. It's anarchy. No one has got the power. It's dangerous
> for the people of Iran. It's dangerous for everybody.[254]

A fissure in the façade of civility between Ahmadinejad and Khamenei also opened up following the 2009 election. The supreme leader objected to the president's choice of Esfandiar Rahim Mashai as first vice president in charge of tourism and culture. He is one of twelve vice presidents in the

Iranian hierarchy. Khamenei issued an order to Ahmadinejad to dismiss the vice president; Ahmadinejad refused. One of the concerns stems from the fact that Mashai is a son-in-law to the president. The president's refusal of a direct order from the supreme leader is a surprising turn of events.

During his first four-year term Ahmadinejad spent his time establishing a network of cronies in the military, law enforcement, and within the media. It is estimated he infiltrated the government with more than ten thousand men loyal to him alone. One analyst wrote, "There is a whole political establishment that has emerged with Ahmadinejad, which is now determined to hold onto power undemocratically. Their ability to resist the outcome of the election means they have a broad base...[including but certainly not limited to] all thirty of the country's governors, all the city managers, and even third- and fourth-level civil servants."[255]

When the so-called "Arab Spring" raced through much of the Middle East in 2011 the uproar all but sidestepped Iran. The few initial protests were quickly quelled by the Revolutionary Guard and the Basij. During a rally in Tehran in February of that year, a slogan surfaced that may have spurred Ahmadinejad to further crackdowns. One sign read, "Whether Cairo or Tehran, death to tyrants!"[256]

— 18 —

IN THE FOOTSTEPS
OF THE MENTOR

"Iran does its utmost to undermine Middle East Peace diplomacy."
—HENRY KISSINGER, 2001[257]

PRESIDENT MAHMOUD AHMADINEJAD SEEMS TO HAVE ADOPTED the motto of his hero, Ruhollah Khomeini regarding Iran's nuclear program. It was Khomeini who said: "America cannot do a damn thing."[258] To many in the Middle East, the US appears to be the "Great Satan" no longer, but is rather cowardly and impotent. The Iranian leader has succeeded in thwarting any efforts made by the US to sanction Iran because of its nuclear program. It seems, all too often, that the Liberal Left is determined to assist Mr. Ahmadinejad in his attempts to discredit the supposedly sinister United States by giving him the benefit of the doubt. Iran, the liberals believe, has justifiable complaints against the "Great Satan." After all, in some minds 9/11 was caused, not by a fanatical hatred for all things American, but by the failure of the US to empathize with the privation and hopelessness in Third World countries. "Along these lines," wrote David Limbaugh, "is it any surprise that Obama… thinks we are at fault for not trying hard enough to meet Iranian tyrant

Mahmoud Ahmadinejad halfway?"[259] This even after Iran's president posted on his website:

> Resistance will continue until Iran sends its enemies
> [Israel and the US] to the morgue.[260]

A precedent was set with Iran under Presidents Jimmy Carter and Bill Clinton which still proves true today. The US appears to cower behind a group of allies that are powerless to implement any viable restrictions on the former Persian Empire. The world is once again being challenged by what may be the best student to emerge from Khomeini's madrasas (Islamic schools), Mahmoud Ahmadinejad.

The global reach of Khomeini is not restricted to Iran. In a treatise by Gen. (Ret.) Moshe Yaalon, he writes, "According to Iranian Supreme Leader Ali Khamenei and Iran's Syrian partners, the Second Lebanon War [August 2006] was launched by Hezbollah—Iran's proxy—as a hostile probe of US reflexes via the engagement of Israel, which for Iran and Syria is a direct extension of Washington in the Middle East."[261] It is apparent that Tehran wishes to neutralize America's influence in the Middle East as a major step in the plan to defeat Western civilization. Foremost in that effort is the funding, training, and arming of Hezbollah in Lebanon, and not just with pistols and ammunition.

Not only does Iran directly support Hezbollah, it also supplies Hamas with funds, arms, and training. For years Lebanon has played host to about 250 members of the Islamic Revolutionary Guard Corps, the elite of the Iranian military, and is best at training other terror units. It is obvious to me that Iran has a long-term plan to take control of the Middle East by using proxies: Hamas, Hezbollah, and Palestinian Islamic Jihad, along with Muktada al-Sadr's Shiite Mahdi Army in Iraq.

Ahmadinejad is equally determined to destroy Israel. He was recalling Khomeini's earlier rhetoric when, in October 2005 he declared, "This regime that is occupying Qods [Jerusalem] must be eliminated from the pages of history."[262] Ahmadinejad's idol, rather than being the savior of Iran and the champion of human rights, instead became the personification of Islamic terrorism, a man whose cruelty and hatred knew no bounds.

In an eighteen-page letter to President George W. Bush (43) on May 8, 2006, Ahmadinejad urged the president to convert to Islam. In his epistle to the president, Ahmadinejad issued a veiled warning, perhaps threat: "Those with insights can already hear the sounds of the shattering and fall of the ideology and thoughts of the liberal democratic systems."[263]

Under Presidents Rafsanjani and Khatami, the West seemed to feel that Iran could be moved by pragmatic political considerations, such that compromise and national self-interest were reasonable appeals to move Iranian foreign policy. President Ahmadinejad clearly has embraced principles of expanding a messianic vision of the Iranian revolution, perhaps even more radical than the principles advocated by Ayatollah Khomeini himself. In dealing with a mystical politician of Ahmadinejad's conviction, the West has lost its compass. With a mystic as head of state, ordinary calculations of power politics no longer apply with the same pragmatic force.

As previously mentioned, particularly disturbing about Ahmadinejad is the belief that an apocalypse must occur before the Mahdi returns. An international war triggered by an Iranian nuclear attack on Israel could well be the apocalypse Ahmadinejad believes he has a divine mission to occasion, regardless of the suicidal nature of the decision. There is no higher status than that of martyr in the Iranian version of Shi'ite Islam. A religious fascination with suicide fundamentally changes the definition of the behavior which rests at the center of all calculations—that the risk of mutually assured destruction will deter a head of state from initiating a nuclear war. Ironically, a suicidal leader motivated by religious mysticism might actually be attracted to a nuclear war.

Neither Ahmadinejad's anti-Semitic attacks on Israel nor his Holocaust denials are unique in Iranian history. Iran's fascination with rabid anti-Semantic ideology goes back to World War II.

Nazi Germany reached out to include Iran in the Axis powers. During the pre-war years, Iran welcomed Gestapo agents, allowing Germany to use Tehran as a base against the British and the region's Jews. Hitler and

Ahmadinejad held a belief in a fated mission of world domination that involved the elimination of Jews. Remarkably, that Iran played a role complicit in the Holocaust does not prevent Ahmadinejad from denying that it happened. Ironically, maybe it's because Iran played a complicit role in the Holocaust that zealots like Ahmadinejad want to deny the historic tragedy.

We would be terribly mistaken to think that Ahmadinejad was simply a rabble-rouser, or that his speeches reflect an unsophisticated politician's bumbling efforts to engage in the international arena. By attacking Israel and denying the Holocaust, Ahmadinejad is delivering the exact message the spiritual leaders ruling Iran want delivered.

In December 2006, the Association of Islamic Journalists participated in a conference on the Holocaust. Hehdi Afzali, the spokesperson of the Association, explained to journalists that the conference was being held to support the argument Ahmadinejad had offered:

> "President Ahmadinejad has placed at the center of international attention a very important question on the truthfulness of the version that Europe and the Zionists have imposed on the world on the murder of Jews during the years of the great war. Therefore, we are of the opinion that it is useful and necessary to organize an international conference on the theme, where all the historians and researchers, even those that do not believe in the official version, will be able to express themselves freely."[264]

Ahmadinejad wants to have the argument both ways. If Europe believes the Holocaust happened, then the guilt and responsibility for it should be Europe's. The conclusion here is: so, let's move Israel to Europe. Yet, Iran does not believe the Holocaust happened. So, the conclusion under this contradictory part of the argument is this: Israel has no justification for existing, let alone occupying land that belongs to the Palestinians. Either way, the conclusion is the same—Iran believes Israel must be wiped off the map of the Middle East.

Iran is pursuing this argument with a focused determination, understanding that the first step toward eliminating Israel today is to undermine the intellectual and moral supports that have served to validate the creation of the Jewish State. The inference Ahmadinejad wants to draw for the future is equally clear: If Israel was founded on a lie at the end of World War II, then fighting to preserve Israel today is equally unfounded. As Ahmadinejad tightens his grip on the propaganda that flows from Tehran, it seems obvious that his measures at home are designed to fulfill his early campaign promise to return the Islamic Republic to the days of the Khomeini revolution in 1979.

Since the early days of that revolution, Iran has moved with great determination to become a nuclear weapons power as quickly as possible. The strategy employed to reach this goal has been both subtle and brilliant.

Iranian physicists decided it was important to study just how Israel was able to launch a military strike against Iraq's nuclear reactor at *Osirak*. As Professor Louis Rene Beres noted, because of the courage of Prime Minister Menachem Begin in approving an Israeli attack on Iraq's *Osirak* reactor:

> Israel's citizens, together with Jews and Arabs, American, and other coalition soldiers who fought in the [Persian] Gulf War may owe their lives to Israel's courage, skill, and foresight in June 1981. Had it not been for the brilliant raid at *Osirak*, Saddam's forces might have been equipped with atomic warheads in 1991. Ironically, the Saudis, too, are in Jerusalem's debt. Had it not been for Prime Minister Begin's resolve to protect the Israeli people in 1981, Iraq's SCUDs falling on Saudi Arabia might have spawned immense casualties and lethal irradiation.[265]

The attack, labeled "Operation Opera", was launched on June 7, 1981. The task force included fourteen F-15s and F-16s, which took off from Etzion Air Force base in the Negev. The pilots' route took them over Jordan and Saudi Arabia and into Iraqi airspace. Their mission was to attack and destroy *Osirak*, the nuclear reactor built for Saddam Hussein by the French.

While on vacation in Aqaba, Jordan's King Hussein is said to have seen the Israeli planes as they flew overhead. He attempted to notify the Iraqis, but it was apparent that his message either did not reach its destination, or the Iraqis chose to ignore it as speculation.[266]

Although the surprise attack shocked the Iraqis and the world, it had not been planned overnight. It was the final resort after all diplomatic efforts had failed and the French could not be persuaded by world opinion to halt the construction of the reactor. Prime Minister Begin consulted closely with his cabinet, and a decision of monumental proportions was reached: The only avenue open to insure that Saddam Hussein did not achieve nuclear arms capabilities and thereby carry out his threats against Israel was to attack *Osirak*. Intelligence sources within Israel determined that within one to two years Iraq would have possessed nuclear weapons. Later resources confirmed that Saddam was, in fact, within one year of his goal.[267]

Prime Minister Begin and his cabinet did not take lightly the choice to attack Saddam Hussein's pet project. Moshe Dayan, Begin's foreign minister, worked zealously through diplomatic channels to forestall such an attack. Casper Weinberger and Alexander Haig, defense secretary and secretary of state under Ronald Reagan, agreed with the Israeli evaluation of the seriousness of the circumstances in Iraq. However, the US refused to take the lead in combating the situation. It might have been that the true danger was not evident, or it might have been simply that Iraq was engaged in a war with Iran, an avowed enemy. Had not the Grand Ayatollah Ruhollah Khomeini abandoned the Shah's nuclear program because it drew from the "satanic" West, it is highly likely he would have used any available nuclear weapons against Iraq. The same may be said for Hussein against Iran…or both against the leaders of Israel, an avowed enemy of Islam.

Israeli Minister of Justice Moshe Nissim recorded that Prime Minister Begin was likely swayed to approve the attack because he realized that an unprincipled and irresponsible Arab ruler such as Saddam Hussein would not have thought twice about launching an attack on Israel. Begin realized the exigency to stop Hussein's quest for nuclear arms.

The Israelis explored every option open to them militarily—jets, ground troops, paratroopers, helicopters—before making the final decision to remove a fuel tank on each of their newly-purchased F-16s in order to make them capable of transporting the armament needed to destroy *Osirak*. More importantly, perhaps, they could make the foray flying under Iraq's radar without having to refuel. The date of the attack was set after Begin was notified that Iraq was about to take possession of a shipment of enriched uranium fuel rods from France. This was crucial because once the rods were in place the danger of nuclear fallout from the attack would have been a certainty.

Yitzhak Shamir stated the obvious in Israel's decision to act:

> "Deterrence was not attained by other countries—France and Italy—and even the United States. It was attained by the state of Israel and its prime minister, who decided, acted, and created a fact that no one in the world today—with the exception of our enemies—regrets."[268]

The Israeli attack was relatively simple because Iraq had only one major nuclear facility. Iran has resolved not to make this same mistake. As a defensive move, its leaders decided to decentralize their nuclear facilities around the country. Many nuclear facilities could be embedded in population centers. Thus, to attack successfully Israel or the United States would have to launch a multi-pronged strike which would be more tactically difficult to plan and implement successfully. Even worse, with nuclear facilities inside Iran's cities, a military strike would cause civilian casualties. Would Israel and America be willing to kill thousands of Iranian civilians to take out Iran's nuclear facilities in a preemptive military attack? Clearly, this would raise the stakes among Israel's enemies.

Iran's leaders further determined that each separate nuclear installation would be devoted to a single purpose, a piece that could be fitted into the puzzle. This way, if a particular facility were attacked and destroyed, Iran would lose only the functionality fulfilled at that location. Some operations would be duplicated in other facilities; others might be replaced by out-sourcing the fulfillment of the functionality to a friendly country, perhaps Russia or Pakistan. No successful attack on any one facility would knock offline Iran's total nuclear capabilities for long.

Each step of Iran's nuclear technology has been designed to allow access to the "full fuel cycle," going from uranium ore to weapons-grade uranium. Since 1988 Iran has opened an estimated ten different uranium mines. Exploration at these sites estimates that the uranium resources of Iran are in the range of 20,000—30,000 tons throughout the country, more than enough to fuel Iran's civilian nuclear power plants well into the future.[269]

In early 2003, Iran announced that a uranium mine was opened at Saghand (Sagend), near the central Iranian city of Yazd, in the central Iranian desert of Kavir, some three hundred miles south of Tehran.[270] In September 2004, Iran allowed the international press to tour that mine for the first time. Ghasem Soleimani, the British-trained director of mining operations at the Energy Organization of Iran, reported on plans to begin extracting uranium ore from the mine in the first half of 2006. He claimed, "More than 77 per-cent of the work has been accomplished."[271]

The mine was reported to have a capacity of 132,000 tons of uranium ore per year. Uranium ore is processed into uranium ore concentrate, com-monly called "yellowcake" at a separate production plant located at Ardakan, about sixty kilometers from Yazd.

Iran's uranium processing facility is located at Isfahan, a central Iranian city some 250 miles south of Tehran. This Nuclear Technology and Research Center is said to employ as many as three thousand scientists in a facil-ity constructed about fifteen kilometers southeast of central Isfahan, at a research complex constructed by the French under a 1975 agreement with Iran.[272] Isfahan also houses one of Iran's major universities, with some one thousand graduate students and approximately ten thousand undergradu-ates in fields that include science, social science, and humanities.

On the eastern outskirts of Isfahan is the Uranium Conversion Facility, a cluster of buildings surrounded by razor wire fencing and protected by anti-aircraft guns and military patrols.[273] In this facility yellowcake ore is processed into uranium hexafluoride gas (UF4), the first step required to convert uranium ore to the enriched state needed to run a nuclear power plant or to provide the weapons-grade uranium needed to make an atomic bomb. The *Daily Telegraph* issued an alarming report from Isfahan on September 12, 2008, indicating that enriched uranium sufficient to assemble six atom bombs had been removed from the facility:

> The [International Atomic Energy Agency "IAEA"] inspectors only have limited access at Isfahan, and it looks as though Iranian officials have removed significant quantities of UF6 at a stage in the process that is not being monitored.... If Iran's nuclear intentions are peaceful, then why are they doing this?[274]

From Isfahan, uranium hexafluoride gas is transported to yet another facility, this one at Natanz, about ninety miles to the northeast of Isfahan. Here the uranium hexafluoride gas is enriched in centrifuges to the higher grade, uranium-235. This completes the "full fuel cycle," ending the range of processes needed to get from uranium ore to highly enriched uranium. At lower grades of enrichment, the uranium would doubtless be used to fuel peaceful power plants. Uranium enriched to uranium-235 can be fashioned into the metallic form needed to serve as the fissile core of an atom bomb.

The Fuel Enrichment Plant at Isfahan is located about ten miles to the northeast of the town of Natanz, set off from the surrounding desert by a perimeter security fence and military guards. The Natanz Fuel Enrichment Plant houses two large underground halls built eight meters below ground. The halls are hardened by thick, concrete-reinforced walls built to protect the facility. The construction was designed to house an advanced centrifuge complex of as many as fifty thousand centrifuges.

Experts estimate that the Fuel Enrichment Plant was prepared initially to house some five thousand centrifuges in the preliminary stage of the project.[275] Operating at full capacity, fifty thousand centrifuges would be capable of producing enough weapons-grade uranium to build over twenty weapons per year. When completed, the underground facilities were planned to have no visible above-ground signature, a move designed to complicate precise targeting of any munitions that could be used in an attack.

Precise satellite imagery of the nuclear facilities at both Isfahan and Natanz show the exact location of the operation. The images document various phases of facility construction and concealment, from the time the facilities were first begun to very recently on a continuously updated basis. Inspection of the satellite images reveals that the complexes were designed to include dormitory/housing facilities for those working at the plant. Also visible are various complexes of administrative and scientific buildings needed to operate the facilities.

Even these publicly available satellite images show the military defense and anti-aircraft installations designed to provide security. Inspection of these images makes clear that Isfahan and Natanz are both sophisticated facilities. The Iranians paid careful attention to design, both for the professional operation of nuclear activity and the military preparedness needed to protect the facilities from attack.

In November 2004, Iranian leaders agreed to stop all processing of uranium at both Isfahan and Natanz. They made this decision to comply with a condition set by the EU3 (the European Union countries of France, Germany, and the United Kingdom) for negotiations to begin.

The goal of the EU3 was to settle with Iran the IAEA requirements for facility inspection. The IAEA wanted to determine that Iran was compliant with the provisions of the NPT (Nuclear Non-Proliferation Treaty) prohibiting the development of nuclear weapons. The IAEA was obligated to hold Iran to a standard of "transparency," meaning that all Iranian nuclear facilities and operations should be open to IAEA inspection at times and places of the IAEA's choosing.

— 19 —

NUCLEAR
AMBITIONS

*"What is written clearly is not worth much,
it's the transparency that counts."*
—LOUIS FERDINAND CELINE[276]

A TRANSPARENT NUCLEAR PROGRAM is one that is open to inspection; a non-transparent program is one where restrictions are placed upon inspections. If Iran were allowed to limit inspections to certain times and to certain facilities or particular areas within facilities, the advanced warning requirement would give workers the opportunity to sanitize operations prior to examination.

International skeptics argued that Iran had only agreed to suspend uranium processing because Isfahan and Natanz were not yet complete in November 2004. More time was needed to finish facility construction and resolve technical problems. By agreeing to "stop" operations it seemed apparent that Iran was truly not even ready to begin, it seized the opportunity to appear cooperative. Skeptics argued Iran's primary goal was simply to buy more time.

In September 2004, Iran told the IAEA in a report little noticed at the time that the country planned to process some forty tons of uranium into uranium hexafluoride gas. This notice tended to be forgotten as soon as Iran announced later that processing and enrichment was being voluntarily suspended.

On January 10, 2005, after Iran resumed nuclear "research and development" at Natanz, Mohammad Saeedi, the deputy director of Iran's Atomic Energy Organization, adopted the Iranian leader's new control tactics when he made the announcement in a way that suggested the IAEA had given its approval: "Nuclear research officially resumed at sites agreed upon with IAEA inspectors."[277]

The inspectors had traveled to Natanz to remove the seals from the research installations there; but actually, no approval had been given to Iran's decision to resume uranium enrichment activities there, even if these activities were distinguished by Iran to be only "research and development," not full uranium enrichment. In reality Mohamed El Baradei, head of the IAEA, had asked Iran to agree voluntarily to keep Natanz closed, in order to build international confidence.

After asking Iran to clarify what was meant by "research and development," El Baradei released a 35-page report to the IAEA board revealing that Iran did intend to release uranium hexafluoride gas into the centrifuges in small amounts. It was an attempt by Iran to distinguish "research activities" from "full-scale uranium enrichment."[278]

The pattern Iran's nuclear scientists followed in the resumption of uranium enrichment at Natanz paralleled the one that had been at Isfahan. Both plants had been closed voluntarily in November 2004, in a move designed to pacify the IAEA requirement for negotiations to commence on Iran's nuclear program. In November 2004, critics charged that both plants had been closed because the country's nuclear scientists and engineers were experiencing technical problems.

Then, in February 2005, an IAEA report was leaked to the Associated Press suggesting that Tehran was planning to process thirty-seven tons of yellowcake uranium oxide into uranium hexafluoride gas, estimated to be enough to make about five small atomic bombs once the UF4 gas was enriched to uranium-235. The report caused a blow-up in the press. Ali

Akbar Salehi, a senior advisor to Iran's Foreign Minister Kamal Kharrazi, reacted sharply when questioned about the AP report:

> "That we want to process thirty-seven metric tons of uranium ore into hexafluoride gas is not a discovery," he told the international press. "The IAEA has been aware of Iran's plan to construct the Uranium Conversion Facility in Isfahan since it was a barren land. We haven't constructed the Isfahan facility to produce biscuits but hexafluoride gas."[279]

This type of forced admission raised concerns in the international community that Iran was deliberately lying about its nuclear intentions. Was Iran going to process uranium or not?

Then, in May 2005, international rumors circulated suggesting that Iran had gone ahead with processing the thirty-seven tons of uranium ore, and that work at Isfahan had never been suspended after all. To resolve this conflict, Mohammad Saeedi, the deputy head of the Atomic Energy Organization of Iran (AEOI), came forward. He explained to the international press that thirty-seven tons of uranium ore had been processed but before formally suspending nuclear processing at Isfahan the previous November:

> "We converted all the thirty-seven tons of uranium concentrate known as yellowcake into UF4 at the Isfahan Uranium Conversion Facility before we suspended work there.[280]

In a separate statement Hasan Rowhani, Iran's top nuclear negotiator, admitted that Iran had produced both UF4 and UF6 gas. Rowhani also discussed the suspension of uranium processing in a way that suggested Iran's real intent was work on the Isfahan and Natanz facilities. "It is true that we are currently under suspension," Rowhani commented, "but we conducted a lot of activities in 2004. Today, if we want to start enrichment we have sufficient centrifuges at least for the early stages, while we didn't have such a capacity twenty-five months ago."[281]

Rowhani was responding to internal criticism from Iranians who wanted the country to move ahead; hard-liners who had argued that the suspension of uranium processing had harmed Iran's technological advancement. The problem was that Rowhani's statement sounded like Iran was flip-flopping, claiming it had processed uranium before it stopped processing uranium.

Iran openly resumed processing uranium at Isfahan on August 2005, defiantly breaking the earlier promise to suspend uranium processing while the EU-3 negotiations were proceeding.[282] Iran was beginning to feel the upper hand. Its aggressive defiance was being met by confusion and inaction from the United States and the Europeans.

When Iran defied world diplomats by deciding unilaterally to resume uranium processing at Isfahan, the regime argued that "uranium processing" was not "uranium enrichment" because uranium processing ends with uranium hexafluoride gas, not with actual enriched uranium. Then, virtually verifying that technical problems had been at issue, Iran confirmed on January 1, 2006 that major advances had been made at Isfahan in the development of a "mixer-settler" process to separate yellowcake uranium from uranium ore.[283] Before Natanz was reopened nine days later, reports indicated that the uranium hexafluoride gas being produced at Isfahan was initially of such poor quality that the centrifuges would have been damaged had the gas been fed into the centrifuges.

Isfahan was reopened for full-scale uranium processing when Iran was ready to do so, but only after technical "research and development" problems had been solved. It had been decided unilaterally to reopen the plant, over the objections of the IAEA and world diplomats.

Officials resumed uranium processing, knowing that their unilateral decision would throw a monkey wrench into the US plan to corner them. Yet even here, the Iranians were calculating carefully, taking one step at a time. Re-opening Isfahan meant the Iranians were resuming uranium processing. By not opening Natanz, the Iranians technically were not yet engaging in uranium enrichment. Stealthily, the Iranians moved their pieces on the chessboard; always with a view to soon declare a surprise "checkmate."

In response, the IAEA fell into a series of crisis meetings. On September 24, 2005, the International Atomic Energy Agency voted at the urging of the United States to hold Iran in non-compliance with the Nuclear Non-Proliferation Treaty. This locked in place a key piece of the US strategy.

When the IAEA vote was taken, Iran was celebrating "Sacred Defense Week," marking the 25th anniversary of the Iran-Iraq War. In Tehran Foreign Minister Manouchehr Mottaki called the IAEA resolution "political, illegal, and illogical." On state-run television, Mottaki portrayed the EU-3 as puppets of the United States, claiming, "the three European countries implemented a planned scenario already determined by the United States."[284]

John Bolton, the US ambassador to the UN, spoke of Iran's nuclear program during an on-the-record briefing:

> "There's not a single permanent member of the Security Council that accepts that Iran should have nuclear weapons...I think foreign ministers and indeed, heads of government going back to the Sea Island Summit in 2004 have made that clear. The issue is how to demonstrate to the Iranians that the course they're pursuing is not acceptable."[285]

Reuters reported that Iran was preparing to process a new batch of 250 drums of yellowcake uranium at Isfahan.[286] This left no doubt about Iran's intentions. It evidently did not want to resume negotiations with the EU-3 if that meant forfeiting the right to process uranium. The Iranian decision was particularly defiant, given that the IAEA was expected to meet on November 24 to vote on the September resolution to take Iran to the Security Council.

Immediately, Russia put a proposal of its own on the table. To break the impasse Russia offered to establish a joint venture with Iran to operate a uranium enrichment facility located in Russia.[287] Once again the IAEA postponed a decision to take Iran to the United Nations Security Council for additional sanctions, preferring instead to give Russia time to develop more fully the alternative and to win Iranian acceptance of the idea. And once again, Iran had calculated correctly. By taking this defiant path Iran had thrown the IAEA and the EU-3 into confusion. Rather than confront Iran, the first impulse of the IAEA and the EU-3 was to retreat, hoping they could still work out a diplomatic solution.

Skillfully, the Iranians had gone from enriching uranium to not enriching uranium to *maybe* enriching uranium and finally to enriching uranium again, defiantly. They danced the same dance over negotiations—first the Iranians refused to negotiate, and then they began negotiating, only to defiantly break off talks again.

At that point the Iranians said they would meet but would not give up the right to enrich uranium in their own country, not even to Russia. The Iranians would talk, but only as long as the talks were on their terms. With every move Iran bought more time. With every start and stop, confusion set upon the United States and the Europeans, just as Ayatollah Khomeini had foretold decades earlier.

Finally, after more than a quarter century following the 1979 revolution in Iran, Ayatollah Ali Khamenei was gaining confidence that he had mastered the game of international diplomacy. With his team of radical true believers more firmly in command than ever, Khamenei felt increasingly confident he could get to the end game and win. Iran would have the nuclear weapons needed to fulfill the vision to annihilate Israel just as Ahmadinejad had proclaimed.

By masking its true intentions and giving out inaccurate information, the regime continues to give the distinct impression that Iran is not being truthful. This is far from the "transparency" required by fully-disclosed nuclear activities subject to open inspection by the IAEA. Especially by deciding to proceed in defiance of strongly-expressed world diplomatic objection, the Iranian leaders further fueled concerns that the true purpose for Iran's nuclear industry was to secretively master the production of weapons-grade uranium-235 on Iranian soil without international assistance, even from "friends" such as Russia.

This should come as no surprise, as Ahmadinejad's radical mystical vision is consistent with using the arts of falsehood and duplicity in pursuing international political goals. His justification is derived from his understanding of Shi'ite Islam itself. According to Ayatollah Khomeini:

> People say: "Don't lie!" But the principle is different when we serve the will of Allah. He taught man to lie so that we can save ourselves at moments of difficulty and confuse our enemies. Should we remain truthful at the cost of defeat and danger to the Faith? We say not. People say: "Don't kill!" But the Almighty Himself taught us how to kill. Without such a skill man would have been wiped out long ago by the beasts. So shall we not kill when it is necessary for the triumph of the Faith? ... Deceit, trickery, conspiracy, cheating, stealing and killing are nothing but means. On their own they are neither good nor bad. For no deed is either good or bad, isolated from the intentions that motivated it.[288]

This twisted doctrine indicates that lying even to the people of Iran is justifiable so long as the lying is calculated to advance Islam along its fated path. These considerations further caution that additional sanctions may do little to deter the Iranian regime from proceeding defiantly with the advancement of their nuclear program. Iran's revenue from energy sales will proceed strongly from the investment placed in the energy sector by countries such as India and China, whether or not the United States ever buys any Iranian oil or natural gas.

Khomeini fought an eight-year war with Iraq in the 1980s that virtually destroyed five of Iran's twenty-three provinces, left millions homeless, and killed or maimed an entire generation of Iranian males. Khomeini advised his people in response: "Islam is a tree that needs the blood of martyrs to grow."[289] These are the politics of a religious zealot who believes religion and politics must be joined in a manner that religion drives politics, not the other way around.

With Ahmadinejad openly signifying that his mission is to prepare the way for the second coming of the Mahdi, we can expect that he will follow the path first set forth by Ayatollah Khomeini. Now, Ahmadinejad seemingly cannot be controlled by international diplomacy, even with the backing of the Americans. He is determined to defy attempts at international diplomacy in order to advamce Islam to achieve world domination. The Iranian revolution initially under Ayatollah Khomeini and today under Ahmadinejad's spiritual mentor, Ayatollah Yazdi, gives Shi'ite Islam the same religious-political force for those under its sway as Nazism did for those persuaded by Hitler.

With Israel as his main focus, can we rule out that Ahmadinejad would not use nuclear weapons against Israel and America if the weapons were available, even if the consequences proved suicidal to Iran? Most likely we cannot. So, what is the answer?

Sanctions have made some inroads, but have not achieved the anticipated results: Hadn't worldwide sanctions against South Africa brought down apartheid in the 1990s? Why wouldn't the same approach work against Iran? The idea was tantalizing, but unfortunately there were important differences between South Africa's situation in the 1990s and the Islamic Republic of Iran today. For starters, South Africa may have had ample diamonds, but that country had virtually no oil. Iran's abundant oil and natural gas resources do more than produce a large and continually flowing income for the mullahs. Iran's energy resources give the mullahs important leverage with energy-poor nations, including China and India.

In 2005, both China and India finalized major energy investment agreements with Iran, which offered the mullahs billions in investment capital to develop Iran's oil and natural gas industries. Even more important, by signing these deals with China and India, Iran bought two powerful supporters. With China a permanent member of the Security Council, the mullahs secured a veto, even if the Russians were inclined to hesitate.

Another key difference is that in the 1990s, South Africa was on the politically incorrect side of the equation, while today that is not true. In the US mainstream media, political correctness since the Vietnam War has been defined by the Liberal Left. In the past five decades, the Palestinians have spent billions of dollars, much of which was handed to them by the United Nations, on a massive worldwide public relations campaign. As a direct consequence, the Palestinians have been assisted by some of the world's top legal, political, and media experts, including at least one former US president—Carter. Israel, once a cause of the Liberal Left, has lost its position to the Palestinians. Today, the Left views the Palestinians as the oppressed second-class orphans of the Middle East, rightfully deserving of their own country—whether attained fairly or fraudulently.

However bewildering, the Liberal Left worldwide leans toward Iran, despite Iran's push for nuclear weapons. That may be in part because Iran has been painted as the proverbial underdog—even with the machinations of both Khomeini and Ahmadinejad. The public is invited to forget Iran's aggression and see the country and its leaders as victims of oppression and isolation, struggling under harsh sanctions enforced by the West. Even so, sanctions are easily circumvented by Iran's extensive ties in Europe and Asia, as well as with rogue countries such as North Korea, and dozens of allied nations in the Islamic world.

Following Iranian news sources for any period of time, one quickly realizes how frequently Iranian officials travel the world for diplomatic meetings in other nations, as well as how many representatives of other nations travel to Tehran for official government visits. Unless the United Nations were to restrict the ability of Iranian diplomats to travel worldwide, Iran is unlikely ever to reach total isolation. Even the US has granted President Ahmadinejad the right to enter this country to address the UN General Assembly several times; this despite strong protests from Iranian democracy advocates worldwide.

International diplomats' resolve to bring Iran's nuclear program within genuinely transparent IAEA inspection seems almost non-existant. As clearly as their predecessors seemed to prefer appeasement with Hitler and Germany in the 1930s, today leaders continue to believe that strong admonitions will have a deterrent effect upon the religious zealots who control Iran's radical Islamic regime. Ahmadinejad thinks differently. He believes the moment is imminent for the return of the Mahdi, ushering in the ultimate triumph of Islam Is he right, or as with Hitler, do the Jews once again have great cause for legitimate concern?

— 20 —

NUCLEAR DANGER

"Humanity is entering a radically new epoch in which,
for the first time in history, it has the power to destroy
itself by deliberate or unintended action."
—YEHEZKEL DROR[290]

JANUARY 2006 INTRODUCED NEW DEVELOPMENTS regarding Iran's nuclear pursuits. Israeli Defense Minister Shaul Mofaz indicated that his country was preparing for a raid on Iran's nuclear infrastructure. He said Israel could not tolerate an Iran with nuclear weapons, especially given Ahmadinejad's threat to "wipe Israel off the map" during the "World without Zionism" seminar in Tehran.

Condemnation from the West only seemed to strengthen the resolve of Iran's leaders. The world was informed that the Natanz nuclear facility was back online and small-scale uranium enrichment—the first step in producing fuel for atomic weapons——had been added to the mix. In another apparently subtle challenge to the United States, a member of the Iranian parliament suggested to Venezuelan dictator Hugo Chavez that Iran might assist him in the development of nuclear technology.

The nuclear facility at Natanz was clandestine until the National Council of Resistance for Iran (NCRI), a political resistance group, revealed the site in a press conference held in Washington, D.C., in mid-August 2002. The NCRI press release was highly detailed, revealing for the first time that the Natanz site was being built to contain two large underground structures designed to house the centrifuges necessary to enrich uranium to weapons grade.

The NCRI press release even disclosed the names of the construction companies that had been hired to start building the Natanz facilities. It was made public that the Atomic Energy Organization of Iran (AEIO) had set up a front company through which the AEIO intended to pursue the project's needs for facilities and equipment, including such detail as the street address of the fronting company in Tehran.[291] None of this information was known to the UN International Atomic Energy Agency (IAEA) until the NCRI held the Washington press conference. Afterwards, the IAEA investigated and confirmed the accuracy of the NCRI report.

In November 2004, the NCRI disclosed a major nuclear site in Tehran that had been kept secret. According to the document, the Iranian Ministry of Defense (MD) had set up The Modern Defense Readiness and Technology Center (MDRTC) on a sixty-acre site previously occupied by three heavy transport battalions operating under the Ministry of Defense. The NCRI report listed the street addresses of the facility's entrances and described the buildings and installations on the site in detail. The report explained "activities in nuclear and biological warfare" that had previously been performed elsewhere were moved to the MDRTC. The press release gave the names of commanders and described how the Iranians had deceived IAEA efforts to investigate.

This was an important report. For the first time the NCRI gave a full explanation of how the Iranian government had assigned nuclear work to the military, calculating to keep the military operation secret even to Iran's own atomic energy agency.

> The MD and the AEIO are the two bodies conducting Iran's nuclear activities in a parallel manner. The AEIO is pursuing the nuclear power stations and the fuel cycle, whereas the MD is seeking to achieve nuclear bomb technology and

keeps all its activities secret from the AEIO. For this reason, redoing of works is a major problem in Iran's nuclear project and many research and preparations are carried out repeatedly and in a parallel manner at huge expense.[292]

The NCRI information was obviously obtained from its underground agents operating in Iran. Much of what was reported had been previously unknown by the IAEA, or by US intelligence units, including the CIA.

Regardless of the State Department designation of the NCRI as a "terrorist organization," what is clear is that the MEK or PMOI (People's Mujahedin of Iran) and NCRI hate the Iranian regime controlled by the mullahs. One of the key weapons in this unrelenting attack has been information. The NCRI is determined to expose the lies of the mullahs regarding their nuclear weapons ambitions. NCRI reports have repeatedly revealed to the world the exact nature of the clandestine nuclear weapons activities going on in Iran. This does not mean that all aspects of the NCRI's reports are fully accurate. Still, the vast majority of what it exposes is subsequently verified by the IAEA or one of the major intelligence operations run by the United States or other governments around the world. It has provided ammunition for increased calls for Iran to halt its nuclear program.

On September 2, 2005, the IAEA Board of Governors issued a report concluding:

> "Iran had failed in a number of instances over an extended period of time to meet its obligations under its Safeguards Agreement with respect to the reporting of nuclear material, its processing and its use, as well as the declaration of facilities where such material had been processed and stored."[293]

The multi-page report listed violations of Iran's failure to disclose the importing of uranium going back to 1991.

What the diplomatic language takes pains to gloss over is the international embarrassment caused to the IAEA every time someone else reveals Iran's deception. Third-party disclosures and international press reports are information leaked from within Iran by internal dissidents. These revelations forced IAEA inspectors to go back and look for what they had missed. Finally, the IAEA issued new, corrected reports. The embarrassment to the IAEA is immediate as the world realizes that the Iranians have fed the IAEA lies, half-truths, and outright deceptions.

It took the release of the truth by opposition groups such as the NCRI before Iran's clandestine nuclear activities were disclosed publicly. The obvious conclusion is that the IAEA could not be relied upon to do its job.

In a rare move, the US State Department released a set of briefing slides on Iran that were later presented to foreign diplomats in Vienna.[294] The whole purpose of the slide presentation was to question whether Iran's pursuit of the nuclear fuel cycle was intended for peaceful uses, as Iran maintained, or for the creation of nuclear weapons, as the State Department contended. The slides were meant to make the argument that the way Iran had constructed its nuclear facilities is more consistent with the way a country would build a weapons program and not a peaceful procedure intended to generate electricity.

In the slides, the State Department "confirmed a record of hiding sensitive nuclear fuel activities from the IAEA," charging that "Iran's rationale for a 'peaceful' nuclear fuel cycle does not hold up under scrutiny."[295] With Iran sitting on proven oil reserves of 125.8 million barrels, roughly 10 percent of the world's total, plus 940 trillion cubic feet of proven natural gas reserves, 15.5 percent of the world's total reserves and the world's second largest supply in any country, the State Department doubted that Iran needed nuclear power in order to provide civilian electricity.

Even more damning, the State Department argued that instead of spending $6 billion to develop the seven new nuclear reactors Iran proposed to build, its leaders could have made the same dollar investments in the country's aging and neglected oil and natural gas infrastructures. This investment would have permitted Iran to build one or more new refineries designed to reduce Iran's domestic cost of energy and eliminate the need to import refined gasoline. The State Department slides argued that:

"If Iran were to invest $5.6 billion in a high gasoline yield, Western-type refinery, it could eliminate its dependence on imported gasoline and increase its annual net oil-related revenue by approximately $982 million."[296]

The State Department slides also showed the diplomats in Vienna satellite photographs of Iran's nuclear facilities. Taken over time, the photos showed how Iran had constructed and misrepresented them so as to hide key functions. Some, Iran had simply failed to disclose at all. With regard to the gas centrifuge uranium enrichment at Natanz, for instance, the State Department identified the site as "a covert facility in a remote location, which could be used to enrich uranium for weapons."[297] Satellite and ground photographs showed dummy structures designed to prevent detection and identification, as well as facilities that were concealed underground, hardened and well-defended.

Significant progress constructing the Arak heavy-water reduction complex was shown for the time period of June 2004 through March 2005. These photos demonstrated that the reactor construction was progressing rapidly despite IAEA Board requests to forgo construction altogether. The State Department dismissed Iran's claim that the Arak reactor was needed for medical and industrial isotopes, a capability that Iran already had inherent in its ten megawatt Tehran research reactor. The slides also documented the development of the uranium mine at Gachin, a facility that was larger and more promising than the one at Saghand, the only mine Iranian reports had bothered to disclose prior to 2004.

The State Department concluded that Iran's nuclear program is "well-scaled for a nuclear weapons capability," especially when compared to the progress being made in the nuclear weapons facilities of another rogue state, North Korea. "When one also considers Iran's concealment and deception activities, it is difficult to escape the conclusion that Iran is pursuing nuclear weapons."[298]

Finally, so as to leave no doubt, one of the last slides drove home the point: "Iran's past history of concealment and deception and the nuclear fuel cycle infrastructure are most consistent with an intent to acquire nuclear weapons."[299] (The last part of the sentence was underlined for emphasis in the original State Department slide.)

Whenever the subject of rogue nations sharing nuclear weapons secrets comes up, the name of A.Q. Khan is not far behind. In early 2004, Abdul Qadeer Khan, the father of Pakistan's nuclear weapons program, went on Pakistani television and apologized to the nation for having sold Pakistan's nuclear secrets to other countries. "It pains me to realize that my lifetime achievement could have been placed in jeopardy," he said with an emotion that looked like regret.[300]

This expression of remorse was touching; however, the record shows that Khan profited handsomely from selling nuclear technology. He sold nuclear warhead blueprints and uranium enrichment technology to the "Axis of Evil" states—Iraq under Saddam Hussein, North Korea, and Iran—as well as to Muammar Qaddafi's Libya.

The CIA's "721 Report" emphasized that Iran's nuclear program "received significant assistance" in the past from "the proliferation network headed by Pakistani scientist A.Q. Khan."[301] This report is named for Section 721 of the 1997 Intelligence Authorization Act, which requires unclassified disclosure to Congress regarding the acquisition of nuclear weapons technology by foreign countries during the preceding six months.[302] Suspicion regarding Khan's secret nuclear black market was reinforced when the IAEA released a report disclosing a handwritten, one-page document that constituted an offer made by Khan's network to Iran in 1987. The report, which had been voluntarily turned over to the IAEA by Iran, represented an offer to sell the country nuclear components and equipment. Iran admitted that some components of one or two disassembled centrifuges, as well as supporting drawings and specifications, were delivered by Khan's procurement network, and that various items referred to were obtained from other suppliers.

A solid-fuel engine was successfully tested on Iran's mainstay missile, the Shahab-3, in July 2005.[303] The Shahab-3 is a single-stage missile based on the North Korean "Nodong" missile series, with a reliable range of approximately 995 miles (1,600 kilometers), with a maximum range estimated at

1,250 miles, more than enough to hit Tel Aviv or US military troops stationed in the Middle East. The Shahab-3 was first successfully tested by Iran in August and September 2004.

A Shahab-3 missile was paraded through the streets of Tehran with banners proclaiming "We will crush America under our feet" and "wipe Israel off the map."[304] The significance of equipping the Shahab-3 with a solid-fuel engine is that less time is required to prepare the missile for firing. Anti-missile systems are most effective when they detect early preparations to fire and hit a launched missile when it first leaves the pad. Missiles in full flight are a more difficult ballistics problem, similar to the difficulty of hitting one bullet in flight with another bullet fired at it. Also, solid fuel technology generally adds greater reliability and accuracy to the missile's performance. The acquisition of more sophisticated rocket delivery systems makes the situation in Iran even more ominous. Today, Iran's missiles can reach not only Israel but much of Europe. Within a few years, Iran's ICBMs should be able to strike anywhere on the globe.

Despite pressure from the EU to adjourn its nuclear pursuits, Iran has continued to defy the worldwide call to halt uranium enrichment. Ali Larijani, secretary of Iran's Supreme National Security Council, announced, "If sanctions are imposed on Iran, then we will suspend our relations with the IAEA...If the USA attacks Iran's nuclear facilities, we will stop acting transparently in the nuclear field and continue covert nuclear work at other facilities."[305]

Iran's leaders announced intentions to hasten uranium enrichment by mid-year 2006. A spokesman indicated it was hoped cascades of some three thousand centrifuges would be established by the end of the year or early 2007. A cascade contains 164 centrifuges linked together. According to the Congressional Research Service, Iran has eighteen cascades (2,952 centrifuges) of first generation (IR-1) centrifuges installed in the facility. Iran is feeding uranium hexafluoride into five additional 164-centrifuge cascades and is installing and testing thirteen more cascades.[306]

In typical fashion, Russia reacted to its neighbor's nuclear arms program by rushing to sign an agreement that would provide fuel for a new power plant that opened in 2007. In reaction to Russia's largess, a bill was introduced and approved by the US Congress to sanction any country agreeing to provide supplies or assistance with Iran's quest to purchase "chemical, biological, or nuclear weapons."[307]

Ahmadinejad traveled to Arak, host city to the Khondab plant to preside over the opening of a heavy-water plant. The Atomic Energy Organization of Iran (AEOI) oversaw the construction of the plant at Arak, operated through a fronting company, the Mesbah Energy Company.

The plant was designed to deliver plutonium, a major ingredient in the production of nuclear arms. Although Khondab's reactor was set for start-up sometime in 2009, a cloak of invisibility seems to have fallen over the facility. Even though Tehran has indicated that the Khondab reactor is only to be used to produce isotopes for medical use, a major concern centers on the by-product of spent fuel that contains plutonium.

The only reason Iran would need a heavy-water facility is if the country were planning to build a plutonium bomb. The Russian-built reactor at Bushehr does not use heavy-water, which is required to moderate the nuclear chain reaction needed to produce weapons-grade plutonium. Fission bombs requiring plutonium are more sophisticated to design and detonate than bombs using uranium-235, but the explosive magnitude of plutonium bombs is many times greater.

By focusing the discussion on uranium enrichment, the Iranians were telegraphing their decision to build first a simpler, more reliable uranium bomb. Even when the first nuclear bombs were designed by the Manhattan Project of World War II, scientists had known that the mechanics of building a gun-type uranium device was simpler and more reliable. The first atomic bomb ever exploded in combat, the one dropped on Hiroshima, was a simple gun-type design uranium-235 atomic bomb. That weapon was considered so reliable that no prototype was ever tested. The *Enola Gay* dropped a bomb known as "Little Boy" on Hiroshima. At the time the US did not have a second "Little Boy." Moreover, testing a gun-type nuclear device was considered unnecessary.

Building a heavy-water facility at Arak suggests that Iran is on the same path. First, Iran would build a simple, gun-type design uranium bomb. Yet, not far behind, Iran evidently plans to be able to build a plutonium device of higher yield and greater destructive power.

Not surprisingly, Ahmadinejad threw down yet another gauntlet in his never-ending battle to provoke Israel during the annual Jerusalem Day protest. Not-so-veiled threats erupted as he declared:

> "The Zionist regime, thank God, has lost all reason to exist. The efforts to stabilize Israel's fraudulent regime have failed. Believe me; soon this regime will be no longer. The Zionist regime was established in the heart of Islamic territory for one purpose—to pose a threat to the region through constant attacks and killings. This regime has lost its way of existence. Today, there is no reason left for it to remain, and it is about to disappear."[308]

Just days later, Ahmadinejad had another startling announcement for the Western world and for his Arab neighbors:

> "Today the Iranian nation possesses the full nuclear fuel cycle and time is completely running in our favor in terms of diplomacy."[309]

He later told a cadre of Iranian reporters:

> "We will commission three thousand centrifuges by the year-end. We are determined to master the nuclear fuel cycle and commission some sixty thousand centrifuges to meet our demands."[310]

Though handed various sanctions and threats of sanctions, Iran has not waivered from its nuclear arms race. Ahmadinejad and the International Atomic Energy Commission danced around each other like fencers exchanging parries and thrusts. The National Intelligence Estimate published in 2007 indicated:

> We assess with moderate confidence that convincing the Iranian leadership to forgo the eventual development of nuclear weapons will be difficult given the linkage many within the leadership probably see between nuclear weapons development and Iran's key national security and foreign policy objectives, and given Iran's considerable effort from at least the late 1980s to 2003 to develop such weapons. In our judgment, only an Iranian political decision to abandon a nuclear weapons objective would plausibly keep Iran from eventually producing nuclear weapons—and such a decision is inherently reversible.
>
> We assess with moderate confidence that Iran probably would use covert facilities—rather than its declared nuclear sites—for the production of highly enriched uranium for a weapon. A growing amount of intelligence indicates Iran was engaged in covert uranium conversion and uranium enrichment activity, but we judge that these efforts probably were halted in response to the fall 2003 halt, and that these efforts probably had not been restarted through at least mid-2007.[311]

By September 2008, the IAEA still had not been able to make any inroads in its mission to determine the magnitude of Iran's nuclear program. Ahmadinejad's penchant for overstating facts further clouded the issue. In one statement Iran's president revealed that Iran had "five thousand operational centrifuges." When his duplicity was uncovered, another official explained that some three thousand centrifuges were coming online. In November Gholam Reza Aghazadeh, the chief of Iran's Atomic Energy Organization, confirmed that the five-thousand number was correct with more to come. He audaciously explained, "Suspension has not been defined in our lexicon."[312]

Following the 2009 elections in Iran, Aghazadeh resigned his post in a shocking move that was viewed as a key hindrance to Ahmadinejad. Aghazadeh is an accomplished technical expert whose administrative skills helped to quickly develop Iran's nuclear program.

The UN Security Council persists in passing resolutions denouncing Iran's nuclear proliferation, while Ahmadinejad and Khamenei continue to thumb their collective noses at its actions. Uranium enrichment is still the main focus at the Natanz facility. The IAEA indicated in February 2009 that Iran possesses "839 kilograms of low enriched uranium," which can be further enriched to produce weapons-grade uranium.[313] Estimates vary on how long it would take Iran to produce a quantity sufficient to produce weapons.

An announcement from Tehran then signified that the much-awaited Bushehr reactor would be capable of producing electricity at half its capacity in March. The reactor was still offline in April of that year.

The G8—a group composed of Great Britain, the United States, Germany, France, Italy, Canada, Japan, and Russia—met in L'Aquila, Italy in July. One of the topics discussed was Iran's nuclear program. A communiqué issued by the leaders defined their concerns regarding the rogue country but stopped short of taking a definitive stand:

> We remain deeply concerned over proliferation risks posed by Iran's nuclear program.... We strongly urge Iran to co-operate fully with the International Atomic Energy Agency and to comply with the relevant UN Security Council resolutions without further delay.[314]

Ahmadinejad is such a rabid follower that he has claimed to have been contacted by the Mahdi—much to the chagrin of some of the clerics in Iran. Why does his belief in the Mahdi make Ahmadinejad so dangerous? According to Shi'a theology, only Allah has the knowledge of when the Mahdi will return to Qom, a city southwest of Tehran. In the company of Jesus, the Mahdi will travel along the new roads constructed under Ahmadinejad's auspices to the capital, Tehran, where he will assume his rightful role as worldwide caliph.

If or when Iran acquires a nuclear device, it could well provide the impetus for other Arab countries in the Middle East to follow suit. Even now the race is on to build reactors in Jordan, the UAE, and Abu Dhabi for the production of nuclear power stations. Like Jordan, Egypt has a treaty in place with Israel to build a reactor. Britain has inked an agreement with Jordan; the US with the UAE (a country with strong ties to Iran); and France signed a multi-billion dollar agreement with Abu Dhabi, which will, in the words of British Foreign Secretary David Miliband, "move the world to a low-carbon economy." He added that nuclear power is needed to be a strong part of the mix.[315] Russia, not wanting to be left out, is courting Egypt with its nuclear stores.

Currently Israel is the only country in the Middle East with known nuclear capabilities. The world is still waiting to see if the Israelis will halt the nuclear arms race by attacking Iran's nuclear reactors. If not, the balance of power may shift to its Arab neighbors who fear Iran's global intentions.

While the world waits, the IAEA continues to prove that it is but a toothless tiger on the world stage. Repeated efforts to gain access to Iran's nuclear facilities in an attempt to enforce nuclear compliance have failed. As late as December 2012, Yukiya Amano, the organizations' head reported:

> "We have intensified our dialogue with Iran this year, but
> no concrete results have been made yet. What we are asking
> in the negotiations is to have access to sites, information and
> people."[316]

The inspectors were cleared to travel to Iran before the end of 2012 to inspect the Parchin test facility. Their aim was to confirm whether Iran has expanded its research specifically on the acquisition of a nuclear bomb for military use. Enough time has elapsed since the request was first made to Iranian leaders that images from space satellites indicate all traces of nuclear activity have been cleansed from the site. Buildings have been razed and soil has been carted away in an obvious attempt to deceive the inspectors. Access to the site was denied on the basis that it had "no connection with Iran's nuclear activities."[317]

—21—

IF ISRAEL
INTERVENES

*"It would only take three nuclear weapons in the hands
of terrorist groups or a government to destroy Israel.
The United States has a compelling interest in preventing
nuclear proliferation and nuclear terrorism."*
—BENJAMIN NETANYAHU[318]

THE MOST FORMIDABLE OPTION WOULD BE AN ATTACK BY ISRAEL on Iran's reactors.
Israeli officials have indicated they would do whatever was expedient to halt
Iran's pursuit of nuclear weapons. A preemptive strike by Israel has always
been a possibility as a deterrent to Iran's open defiance of the IAEA and the
UN. Israeli Defense Minister Ehud Barak indicates that his country would
consider all options:

> "We clearly believe that no option should be removed
> from the table. This is our policy. We mean it. We recom-
> mend to others to take the same position, but we cannot
> dictate it to anyone."[319]

Israel has been placed in the uncomfortable position of having to decipher whether the administration of Barak Obama is more interested in courting the mullahs in Iran than in supporting America's long-time Middle East ally. The president, taking a much harsher approach toward Israel than did George Bush, has rejected that interpretation of his foreign policy towards Iran, while at the same time taking covert steps to discourage an Israeli attack.

In a statement issued by Prime Minister Netanyahu's office, the prime minister "reiterated the seriousness (with) which Israel views Iran's nuclear ambitions and the need to utilize all available means to prevent Iran from achieving a nuclear weapons capability."[320]

While some believe Iran is as much as two to three years from nuclear arms capabilities, some intelligence sources have predicted that it would only require approval from Supreme Leader Ayatollah Ali Khamenei to begin production on its first nuclear arms device. The technology, say the sources, has been in place since 2003:

> A US National Intelligence Estimate...concluded that Iran had ended its nuclear arms research program in 2003 because of the threat from the American invasion of Iraq. But intelligence sources have told *The Times* that Tehran had halted the research because it had achieved its aim—to find a way of detonating a warhead that could be launched on its long-range Shehab-3 missiles...The Iranian Defense Ministry has been running a covert nuclear research department for years, employing hundreds of scientists, researchers, and metallurgists in a multibillion-dollar program to develop nuclear technology alongside the civilian nuclear program... "If the Supreme Leader takes the decision [to build a bomb], we assess they have to enrich low-enriched uranium to highly-enriched uranium at the Natanz plant, which could take six months, depending on how many centrifuges are operating. We don't know if the decision was made yet,"

said the intelligence sources, adding that Iran could have created smaller, secret facilities, other than those at the heavily guarded bunker at Natanz to develop materials for a first bomb.[321]

In my book, *Showdown with Nuclear Iran*, I outlined in detail how Israel might launch a strike against Iran. In the ensuing years since the book's release, Iran has made enormous progress on its nuclear program and in its air defense systems, which has not escaped the attention of the Israeli government.

Time is not on Israel's side; a decision must be made soon. Will Israel attack, or will she accept the inevitable—a nuclear-armed Iran? It would surprise few people should Israel decide to strike before Iran reaches the critical point in developing a nuclear bomb.

The refugee crisis faced by the Palestinians should be dealt with as such by the Arab world. The terror camps in Lebanon must be shut down, and refugees absorbed by Arab countries. All arms being sent to terrorists must be halted. Of those living within the Palestinian Territory, the majority is Jordanian, and should become part of the Hashemite Kingdom of Jordan. An economic summit on the Palestinian refugee issue would provide funds donated from the nations of the world, especially the Arab countries, in order to assist Jordan in building an army, police force, schools, hospitals, housing, and other needs. The suffering of the Palestinian people could be resolved once and for all.

Unable to focus world opinion on Iran and its proxies, Hezbollah and Hamas, Israel is becoming more isolated in her determination to stop Iran's march toward the means to decimate the Jewish state. World opinion seems to focus more on the saccharine explanation that Hamas, Hezbollah, and other terrorist groups are "freedom fighters" even while they target innocent civilians, not just in Israel but in countries around the world. Iran, one of the largest suppliers of arms, funding, and training to would-be terrorist states, is allowed to escape almost unscathed for the choices its leaders make.

In fact, many Arab heads of state would secretly applaud an Israeli solution to the Iran threat.

While the US continues to support sanctions as the most viable alternative to halting Iran's nuclear program, Israeli leaders believe their country's very existence is being threatened—and with good reason. Infighting among Iran's radical conservatives could produce an even more rogue regime determined to use any means necessary to regain total control in the nation—even its outright attack on Israel or through one of its proxies.

The window of opportunity to eliminate the menace posed by Iran is closing sooner than expected. While the Obama administration is working overtime to restrict available options, the Israelis will not allow themselves to be boxed in by the president or anyone else. The tiny nation doesn't have the long-term alternative of waiting for negotiations and sanctions to be effective; her very existence is at stake. Benjamin Netanyahu has said, "The Obama presidency has two great missions: fixing the economy and preventing Iran from gaining nuclear weapons."[322]

It seems obvious that the world is threatened by Iran's resolve to complete the nuclear cycle on its mission to possess an atomic bomb. It would seem equally evident that global measures could and should be initiated to stop the radical Islamic Republic from achieving its purpose. Czechoslovakian psychologist Stanislav Grof said, "At a time when unbridled greed, malignant aggression, and existence of weapons of mass destruction threaten the survival of humanity, we should seriously consider any avenue that offers some hope."[323]

We have explored a number of options, but perhaps the most vital ingredient in the survival of the West is best described by E. M. Bounds who wrote:

> God shapes the world by prayer. The more praying there
> is in the world the better the world will be...the mightier the
> forces against evil.[324]

The West can be saved, but only if we have the courage to respond to this crisis swiftly and with moral clarity.

The alternatives outlined here can work and save the West, but that success is dependant upon the cooperation of world leaders. No one is immune from an attack by Iran or its proxies. No country is exempt from the wrath of the radical Islamists who govern Iran—not its Arab neighbors, not Europe, not Russia, not China, not the US, and especially not Israel.

More than two decades ago Benjamin Netanyahu warned of the threat posed by Iran:

> "The spread of lawlessness and the blatant disregard of any constraints by governments are, as in the thirties, gradually becoming accepted norms again, and the consequences could be intolerable. By far the most disconcerting prospect would be acquisition of weapons of mass destruction by the principal terrorist states in the Middle East—Iran, Libya, and Syria. These regimes pose a much greater threat to their neighbors, and to the democratic world generally, than has yet been acknowledged."[325]

Mr. Netanyahu was correct in 1986; let us hope and pray that his current assessment of Iran's nuclear threat is wrong. The security of the global community depends upon it.

The Wisdom of Solomon resonates:

> For everything there is a season, And a time for every matter under heaven…A time for war, and a time for peace.[326]

What time is it? It is time to take a stand against the apocalyptic threat posed by Iran. The father of our country, George Washington, said, "There is nothing so likely to produce peace as to be well prepared to meet the enemy."[327] Are we prepared? In the words of President Ronald Reagan:

> "We must make it clear to any country that is tempted to use violence to undermine democratic governments, destabilize our friends, thwart efforts to promote democratic

governments, or disrupt our lives that it has nothing to gain and much to lose."[328]

The Western World has not yet made that clear to Iran.

— 22 —

SAMSON ARISES

"I made clear that once Iran crosses that enrichment threshold, the chances of us effectively stopping Iran's nuclear weapons programme would be reduced dramatically.Iran is...closer to crossing this line and there is no doubt that this will be a major challenge that will have to be addressed next year [in 2013]."
—PRIME MINISTER BENJAMIN NETANYAHU[329]

ISRAEL, ALONG WITH INDIA AND PAKISTAN, ARE THE THREE SOVEREIGN STATES in the Middle East possessing nuclear weapons, which have not signed the Nuclear Non-Proliferation Treaty (NPT). Israel made this decision simply to avoid discussion about the program the world knows it has.

Before her death in 1978, Prime Minister Golda Meir told friends that suicidal thoughts had plagued her during the Yom Kippur War. Yom Kippur is the Day of Atonement for the Jewish people. It is the year's holiest day. Prime Minister Meir referred to the surprise attack by Egypt and Syria. The initial forays by Israel's two enemies were disastrous. Moshe Dayan, the Minister of Defense, is said to have called for nuclear bombs to be put aboard fighter planes and nuclear warheads placed on Israel's Jericho missiles. He wanted to be ready should the attacking Arab states reach the point-of-no-return in endangering the State of Israel.

Dayan was gravely fearful that the attack would result in the destruction of what he referred to as the "third Commonwealth." The first had been destroyed by the Babylonians and the second by the Romans.

Israel's nuclear weapons have always been considered the core of what has commonly been known as the *Sampson Option*. The strategy is named after the biblical character of Sampson who used his great strength to bring down a temple, killing a great number of enemy Philistines, and himself, in the process (Judges 16: 4-30). Israel has sworn "never again" in relation to the possibility of another Holocaust. Given this determination, the *Sampson Option* postulates that Israel would be willing to use extreme measures if the country's survival were at stake.

In the crisis with Iran, the *Sampson Option* has been cited to mean that Israel would attack Iran in a preemptive war and would be willing to use nuclear weapons. Iran's acquisition of nuclear weapons is a threat to Israel's continued existence, but Israel would be willing to attack Iran even if the result of a strike might end in the destruction of both.

The Israelis judge that destruction in a military conflict with an aggressor like Iran would be better than doing nothing and waiting to be destroyed. Passivity in the face of aggression has always been judged the mistake the European Jews made against Hitler.

"Never again!" is the oath the Israelis swear to make clear to aggressors that they will not hesitate to respond. In extreme situations, Israel can be expected to attack, rather than to delay. This is why Israel's patience for negotiations with Iran's religious leaders can be expected to run out. Israel knows the mullahs are trying to buy time, and that time in this crisis works against Israel. Analysts argue that Israel's current nuclear arsenal opens up many strategic possibilities short of the *Sampson Option*.

Israel has the type of relatively low-yield tactical nuclear weapons that can be selectively fired to eliminate specific targets. Low-yield "tactical nukes" could be used to hit the type of hardened underground centrifuge farm which Iran has built at Natanz to enrich uranium.

Israel's larger nuclear warheads have been adapted for the Jericho series of missiles. Israel first began developing these missiles with French assistance in the 1960s. The Jericho II is a solid fuel, two-stage missile that Israel has test fired into the Mediterranean Sea at ranges estimated at around 1,300 kilometers (800 miles). Reportedly, Israel has had a multi-stage Jericho III under development; more truly an intercontinental ballistic missile (ICBM) with a range of around 4,800 kilometers (3,000 miles).

Israel also has cruise missiles which can be adapted with nuclear warheads, such as the Popeye Turbo which is designed to be air-launched from Israel's F-15 and F-16 fighter jets.[330] It can also be launched from the three Dolphin-class submarines the Germans built for Israel.[331]

While details of the Israeli nuclear arsenal remain highly classified, analysts believe Israel can launch a mix of tactical nuclear weapons delivered via fighter aircraft and cruise missiles fired from sea. Higher-yield nuclear warheads deliverable by Israel's Jericho II missiles would most likely be held in reserve, waiting to see what retaliatory responses Iran launches and how the war escalates from the initial attack.

Iran continually points to the one-sided nature of US foreign policy in the Middle East: We accept Israel's nuclear weapons program, but government officials have repeatedly stated their clear determination that Iran will not be permitted to develop nuclear weapons capability.

Iran's president has retorted that their developing nuclear weapons would be a counter-force to Israel's nuclear weapons, much as Pakistan's nuclear arsenal keeps India in check. Pursuing this logic, the Iranians have argued that their development of nuclear weapons capability would stabilize the region. The point would be to take away Israel's ability to act unilaterally. Clearly, Israel has a tactical advantage as the only nuclear-armed Middle Eastern state.

Still, the US objects. Iran's history of supporting terrorism and the country's openly belligerent posture removes it from the column of peace-keeping states. Iran's goal is to destabilize the Middle East, while the Jewish State's goal is regional stability.

Iran's leaders have also suggested that their nuclear weapons capabilities might be developed, but not fully. In other words, Iran would pursue nuclear weapons expansion to "within the turn of a screw" from being completely functional, but would stop. This way Iran would never actually make an atomic bomb, even though it would be capable of making one relatively quickly.

Again, the US has not been reassured. Iran's well-documented attempts to repeatedly conceal material aspects of their nuclear program have given experts pause. Who knows if Iranian leaders would keep their word on this promise? What would happen if Iran did make a few atomic weapons? Zealots among the mullahs might insist that nuclear weapons be produced clandestinely and stockpiled for future use.

The Iranian nuclear facilities were constructed in the anticipation that at some point Israel or the United States might launch a preemptive strike. Its sites are geographically dispersed, with several important research facilities embedded in population areas. Still, Israel could target five or six major locations, such as the uranium processing plant at Isfahan, the enrichment plant at Natanz, the heavy water facility at Arak or the Russian-built reactor at Bushehr.

Military exercises as far back as the massive allied strategic bombing campaign against the Nazis in World War II, demonstrate how quickly bombed machinery can again be made operational. At best, an Israeli attack would only slow the progress of the Iranian nuclear weapons program. At worst, adverse world reaction against Israel might escalate.

In the face of an Israeli attack, Iran might easily win world consensus that it now had a clear case justifying the pursuit of nuclear weapons for self-defense. European countries now trying to contain Iran's nuclear efforts might reverse their positions. Besides, the Europeans would inevitably see opportunities to seize lucrative Iranian nuclear technology contracts. Iran might quickly rebuild better or newer models, whichever nuclear facilities an Israeli preemptive military strike managed to destroy.

Important lessons can be derived from Israel's 1982 war with Syria at the onset of Israel's invasion into Lebanon. From June 6-11, 1982, Israel's Air Force "scored one of the most impressive military achievements in the history of modern warfare" against Syria.[332] Within a matter of hours, the IAF (Israeli Air force) destroyed Syria's Soviet-built surface-to-air missile defense system in the Bakaa Valley. Then Israel downed 25 Syrian fighter planes, most of them MIG-23s, again attesting to Russia's support for Middle Eastern client-states.

Over the following days, Israel virtually wiped out the Syrian Air Force by shooting down what amounted to approximately 80 more Syrian fighter planes in dogfights. Remarkably, Israel did not suffer the loss of a single Israeli fighter plane in the course of the entire war. With this stunning air victory, Israel effectively controlled the skies.

Neither Syria nor Lebanon wanted to confront Israel in a conventional ground war. Instead, with the assistance of Iran, a guerilla war broke out. Various Lebanese Shiite militias joined forces with the Lebanese Islamic Jihad, the Palestine Liberation Army (PLO) and Hezbollah. Together, they attacked Israeli forces and bombed the US Marine barracks in Beirut.

In response, President Reagan ordered the withdrawal of US forces from Lebanon in 1985. Later, the IDF (Israeli Defense Force) also left Lebanon, unable to contain what amounted to a radical Islamic insurrection.

What began as a great victory for Israel ended up being a *coup* for radical Islam. Terrorism tactics, including the type of signature suicide bombings developed by Hezbollah with the assistance of Iran, proved to be highly effective.

Throughout the Muslim world, the war in Lebanon was ultimately seen as a major defeat for the US and Israel. The defeat encouraged radical Islamic terrorists to continue their war against Israel. Iran provided additional funding for the Islamic radicals fighting in Lebanon, and the alliance between Iran and Syria grew closer.

When Israel finally pulled out of Lebanon, Syrian troops and intelligence agents moved in. As a result, Lebanon became a client-state of Syria. Instead of removing the risk of rocket attacks on Israel from Lebanon, the risk has increased. Today the stockpile of rockets, largely Iranian-supplied, is available to Hezbollah in Lebanon and another of Iran's proxies, Hamas in Gaza, and are positioned for launch against Israel.

In retaliation for a military strike on Iran, Hezbollah would undoubtedly launch rockets into Israel from Lebanon, and Hamas would follow suit from Gaza. We might even see a proliferation of the suicide bombings that marked Palestinian *intifadas* under Arafat.

US troops in the region could also expect retaliation, even if Israel unleashed a solo strike. Militant groups within the region would be doubly motivated, attacking to avenge the Israeli assault on Iran. In summation, an Israeli attack on Iran can be counted on to energize every radical Islamic terrorist organization in the region to renewed attacks, including al-Qaeda groups affiliated with the late leaders Abu Musab al-Zarqawi and Osama bin Laden.

Even if the United States did not directly participate in an Israeli air strike on Iran, it would have to provide some support during the initial attack and ensuing conflict. Israel would use its F-15 and F-16 fighter jets sold to the nation by the US. The US might also be called upon to refuel Israeli jets involved in an air strike on Iran. The newest fighters in Israel's attack force are the Lockheed-Martin manufactured F-16I Soufa ("Storm") fighters. The second mainstay of the IAF is the 1990s Boeing-built (originally McDonnell Douglas) F-15I Ra'am ("Eagle") fighter planes. Both aircraft have a strike radius that should extend to targets in Iran without having to be refueled. However, the distances involved would not leave much room for error.

The F-16Is can be fitted with a pair of removable conformable fuel tanks mounted on both sides of the upper fuselage, to hold 450 gallons of extra fuel, plus detachable wing tanks carrying another 600 gallons of fuel.[333] The F-15Is carry 4.5 tons of fuel in the internal tanks, conformal tanks, and detachable tanks, giving the F-15I an unprecedented range of 4,450 kilometers (2,765 miles).[334] Still, a mission without refueling would be pushing the performance window of the aircraft.

Iran's military is no match for the US or Israel in any type of a conventional war. The Iranian military is still recovering from the 1980-1988 war with Iraq.[335] The ease with which the US military defeated Saddam Hussein is a good indication of Iran's conventional military strength; Iran had not been able to beat Iraq in a conventional war in the 1980s. Today, the US military could easily defeat Iran's military in the field, though a land invasion would be costly—both in lives and dollars—to the US, as well as being extremely unpopular.

The Iranians would most likely retaliate with missile attacks which could be quite harmful both to the US and Israel. Conventionally armed Shahab-3 missiles could cause considerable casualties on US military bases throughout the Gulf Region. All of Israel's cities, as well as her nuclear facilities at Dimona in the Negev Desert are within range of Iran's Shahab-3.

Joint military exercises held between the IDF and the US Army stationed in Europe demonstrated that a Shahab-3 missile could be intercepted by the combination of the Israeli Arrow anti-missile defense system, working together with the US Patriot anti-missile system, backed up by the US Navy's Aegis anti-missile system. But while these anti-missile defenses might be effective in stopping one Shahab-3 attack, the defense system would have trouble taking down multiple missiles.

Should Iran fire a barrage attack of multiple Shahab-3 missiles at the same target, one or more missiles would most likely get through to hit their targets. Russia, as we have noted, has already agreed to supply Iran with $1 billion worth of new TOR-M1 anti-missile SAM defense systems. Once these are in place, an Israeli attack on Iran's nuclear facilities would be much more difficult. Moreover, after an Israeli strike on Iran, Russia could decide to enter the conflict on the side of Iran. This would pit the US and Russia head-to-head for the first time since the end of the Cold War.

In the November 2012 clash between Israel and Hamas in Gaza, another arrow in Israel's arsenal, the Iron Dome anti-missile defense battery, got a workout. The prototype, designed by the state-owned company Rafael Advanced Defense Systems, has the capability to intercept short-range rockets and mortars. With its use, Israel was able to stop 85 percent of the missiles launched from Gaza.

Following the cease-fire, the US Congress was petitioned by the Pentagon to boost military assistance to Israel by $647 million. Its purpose according to the *Blumberg* report is to "arm the IDF with a tail kit system used to convert free-fall bombs into satellite guided ordnance, as well as with missiles that can be mounted on F-15 and F-16 fighter jets and are capable of penetrating underground or fortified targets." The military aid includes 1,725 JDAM tail kits together with BLU-109 bombs, also dubbed "bunker-buster" and weighing in at more than 900kg. By definition, the bombs are intended to "defeat an enemy's most critical and hardened targets such as protected weapons storage sites, and penetrate as much as six feet of reinforced concrete."[336]

Concern that Israel had seriously depleted its military materiel stockpile in November 2011 is said to be the motivation for the move by the Pentagon. However, the supplies would not increase Israel's ability to target Iran's nuclear facilities buried deep below the ground and secured by quantities of reinforced concrete.

The escalation in aid could very well give Israel the boost it needs to move forward with planning an attack. There has been a buildup of military and naval personnel and equipment in the Persian Gulf area over the past year as US carriers have been bicycled into and out of the region. Bahrain, which lies just 120 miles from Iran, is the base for the US Fifth Fleet. In April 2012 the USS Abraham Lincoln was dispatched to the north Arabian Sea, and the USS Enterprise to the Gulf of Aden. A squadron of F-22 fighters has also been posted to the Persian Gulf, and two US army brigades are stationed in Kuwait. The Navy also deployed the tiny SeaFox, a four-foot-long submersible that aids in the detection and destruction of the floating mines which Iran has deployed in the Strait of Hormuz in the past. Also in the mix is the Ponce, a converted naval amphibious transport and docking vessel. It is equipped with a medical facility, a helipad, and living quarters for troops.

The presence of added fire power is to prevent a move by Iran that could cripple oil flow worldwide by attacking shipping in the Strait of Hormuz. This would be a perfect example of "asymmetric warfare," wherein disproportionate damage is inflicted by a weaker enemy using minimal force at a strategic point of attack.

Iran currently operates four anti-ship missile systems acquired from China. One of these, the CS-801K is a Chinese-supplied, air-launched, anti-ship missile that Iran has test fired from its air force F-4E fighters.[337]

Iran reportedly purchased eight Russian-built "Sunburn" anti-ship missiles (SS-N-22) from the Ukraine and has deployed them for use around the

Strait of Hormuz. The Sunburn missile represents a significant increase in the threat level, in that it accelerates to a speed of Mach 2.2 (1,520 mph, over twice the speed of sound) in 30 seconds. The missile has a sophisticated guidance system and can carry a 200 kiloton nuclear warhead or a 750-pound conventional warhead.

For the purposes of a tanker war, a Sunburn missile with a conventional warhead traveling at Mach 2.2 would completely destroy any vessel it hits. The tankers are slow-moving targets with no defense against missiles. Truthfully, there is enough kinetic energy in a cruise missile traveling at Mach 2 to destroy a tanker, even without an explosive warhead.

US experts acknowledge that Iran has been in the market to buy these cruise missiles.[338] In the 1980s war with Iran, Iraq engaged in a limited tanker war, using French Mirage fighter planes and Exocet missiles.[339] Iraq suffered two disadvantages: the Exocet missiles were not sufficiently powerful to damage Iranian supertankers seriously and the Iraqi pilots were poorly trained. Still, Iran has been well-schooled on the Iraqi tactic.

The key insight in evaluating *Sampson Option* thinking is that Israel remains a one-bomb state. As Iran advances to develop an atomic bomb covertly, Israel may have no recourse but to attack. The point is that Israel must be willing to use desperate tactics if there is no other way to stop an enemy set on the destruction of the Jewish state.

On September 27, 2012, Benjamin Netanyahu faced an unsympathetic audience as he took the podium at the UN General Assembly in New York City. Holding up a simple drawing, the prime minister drew a red line near the top of the depiction of a nuclear bomb. He admonished those present, "The red line must be drawn on Iran's nuclear enrichment program. I believe that faced with a clear red line, Iran will back down." He further warned, "Nothing could imperil the world more than a nuclear-armed Iran."[340]

Remember, at the moment Israel has the only nuclear arsenal in the Middle East. In the metaphor of poker, we have suggested that this is like being dealt an ace-high royal flush in the first five cards in a game of seven card stud. Israel today is the strongest military power in the Middle East. It could destroy Iran's most important nuclear facilities by launching a massive air strike designed to last a few days at most. If Iran retaliated in a massive way, Israel could expand its attack on Iran, suggesting her willingness to escalate the conflict.

A ground invasion of Iran would likely mobilize the entire Islamic world, and produce a tactical dilemma to even get inside the country. No Arab naiton would cooperate in any way. The opposite is also true; everything would be done to obstruct an attempted invasion by Israeli forces. If Israel did decide to launch a preemptive air strike on Iran, the *Sampson Option* would be implemented, and Israel would be on nuclear alert. Iran would most certainly retaliate with missiles from Lebanon and terrorist attacks on Jews worldwide. The most chilling scenario of all is the fear that Iran may possess one of the Soviet's suitcase nuclear bombs and would attempt to smuggle it into Tel Aviv.

Every day that passes means another day with Iran's centrifuges whirling at near capacity, another hour for Israel to be held up to global ridicule without reason, and another minute to inch closer to the red line of no return.

—23—

A Broken Olive Branch

"I hope military force is not necessary to stop the Iranian regime marching toward a nuclear capability, but I do know this: that if force is to be used, [US] capabilities need to be such that it would be decisive."
—SENATOR LINDSEY GRAHAM,
REPUBLICAN, SOUTH CAROLINA[341]

AFTER HIS INAUGURATION IN 2009, President Barack Obama extended an olive branch to Iranian leaders with his offer of "unconditional" talks. The included wording closely resembled that of Jimmy Carter when, in his 1981 State of the Union address, he made an offer to Khomeini, the mad mullah of Tehran:

> "We are prepared to work with the government of Iran to develop a new and mutually beneficial relationship."[342] The latest, almost identical offer to Iran's government came from international envoy Javier Solana. In typical fashion Ahmadinejad responded not by decreasing but by increasing the enrichment of uranium.

In an article for *The Wall Street Journal*, Bret Stephens offered this observation:

> For three years, the administration has deferred to European and U.N. diplomacy while seeking to build consensus around the idea that a nuclear-armed Iran poses unacceptable risks to global security…*Today, the international community is less intent on stopping Tehran from getting the bomb than it is on stopping Washington from stopping Tehran.*[343] (Emphasis is mine.)

As a lame duck president now in his second term in office, Obama seems more intent on negotiating with the sworn enemies of the United States, i.e., Ayatollah Ali Khamenei and his purveyors of terror, than with those who seek freedom in the Middle East. In December 2012, the president reportedly proposed a plan to the Iranians that the two sides hold face-to-face dialogue regarding Iran's nuclear program—without consulting or coordinating with Israel. The report also stated that the US was likely to close the window on negotiations after four to five months if no progress had been made. The next move could then be a military option.[344]

At the same time the Obama administration was making an attempt to draw Iran to the negotiating table, North Korea launched a satellite-carrying missile. The latest move from Pyongyang is further proof that the rogue nation, with which the US is still technically at war, has the capability to deliver a nuclear device to the west coast of the US. Iranian armed forces deputy chief, Brigadier General Masoud Jazayeri was quick to acknowledge that Tehran "congratulates the people and the government [of North Korea] on the successful launching of the satellite-carrying rocket."[345] Despite reports that Iranian experts were in North Korea, Tehran was equally swift to deny any collusion with that country. If those statements prove to be valid, Iran could be closer than was thought to having access to a missile delivery system that could endanger the Middle East, Europe, and the United States.

Among the options for dealing with Iran are sanctions—which have had some limited effect on the economy there—and regime change, which is not the policy of the Obama administration. This was made patently obvious in 2009. President Obama had a legitimate chance to support change for good, but he turned a blind eye to the freedom-seekers who took to the streets of Tehran to protest Ahmadinajad's debatable presidential victory. He had the opportunity to respond vigorously in support of the Iranian people, but failed to do so, and his silence was most telling. As Iranians risked their lives, Obama took a neutral stance. Dante Alighieri said, "The hottest places in Hell are reserved for those who, in time of great moral crises, retained their neutrality."[346]

It seemed that President Obama was determined to remain aloof to the cries of the people of Iran in favor of doing nothing in what appeared to be an attempt to preserve the possibility of negotiating with the very man who holds the Iranian people under his thumb...Ayatollah Ali Khamenei.

The young men and women of Iran who stood up to Ahmadinejad and had their votes stolen waited eight days before President Obama finally issued a statement. Even then, he offered no hope of any kind to the protestors. Did President Obama understand men and women weren't willing to die simply for a vote recount; but that they were willing to lay down their lives for the right to be heard, for the right to life, liberty, and the pursuit of freedom? They were not protesting faux ballots; they were protesting the despotic limitations imposed on them by the tyrannical clerics who really run the country.

The Islamic Republic in Iran was exposed as a fraud. If President Obama could not use diplomacy to support democracy, any hand he might extend to Iran's ruling mullahs had better have a whole lot of *baksheesh* (bribery money) in it.

According to Education Views website, Mr. Obama's reputation in Arab countries has suffered:

> Despite intense and sustained efforts to woo the Arab
> world with money and nice words, a newly-released survey

of the region finds that President Obama is at the bottom of a list Arabs admire most. Obama is admired by just 4 percent of Middle East Arabs in the new survey released by Brookings Institution and University of Maryland. Above him:

✧   13 percent prefer Iranian leader Mahmoud Ahmadinejad.

✧   6 percent prefer dead Iraqi dictator Saddam Hussein.

✧   5 percent chose Venezuelan strongman Hugo Chavez.

Even 5 percent chose French President Nicolas Sarkozy over Obama.

And when asked if there could be just one superpower, who would they like it to be, Arabs snubbed Obama again. The top choice, with 22 percent, was China...the United States came in at 7 percent.[347]

Should all of the administration's attempts to force an agreement from the mullahs in Iran fail, the US (and Israel) are left with just one response—the military. There are a multitude of scenarios that could prove effective. For the sake of brevity, only the minimum will be outlined here.

First: What steps might be taken in advance preparation for an attack? The US could position its aircraft carriers in strategic locations from which they could steam toward the Arabian Sea and the Persian Gulf on a moment's notice. Possibilities for combat duty would be Nimitz class carriers:

✧   *USS Ronald Reagan* (CVN 76) with Carrier Air Wing One Four (CVW-14).

✧   *USS Abraham Lincoln* (CVN 72) with Carrier Strike Group Nine and host to Carrier Air Wing Two.

✧   *USS John C. Stennis* (CVN 74) with an embarked Air Wing (CVW-9) including eight or nine squadrons consisting of Navy and Marine F/A-18 Hornet, EA-6B Prowler, MH-60R, MH-60S, and E-2C Hawkeye.

❖ The *USS Kitty Hawk* was decommissioned in 2009, but the *USS George H.W. Bush* could be called into service in the Persian Gulf Region.

If the United States were to move two carrier task forces into the Persian Gulf region, it would deliver a clear signal to Tehran of increased firepower in the region available to launch a sea-based air strike.

The carriers would be supported by the US underwater fleet that includes:

The *USS Ohio* (SSGN 726), the first ballistic missile submarine to complete conversion to a new class of guided missile submarines (re-designated SSGN from SSBN). With guided missile capability, this new class of submarine is being reconfigured to support Special Forces capabilities on the ground. Three other submarines are undergoing the SSGN conversion process, including the *USS Michigan*, the *USS Florida*, and the *USS Georgia*. The US Navy could deploy any of these attack subs to the Persian Gulf region to support Special Forces operations that might be involved in a strike on Iran.

Additionally, the US Navy could announce any task force assignments that would deploy additional Tomahawk cruise missile resources in the Persian Gulf. Knowing that the US Navy was deploying additional military resources to the region would clearly signal an attack on Iran.[348]

If the use of ground forces became necessary, there are several US military bases that observers could watch closely for activity that might signal an attack on Iran.[349] Fort Rucker, Alabama, is where the Army has consolidated air support operations, including the Apache (AH-64A) attack helicopter, the Blackhawk (UH-60A) and the Kiowa (OH-58D) that is used in reconnaissance as well as target acquisition/designation missions.

The 16th Special Operations Wing (SOW) is stationed at Hulburt Field in Florida. That is the largest Air Force unit assigned to US Special Operations Command, and is uniquely equipped to undertake missions in an enemy-controlled area or with politically sensitive objectives, such as Iran's nuclear facilities. Rather than launch a full-scale invasion of Iran, the unit could hit designated targets. Its motto is "Any Time, Any Place." The unit was responsible for the capture of Manuel Noriega in Panama and Operation Uphold Democracy in Haiti.

A third key base is Twenty-Nine Palms, the Marine Corps Air Ground Combat Center near Palm Springs, California. It is located in a mountainous desert area that would be ideal for training in a physical terrain that resembles the sites of several key nuclear installations in Iran. Units from these three bases would be ideal to support a limited military incursion that could accompany a US air strike on Iran.

We should also expect that the CIA director and the US secretary of state might make trips to confer with NATO allies prior to any US preemptive strike on Iran. The point is that prior to actually launching an attack, the ramp-up to any action could be used as an additional, final opportunity to increase pressure on the regime in Iran.

If the Security Council and the Obama administration are totally ineffective in halting Iran's forward momentum in the nuclear race, the scenario will certainly shift to military preparedness.

It is expected that a reasonably short period will precede an attack, to issue a final ultimatum to Iran and to prepare the US public for yet another preemptive war in the Middle East. Even in this final stage, when the US military is positioning for attack, Iran still will have a last opportunity to realize the seriousness of the situation and recant. The probability of Iran reversing course after Security Council failures is small. If anything, Iran may become even more defiant.

As we have repeatedly noted, the religious zealots ruling Iran believe war and destruction are a necessary precondition for the second coming of the Mahdi. Moreover, the hard-liners in the Iranian regime judge that the United States will over-extend by attacking Iran, believing that Iran is destined to defeat the US in a Middle East war. The religious zealots ruling Iran may see a war as the beginning of the fulfillment of Ayatollah Khomeini's prediction that Israel and the United States will fall, just as he had envisioned that the Shah, the Soviet Union, and Saddam Hussein would fall.

The US attack on Iraq involved a military invasion with the intention to move on Baghdad and depose the regime of Saddam Hussein. Let us assume, at least initially, that the US strike on Iran would be more limited, consisting primarily of an air attack combined with Special Forces Operations on the ground. A move to a full-scale invasion would only follow an official US acceptance that regime change was the official foreign policy with regard to Iran. The goal in a more limited military attack would be to knock out Iran's major nuclear facilities, causing a major setback in Iran's ability to manufacture nuclear weapons.

Should an attack become imminent, the following Iranian nuclear facilities would likely be primary targets: [350]

✧ Arak, the heavy water plant about
154 miles southwest of Tehran.

✧ Bushehr nuclear reactor, located along the Persian
Gulf, approximately 250 miles south of Tehran.

✧ Isfahan nuclear processing plant.

✧ Natanz nuclear enrichment plant.

✧ Saghand uranium mine.

✧ Fordow, uranium enrichment plant.

About a dozen smaller facilities devoted to Iran's nuclear efforts would also be targeted, some of which are imbedded within cities and will require precision bombing. While several hundred sites may play some role contributing to Iran's nuclear technologies, the goal would be to target the major facilities which would need to be destroyed to stop Iran's progress toward enriching uranium and pursuing nuclear weapons technology.

Iran's missile facilities have also been systematically catalogued and studied by US military intelligence. Fairly comprehensive surveys are publicly available on the Internet. The National Threat Initiative (NTI), for instance, lists 29 Iranian missile production facilities by name, location, and function.[351]

Iran's military air bases, including army, navy, and air force are also well known to US intelligence services; again, Internet resources make available many detailed descriptions of Iran's military forces and their base locations.[352] Iran's Shahab missiles are launched from mobile carriers; a satellite intelligence effort will have to be made in the days immediately prior to an attack to see if their current locations can be identified.

Secondary targets would be comprised of government buildings, including military facilities; Iran's media and telecommunications infrastructure, also radio and television stations; telephone switching facilities; government buildings; conventional power plants; bridges and highways; rail lines; port facilities.

Hardened structures, such as the underground centrifuge plants at Natanz, might be attacked with tactical nuclear weapons, either from ship-launched Tomahawk cruise missiles, or launched via air strike. Otherwise, the munitions utilized would be conventional, largely precision-guided bombs, such as those used in the 2003 attack on Iraq. Most likely, tactical nuclear weapons would not be employed, so as to keep the weapons threshold conventional only.

A more limited attack would see multiple waves of air strikes and cruise missile attacks. In a noted book about John Boyd, the fighter pilot whose ideas on air combat fundamentally changed the tactics of air warfare, author Robert Coram notes that air combat is a blood sport:

> Many civilians and those who have never looked through
> the gun sight—then called a pipper—at an enemy aircraft
> have a romantic perception, no doubt influenced by books

and movies about World War I, that pilots are knights of the air, chivalrous men who salute their opponents before engaging in a fight that always is fair. They believe that elaborate rules of aerial courtesy prevail and that battle in the clear pure upper regions somehow is different, more glorified and rarefied, than battle in the mud. This is total nonsense. Aerial combat, according to those who have participated, is a basic and primitive form of battle that happens to take place in the air. Fighter pilots—that is, the ones who survive air combat—are not gentlemen; they are backstabbing assassins. They come out of the sun and attack an enemy when he is blind. They sneak up behind or underneath or "bounce" the enemy from above or flop into position on his tail—his six-o'clock position—and "tap" him before he knows they are there.[353]

Coram comments that effective aerial combat is a "knife in the dark." The same principle that makes one-on-one dog-fighting effective applies to massive air attacks. The goal is to exert enormous air power to destroy key targets as rapidly as possible; catching the enemy unprepared, even surprised, is most effective in what amounts to a modern application of Nazi Germany's World War II *blitzkrieg* tactic.

As with the "shock and awe" strike on Iraq in 2003, the attack could involve submarine and ship-launched Tomahawk cruise missiles, B-2 stealth bombers and F-117 stealth fighters, using precision-guided bombs and bunker-busters.[354] This same type of massive airpower could be launched against Iran, with a focus on Iran's nuclear facilities and military bases.

If the goal is not regime-change, the attacks on the government infrastructure could be aimed at reducing its ability to communicate internally or organize an effective counter-attack. The air attack could occur over the span of a few days, with no plan to launch a ground invasion, unless Iranian counter-attack measures required an expanded war effort. While the air attack most likely would not eliminate Iran's ability to produce nuclear weapons permanently, the program could be significantly set back, perhaps to a point where recovery would be extremely costly, requiring several years to reach a pre-attack status.

Helicopter-delivered Special Operations assaults could supplement the air attacks by going after installations embedded in population areas or hardened targets that might be better destroyed by troops on the ground. The Special Operations strikes would most likely be defined as hit-and-destroy missions where there was no anticipation of a sustained campaign.

The overall design of such an offensive would be to inflict a hard blow over a limited time, with no expectation of launching a sustained invasion aimed at regime change. The goal would be to destroy as much of Iran's nuclear technology as possible, so we could set back any nuclear weapons program and gain more time to deal with the government in Tehran.

Inflicting major damage to Iran's nuclear facilities could be accomplished by the US launching a blitz air attack. Unless Iran's military capabilities were destroyed in the first few hours, however, a counter-attack would be costly.

Many, if not the majority of the mobile Shahab missile launchers might survive air strikes, and be prepared to hit selected targets, including the many US military bases in surrounding nations, including in Iraq, Kuwait, Qatar, Azerbaijan, and Oman. Thousands of US military personnel could be killed in missile raids organized by Iran in the days and weeks after a US air attack.

Additionally, Hezbollah terrorists in Lebanon as well as Hamas and the Islamic Jihad in Gaza would most likely launch retaliatory missile strikes on Israel. Iran, as well, could launch conventionally-armed Shahab missiles against Israel's major cities, with the likelihood of inflicting thousands of human casualties and causing substantial infrastructure damage.

If any Iranian military fighter planes survived, a missile war could be supplemented by Iranian fighter sorties against US bases in the area and against Israel. Even a conventional missile war would cost thousands of lives on all sides and would almost certainly draw Israel into the conflict, even if the United States labeled the war a preemptive strike.

Within Iran today, there is a considerable base of opposition to the current regime, especially among Iran's youth and student populations. A tactical military strike launched by the United States against Iran risks backfiring. In reaction to the attack, the US might stir up Iranian nationalism, even among the nation's dissidents. Following an attack, internal support for the Iranian regime might actually intensify. Iranians could oppose what would be portrayed as US aggression against Iran, with the regime certainly arguing that the attack was completely unjustified.

If America were seen as opposing Islam, not simply going after Iran's nuclear facilities, a region-wide uprising might unify in support of Iran, regardless whether the Muslims involved were Shiite or Sunni. Right now many of Iran's Muslim neighbors, including Turkey, are concerned about their own national security as Iran pursues nuclear technology aggressively. Even Saudi Arabia has taken a position opposing Iran's defiant pursuit of nuclear technology.

Following a US strategic strike against Iran, many Islamic nations, including even Sunni Saudi Arabia, might reverse their policy, to express sympathy with Iran, if not offering outright support. By launching a preemptive attack against Iran, anti-American sentiment throughout the Islamic world could intensify.

Wherever terrorist sleeper cells have operational capabilities, a US military attack against Iran would provide an occasion for renewed incidents. If the strikes were only limited to the type of rail transportation and subway bombs we saw in Spain and London, terrorists could cause havoc by launching raids in several Western countries simultaneously.

The US would be blamed by those in the West predisposed to be sympathetic with Iran's argument that its nuclear program is for peaceful purposes only. As the world's only remaining superpower, the US would then be cast in the role of an international aggressor.

If the war against Iran were characterized as a war of self-defense, worldwide public opinion would most likely turn against the United States. A preemptive attack on Iran would bear heavy political consequences for the United States, not only in the Islamic world, but among many traditional allies as well. In the extreme, an attack against Iran could backfire, causing a rise of Islamic unity across the globe.

The aftermath of a military strike against Iran would be risky for the US, even if it achieved the objective of knocking out or slowing Iran's nuclear capabilities. A long war in Iran would be disastrous, given the potential to stir up anti-American terrorism and insurgencies in the aftermath. As we learned in Afghanistan and Iraq, a rapid military victory may only be the first chapter to managing a successful peace. Rather than stabilizing the Middle East, an attack on Iran might further destabilize the region, such that Israel's ultimate survival was even more at risk than before the attack.

Should the Palestinians unite behind Hamas and Islamic Jihad in reaction to a US strike on Iran, it might well portend intensified political pressure against Israel for further concessions. In the extreme, the US attack might occasion a new wave of terrorist attacks launched against Israel.

The following reasons, then, are an argument for the regime-change solution:

✧   If Ayatollah Khamenei and President Ahmadinejad remain in power after a US preemptive military strike, a move toward declaring war on the United States might be the next step. The military strike might bring Iran's nuclear program to a halt, but that halt would only be temporary. The radical regime under the mullahs would move to reconstitute its nuclear program immediately. Moreover, those countries who feel the US attack was unjustified might provide increased technical and financial support to Iran.

✧   •   A US military attack on Iran undoubtedly would cause world oil prices to spike. Oil would likely increase to much more than $100 a barrel, pushing US gasoline costs even higher. If the Iranian regime withstands a US military preemptive attack, it would most certainly urge OPEC to restrict supplies. Approximately 40 percent of the world's oil supply passes through the Strait of Hormuz.

✧ The decision to depose the current Iranian government would avoid leaving in place a regime that would declare the United States an enemy to be destroyed at all costs.

✧ Once rebuilt, Iran's nuclear program would be harder to control. Having once defied the world community, Iran would not hesitate the second time to present the world with the choice of deposing the regime or facing the prospect of an atomic Iran armed with nuclear weapons. Having survived one attack, the Iranian regime would resolve to build a coalition of international allies into what could amount to a mutual security pact, where the allies declare that any further attacks will be considered an attack on Iran's allies.

✧ Terrorist organizations would use the US preemptive attack as the justification for their open declaration to obtain nuclear weapons and trigger a nuclear arms race in the region. Intensified terrorism in support of Iran would be aimed at further destabilizing the Middle East, Europe, and America.

✧ The Iranian regime would have to rebuild the physical facilities destroyed in the attack. The human talent of Iran's nuclear scientists and engineers, however, would remain in place, unless a large percentage of Iran's nuclear experts were killed at facilities which the attack damaged or destroyed.

✧ The second time the facilities are constructed would be easier than the first. Conceivably, better facilities would be reconstructed faster, cheaper, and be made more secure from future attack. Ironically, Iran's nuclear infrastructure might emerge superior to those destroyed.

In rebuilding its nuclear infrastructure, Iran could go immediately to advanced-generation nuclear technologies. Ironically, in the longer run, we might have done Iran a favor by eliminating old and experimental nuclear facilities, so the regime could rebuild its nuclear program with new, state-of-the-art technologies. Within a short time, Iran's nuclear program could be back, fully functioning, possibly even more advanced than it had been before the attack.

On January 16, 2006, Davoud Danesh-Jafari, Iran's economy minister, said that the country's role as the world's fourth-largest producer of oil gave Iran a position of power in the world oil economy. "Any possible sanctions from the west," he warned, "could possibly, by disturbing Iran's political and economic situation, raise oil prices beyond levels the West expects."[355]

This thinly-veiled threat of oil retaliation was intended to put the US, the EU-3, and the IAEA on notice. If this is Iran's response to possible Security Council review, how much more severe would the regime's response be to a military strike aimed at Iran's nuclear facilities?

A preemptive strike involves attacking the symptoms, not solving the problem. If this realization can be communicated to the political Left, especially to key Democratic Senators, and to the American people, an attack aimed at creating regime change in Iran offers a more realistic chance that the nuclear threat can be removed altogether, not just postponed.

Ironically, the political repercussions on the US from a full-scale invasion of Iran might be less than would be realized from a more limited attack. With the Iranian regime left in place, the mullahs and their supporters would have a continuing podium from which to project their anti-American grievances.

Dissidents within Iran, as well as expatriate opponents of the regime worldwide, will have to come forward to reorganize what could hopefully emerge as a more democratic Iran. US leaders would need to demonstrate a desire to withdraw once a new Iranian government had been installed. This is the same model the US followed at the end of World War II, where the goal was to establish democratic governments in Germany and Japan, as a pre-condition for withdrawal.

The current regime in Iran is a central instigator of terrorism worldwide. As has been noted repeatedly, Hezbollah, Hamas, and the Islamic Jihad virtually owe their financial survival to the mullahs in Iran. Al Qaeda operatives work actively with the Iranian government to further mutually-held aims.

By eliminating the Iranian regime of the mullahs, a central part of the War on Terrorism would be won. Without support from the mullahs in Tehran, Syria would have a much more difficult time dominating Lebanon. Without the constant discouragement from Tehran, the Palestinian Authority might have an easier time reaching a final agreement with Israel to implement a "two-state" solution.

The mullahs in Tehran have been a roadblock to Middle East peace since the 1979 revolution. As long as the current leaders remain in power, one cannot expect the War on Terrorism to end. With the regime of the mullahs gone, however, substantial sums from Iran's abundant oil profits would no longer be available to fund terrorism. With such interference removed, the War on Terrorism might make important strides towards reaching a successful conclusion.

Eliminating the regime of the mullahs would represent an important movement toward freedom and democracy in the Middle East, as well as provide the potential for a more complete reconciliation of Islamic peoples worldwide with the US and the West.

From this perspective, the United States might well calculate that rather than launch a limited strike on Iran's nuclear facilities, more would be gained by going after the regime itself.

Obviously, solving the Iranian nuclear crisis involves no easy choices. Rather, as I have noted, all options have negative consequences. The choice then is to find the best among admittedly undesirable choices.

Russia and China, while opposed to any US invasion of Iran, would likely stand aside, having decided not to provide direct military assistance to save the regime of the mullahs. Skeptics worldwide will argue that an invasion of Iran would overstretch the US military and prove too costly an undertaking. Yet, with US military force levels having been reduced in Iraq and Afghanistan, redeployment to Iran is more achievable now. Clearly, a military invasion of Iran would not be the option first considered by any US administration.

Yet, after a serious attempt is made to deal with the Iranian regime on a more limited basis of engagement, the Obama Administration may come to the conclusion that regime-change is the only option that truly makes sense. However, all other options should be explored first. Still, after months of pursuing more limited objectives and tactical methodologies, the fundamental choice may well be: remove the regime of the mullahs once and for all, or accept the reality that sooner or later the Iranians will end up with nuclear weapons.

If the mullahs wanted to be sure that no single country could deny access to the enriched uranium needed to run a peaceful program, then the IAEA could create a multi-nation "uranium bank" from which enriched uranium could be withdrawn. The Iranian nuclear crisis could be resolved fairly easily and quickly by mature and experienced international diplomats, provided that Iran's intentions are truly peaceful and that all defiance would cease. This includes attacking Israel with verbal threats and halting financial and war materiel support to terrorist organizations such as Hezbollah and Hamas.

In conclusion, the leaders in Iran have an easy solution to the entire crisis. If Iran's only intent with its nuclear program is peaceful as claimed, then all it has to do is comply with the IAEA's request for verifiable inspections.

— 24 —

ISRAEL IN THE CROSSHAIRS

"September 11ᵗʰ was a wake-up call from hell that has opened our eyes to the horrors that await us tomorrow if we fail to act today."
—BENJAMIN NETANYAHU[356]

ROLE-PLAYING IS EASY—as we've seen in the last two chapters outlining two attack scenarios. However, it is much more difficult to make the decisions that affect the world as a whole; issues that involve war and peace, sacrificing the lives of men and women, surviving the global economy, and other vital concerns.

The world is more than a decade into the twenty-first century. At the conclusion of the twentieth century Americans could look back on the end of two World Wars and the Cold War, the collapse of the Berlin Wall, the close of the first Persian Gulf War, and a time of prosperity. As the clock struck midnight on New Year's Eve, December 31, 1999, we discovered that some imagined catastrophe had been averted. The world had not come to a standstill either technologically or mechanically. Folks did not need to hole up in their homes with shelves of canned goods, bottled water, and weapons to protect their property from the midnight marauders of a new millennium. It was, surprisingly, business as usual.

However, the eyes of our enemies never strayed from their focus upon the US; they simply waited to determine our next move in order to calculate theirs. On September 11, 2001, the hammer fell and the US felt the devastation of terrorism as never before.

Despite the tragic warning of 9/11 and the certainty that there are still those who want only to see the US decimated, we returned too quickly and easily to the monotony of everyday life and the belief that the US is somehow immune to future devastating terrorist attacks.

When I see such apathy, I am reminded of an encounter I had with Isser Harel, the head of Mossad from 1947-1963, at a dinner in his home on September 23, 1980. It was just a few months before the US presidential election. On that night I asked Harel, "Who do you think will be the next president?"

Harel responded, "The word on the street is that terrorists might have a say about the outcome. They will attempt to influence the election by releasing the hostages precisely when Reagan is sworn into office. They want Carter out because of his challenges to Islam." The former intelligence officer was referring to the Camp David accords and Carter's insistence that Egyptian President Anwar Sadat give a speech in his home country stating that religion and politics must be separate. This speech was heard by a blind cleric named al-Rahman who issued the Fatwa to assassinate Sadat; the same cleric was later indicted for his part in the first bombing of the World Trade Center in 1993.

Later on that same evening, I asked Harel another question: "Will terrorism ever come to America?"

He repeated my question back to me, and then responded, "America is developing a tolerance for terrorism. America has the power to fight terrorism but not the will; the terrorists have the will, but not the power. That could change in time. Oil buys more than tents. You in the West kill a fly and rejoice. In the Middle East, we kill one, and one hundred flies come to the funeral. Yes, I fear America will experience terrorism in time."

"Where will it come?" I asked him.

He thought for a moment. "New York is the symbol of your freedom and capitalism. It's likely they will strike there first—at your tallest building, which is symbolic of your power."

Little did I know that both of Harel's predictions—the release of the hostages at the exact hour of President Reagan's inauguration and the terrorist strikes against the tallest building in New York—would come to pass. After Reagan's victory, the hostages were released, and on September 11, 2001, the United States would plunge headfirst into an apocalyptic tornado.

There are many who think the West cannot survive the onslaught of fanatical Islam of which Iran is only one, but the primary example. In spite of the tremendous upheaval we are witnessing with the rise of terrorism worldwide, we have failed to fully comprehend the danger. Surrounded by those who wish to see both America and Israel wiped off the map, one must ask: How can the West survive?

Just as the world in Hitler's day did not recognize the process by which that cruel dictator began to dehumanize the Jews in Europe, so it does not recognize that Iran has, for decades, been using those same guidelines to question the legality of the State of Israel and the proprietary claim of the Jewish people in that small spot in the Middle East. The Supreme leader Ayatollah Ali Khamenei has questioned:

> Who are the Israelis? They are responsible for usurping houses, territory, farmlands, and businesses. They are combatants at the disposal of Zionist operatives. A Muslim nation cannot remain indifferent vis-à-vis such people who are stooges at the service of the arch-foes of the Muslim world.[357]

Khamenei's intent toward Israel cannot be more obvious than in his following statement printed in the *Daily Telegraph* in 2006:

> There is only one solution to the Middle East prob-
> lem, namely the annihilation and destruction of the Jewish
> state.[358]

One of the most powerful strategies that can save the West is a zero-tolerance for terror policy. After Harel's warning, it became clear that America
did, indeed, have a tolerance for terror. Today, it is still operating under that
policy. Iran is responsible for more deaths through IEDs and the injuring of
more US soldiers than anyone in Iraq. Through its proxies, Hezbollah and
Hamas, it is responsible for killing more Jews in the State of Israel than any
other supporter of organized terror, and still US presidents have sidestepped
that issue when trying to coerce Israel to the bargaining table.

Syria, too, is in the business of terror—even to turning its weapons on
its own people who disagree with the regime's policies. Iran is cleared to fly
its planes into Syrian air space in order to arm Hezbollah and Hamas proxies in Lebanon and Gaza. The US must immediately establish a policy by
which it will not, under any circumstances, negotiate with any regime that
supports, aids or funds terror—including the PA, Syria, Iran, and virtually
any nation aligned with radical Islam. A zero-tolerance policy will shut down
the engine of terror. All US funding and diplomatic relations with terror-
supporting states need to cease. The diplomatic missions for those countries
in the US should be closed, and the harshest penalties imposed for sustain-
ing terrorist factions. They should be isolated from the world.

In addition, the US government must stop the hypocrisy of Jew-baiting.
It's appalling to continually promise Muslim, Jew-hating bigots an Islamic
state with its capital in Jerusalem. An ironclad bond needs to be established
between Israel and the US, with Jerusalem recognized as the undivided capital and Judea and Samaria acknowledged as Israel's land.

A secure and strong Israel is in the United States' self-interest. Israel is
not a client state, but a very reliable friend and a strategic ally. To weaken
Israel is to destabilize the region and risk the peace of the world, for the road
to world peace runs through the Middle East.

God deals with nations in accordance with how those nations deal with Israel. Israel does not have to offer an excuse for its existence; Israel lives today as a right that has been hallowed by the Bible, by history, by sacrifice, by prayer, by the yearnings of the Jewish people for peace.

It seems the tyrants of this world must always have a scapegoat, someone or some ethnic group to blame for their own inequities. All too often those people have been the Jews. Iran's President Mahmoud Ahmadinejad has joined his supreme leader in castigating Israel as a puppet regime planted in the Middle East by Western Zionists simply to usurp Muslim claims to the land. Khamenei once again threw down the gauntlet when he asked:

> What are you? A forged government and a false nation. They gather wicked people from all over the world and made something called the Israeli nation. Is that a nation? Those [Jews] who went to Israel were malevolent, evil, greedy thieves, and murderers.[359]

Both of Iran's most visible leaders have further characterized Israel, at varying times, as a "filthy germ," a "cancerous tumor," a "stinking corpse," and a "stain of disgrace [on the] garment of Islam." The intent is to demonize the Jewish people and mark them a tool of the devil, a "manifestation of Satan"[360] to be used against the poor, unsuspecting Muslim people. They are dedicated to make the Jewish people seem subhuman—thus the moniker "monkeys and apes" is often ascribed to Jews.

In my interview with Prime Minister Benjamin Netanyahu, he alluded to Iran's determination to destroy Israel:

> "Israel could be in great jeopardy; so will everybody else. In short order, the Western-oriented regimes of the Middle East would fall by the wayside. That is why you see the Arab countries siding against Iran, against Hezbollah; they understand what I am saying. The Middle East could be taken over, and that means the oil fields—the oil spigot of the world—would be in Iranian hands."[361]

He further stated:

> "Imagine what would happen later if Iran were to have missiles that would reach into every European capital. Within a decade into the Eastern coast of the US, and would be armed not with explosives, but with nuclear weapons.
>
> Iran could inspire the 200 million…300 million Shi'ites… That's what it intends to do—inspire them into a religious war, first against other Muslims, then against Israel and the West. The reason they despise us so much, the reason they want to eradicate us is that they don't hate you because of us, they hate us because of you. They say we are the 'Small Satan' and that America is the 'Great Satan.'"[362]

Iran is obviously the greatest immediate threat to the State of Israel, as it is the Iranian rial that funds many of the major terrorist movements determined to decimate the Jewish people and wrest their homeland from them. When the fundamentalism that fuels the likes of Mahmoud Ahmadinejad is married to the proliferation of its nuclear program, the threat to Israel grows exponentially.

What Ahmadinejad and the mullahs who rule Iran seem to overlook is that Israel possesses the capacity to retaliate on a large scale. It boasts an advanced anti-missile system in collaboration with the US and has the capability of crippling Iran's growing nuclear program. "Israel has a whole arsenal of capabilities to make sure the Iranians don't achieve their result," said Efraim Halevy, former head of Mossad.[363]

Following the death of the Ayatollah Ruhollah Khomeini, it seemed that the mullahs and ayatollahs were simply waiting for the likes of a Mahmoud Ahmadinejad to burst upon the scene and verbalize their hateful rhetoric. Today it doesn't take much insight to determine the identity of the one out to destroy Israel, or in his own words to "wipe Israel off the map."

What, I wonder, does the world really think of Mahmoud Ahmadinejad? Are most people aware of his devotion to the Mahdi? Do most understand that he is an ardent Twelver, a dedicated disciple of the Twelfth Imam, who will do anything to insure that the world is made ready for the second coming of a false messiah—even if it requires manufacturing his own apocalyptic event to insure a rush to Armageddon? When I met Mahmoud Ahmadinejad's spiritual advisor in New York City in 2007, he declared to me that his leader would usher in the Mahdi—the twelfth descendant of Mohammad—through an apocalyptic event within three years.

Unfortunately, one need look no further than Ahmadinejad's speech at the United Nations on September 17, 2005, when he closed with the words: "O mighty Lord, I pray to you to hasten the emergence of your last repository, the promised one, that perfect and pure human being, the one that will fill this world with justice and peace."[364] No, he was not speaking of the return of Jesus Christ. He was speaking of the coming of the Mahdi. Ahmadinejad went home to Tehran and regaled his compatriots with a story about how mesmerized his listeners were when he spoke:

> "On the last day when I was speaking, one person in our group told me that when I started to say *"bismullah Muhammad"'* he saw a green light come from around me, and I was placed inside this aura...I felt it myself. I felt that the atmosphere suddenly changed and for those twenty-seven to twenty-eight minutes, all the leaders of the world did not blink. When I say they didn't move an eyelid, I am not exaggerating. They were looking as if a hand were holding them there, and had just opened their eyes."[365]

The miniature martinet that leads Iran had the audacity to write a letter to President George W. Bush and one to the American people. If I were to put the message of each into a nutshell, they were both basically saying, "Become Muslim and we shall all live at peace."

The intentions of its leaders are deadly serious; they can neither be taken for granted nor underestimated. They seek converts to their fanatical lifestyle from every nation, not just from among the Arabs. Remember, after all, Iranians are not Arabs but Persians. Theirs is not a racial war but a religious one. Ahmadinejad reveres terrorists, whom he defines as "martyrs": "Is there an art that is more beautiful, more divine, more eternal than the art of the martyr's death?" he asks.[366] He wants nothing more than that every knee on earth should bow to the Mahdi, and warns that there will be no real peace in the world until the whole world is Muslim.

It is belief in the Mahdi that drives Ahmadinejad and his fellow Twelvers in Iran. They are by far the largest group of Shi'as, compiling approximately 80 percent of the total worldwide group. Twelvers represent the majority of Muslims in Iran, Iraq, and Bahrain. They also make up large communities in Lebanon, Syria, and Saudi Arabia.[367] Ahmadinejad believes the return of this descendant of Mohammad will come in a mushroom cloud suspended over Israel and America. His regime is a suicidal one, and reminiscent of the statement made by Ayatollah Ruhollah Khomeini: "I say let this land burn. I say let it go up in smoke, provided Islam emerges triumphant in the rest of the world."[368]

Given his determination to usher in the Mahdi, it is likely that Iran's fiery president will, with Ayatollah Ali Khamenei's blessing, continue his defiance against the Western world and forge ahead with Iran's nuclear program. According to Israel's Prime Minister Benjamin Netanyahu, Iran is the greatest threat to Israel since that nation was founded in 1948. This is true not only regarding the Islamic Republic's atomic aspirations, but because Iran fully undergirds the fanatical groups that surround Israel—Hezbollah in Lebanon and Hamas in Gaza. Both groups have drawn Israel into wars to defend her citizens. Netanyahu has not ruled out a military strike against Iran's nuclear sites, and after a meeting with President Obama in May 2009, the prime minister reiterated that Israel reserves the right to defend herself.

Iran seems intent on standing aloof from the world community. Its leaders thumb their noses at calls from the UN Security Council to halt the enrichment of uranium in the quest of nuclear arms. And yet, this same entity that is entrusted with peacekeeping has failed to recognize the link between Iran's pursuit of weapons of mass destruction and its persistent threats to Israel and the United States. The Security Council has become the proverbial ostrich that buries its head in the sand in order not to see the approaching threat to global safety. Its refusal to recognize this danger has made the United Nations an even more ineffective body. The leaders in Iran flaunt their violations of international law, and thus far, no one has been courageous enough to challenge them. No one has made a move to hold them accountable—either for their infractions in the nuclear arena or for their terrorist activities.

The pursuit of nuclear arms has placed the Sunni states in the Gulf region on alert. Leaders are concerned about the vulnerability of their countries should Iran complete the fuel cycle and actually manufacture nuclear weapons. Iran, a Shi'a majority, would then possess the means to intimidate its moderate Sunni Arab neighbors and create a climate of fear throughout the Middle East. The ghost of a nuclear arms race between the more radical Shi'a and the moderate Sunnis hovers over the region and fuels anxieties. This is another obvious reason why an atomic Iran is unacceptable; it will precipitate a trillion-dollar arms race in the Gulf region and provide a nuclear umbrella for a terrorist state.

Given the hatred for Israel and the West demonstrated by the radical Muslim world and Iran's fanatical pursuit of nuclear weapons, the question must again be asked: Can the West be saved, and if so, how? What will checkmate Iran's endgame in the nuclear arena? Will sanctions drive the country into bankruptcy? Will it be pressure from the US, the EU, Russia, or China? Will globalization be the straw that breaks Ahmadinejad and Khamenei's backs? Will an embargo on refined oil be the answer? Will it be a direct strike on their nuclear facilities by Israel? Let's examine these possibilities to see how each might act as a deterrent to Iran's pursuits of nuclear arms.

Will sanctions be a strong deterrent? It has long been apparent that they are not effective. That idea can be supported by gauging their efficacy against Fidel Castro, who quickly established a dictatorship on the island of Cuba despite their imposition.

Why have these newest attempts been more effective? The USA Patriot Act, Section 311, allows the US Treasury to label foreign banks as being of "primary money laundering concern."[369] This prevents an institution from being a clearinghouse for US dollars, disallows any transactions with banks, and halts any affiliation with US financial institutions. This proverbial shot-in-the-arm in applying monetary sanctions effectively quarantines the targeted country and keeps it from infecting other banks worldwide. This is due in large part to globalization, another tool that could be effective in isolating Iran.

In September 2006, the US Treasury department targeted one of Iran's largest government banks—Bank Saderat. It was charged with channeling approximately $50 million in payments to terrorist organizations Hezbollah and Hamas. All contact with the US banking system was shut off. Similar actions were taken in January 2007 against Bank Sepah in order to slow Iran's purchases of ballistic missiles.

Washington Post reporter David Ignatius summed up these moves by the US Treasury:

> The new sanctions are toxic because they effectively limit a country's access to the global ATM. In that sense, they impose—at last—a real price on countries such as North Korea and Iran that have blithely defied UN resolutions on proliferation. "What's the goal?" asks [Treasury spokesperson, Stuart] Levey. "To create an internal debate about whether these policies [of defiance] make sense. And that's happening in Iran. People with business sense realize that this conduct makes it hard to continue normal business relationships."[370]

Although sanctions imposed by the UN have generated little response, that organization has gathered some support from China and Russia, as well as the EU and US, which have all released statements supporting the determination that Iran should be banned from possessing nuclear weapons. Furthermore, financial sanctions, "creatively administered by the Treasury Department, are working to discourage European and Japanese banks from financing important projects in Iran and are having an adverse impact on Iran's economy."[371]

Stronger action needs to be taken to educate the global community as to the threat Iran poses to civilization—to worldwide stability and well-being. Iran has long been described as simply a threat to the Jewish state of Israel and to the United States; that is a complete fallacy. The possession of nuclear arms by a fanatical entity, whether Iran, North Korea, Al-Qaeda, or any of the myriad other radical countries or groups, is a menace of great magnitude and must be addressed with equal alacrity.

One of the avenues which must be explored is what the Western allies might be willing to discuss with Russia and China in order to gain their backing on the Iran question. The US has negotiated with China on separate issues involving currency and Iran; what would be the end result should those become joint discussions? China and Russia have formed what might be loosely described as a protectorate for Iran. This tripartite, back-burner agreement has proven to be reciprocally advantageous for all. Steve Schippert, co-founder of the Center for Threat Awareness, says:

> No nation at the UN Security Council has been more steadfast or consistent in resistance to US and Western sanctions efforts there than either the bear or the dragon. The reasons for this are quite simple: synergistic strategic advancement against a common enemy, oil and money. Iran is rightly portrayed as one of the most pressing threats to the United States and her interests. But Iran remains in many respects a piece on the chessboard of a greater Russian and Chinese game. Iran seeks greater power and regional dominance and enjoys the support of both Russia and China in its pursuits. Both afford Iran the protection of cover and interference at the UN Security Council and other diplomatic endeavors, allowing Iran to continue its nuclear efforts under a fairly comfortable security blanket.

For Russia...the gains are monetary and psychological, with Iran as a major arms client...China...signed a massive long-term energy deal with Iran worth billions. The United States in particular had made...public calls for other nations to specifically stop making energy agreements until Iran complies [with UN calls for halting the nuclear program]. Signing the energy deal...[afforded] the oil-starved dragon energy relief...All seek to weaken the United States to the point where each is enabled to act on their respective interests.[372]

Each of the three nations has a different agenda in seeking relationship with the others in the group: Iran wishes to gain superiority in the Persian Gulf and continue its support for the terrorist groups that act as its proxies; Russia, the once-proud bear, desires to regain a dominant role on the world stage; and China, the Johnny-come-lately to the international political scene, wants to wrest the "superpower" title from the United States and desperately needs the oil flowing to it from Iran. So long as America remains strong politically, economically, and militarily, those wishes will be thwarted. The United States needs to delineate ways to put increased pressure on both Russia and China to bring Iran to heel and force the leaders of that rogue nation to the bargaining table.

Having taken a snake into one's bosom, it is imperative not to think all is well and relax one's vigil. It might behoove both China and Russia to take notice of an event that followed the botched elections in Tehran in June 2009. According to a *Miami Herald* report:

In Tehran University's huge prayer hall, the Islamic regime's most powerful clerics deliver heated Friday sermons to thousands. These diatribes are normally accompanied by the chant, "Death to America!"

But at the last Friday prayers [July 17, 2009]—an electrifying event that will affect the core of President Obama's foreign policy—the loudest chants were, "Death to Russia!" and "Death to China!" Also, "Azadeh!" which means "freedom" in Farsi... Consider the impact of this new list of enemies. Ahmadinejad has been trying to distract attention from rigged elections by blaming the West for stirring up demonstrations.[373]

The next issue to be addressed when contemplating the question of how the West can be saved from an apocalyptic event orchestrated by Iran is that of globalization. What is it and what effect might it have on saving the West from Iran's nuclear pursuits and apocalyptic mission? Globalization is defined as:

> A process of interaction and integration among the people, companies, and governments of different nations, a process driven by international trade and investment and aided by information technology. This process has effects on the environment, on culture, on political systems, on economic development and prosperity, and on human physical well-being in societies around the world.[374]

Globalization knows no borders and crosses international boundaries. That is why the fight against terrorism in any form must first be global. No one is exempt from the hatred and fanaticism that grips those radical Islamic countries such as Iran. Having explored the dangers of nuclear weapons in the hands of leaders such as those in power in Tehran, we must define ways in which the world community can halt the forward progress of an atomic Iran.

A unified world marketplace would have a major impact on the economy of Iran. Such global tools as the Internet, Twitter, Facebook, and others are used by terrorist groups to plot and plan strikes, to fundraise, and to engage new members; those same tools could be used to discourage trade with Iran. Globalization could be a vital tool in halting the forward march toward an apocalypse, but only if world leaders are engaged. It directly affects markets, economies, communications, transportation, trade, service industries, and capital. It clearly could be a determining factor in whether or not sanctions against Iran were effective. It could be used to leverage Iran's oil-based economy.

In a speech delivered at the National Defense College graduation ceremony in July 2009, Benjamin Netanyahu addressed the effectiveness of globalization:

> Eventually radical Islam will be defeated by the global information revolution, by the freedom of ideas which are breaking out, through technology and through ideas of freedom. This won't happen immediately, but it will happen... The only thing that can postpone and disrupt the rate of the extinguishing of radical Islam is the possibility that it will be armed with a nuclear weapon.[375]

Another action that would require a global response centers on the credit card industry. The director of the Israel Atomic Energy Commission told me one of the greatest weapons the world has against Iran's nuclear program is the credit card. If the credit cards and bank accounts used by mullahs and members of the Revolutionary Guard were frozen, it would have an enormous and immediate impact on their nuclear ambitions. This would amount to tens of billions of dollars.

While there are those who feel that "globalization" is a word not to be used in polite company or in political circles, it might well be a most effective weapon against Khamenei and Ahmadinejad if wielded unilaterally. It would require a united front, which would of necessity include China and Russia, not to mention a decline in the purchase of crude from Iranian oil wells.

Is oil a possible key to halting an atomic Iran? In 2008, an analysis of the Iranian oil industry began:

> The Iranian oil and gas industry approaches its 100th anniversary bloated, corrupt, and nearly bankrupt, managing four times the employees but two thirds of the oil production it had before the Islamic Revolution of 1978-79.[376]

Even with that gloomy report, Iran continues to export 2.1 million barrels of oil per day. The majority of its exports go to Asia, with Europe taking the leftovers. Japan is the largest consumer of Iranian oil, with China a close second. While it is able to export crude oil, Iran is forced to import 40 percent of its refined petroleum because of increased demands, which its refineries are unable to meet. Iran is, however, spending its oil and gas revenues to fund terrorism. Some estimates indicate that Hezbollah receives as much as $200 million annually from Tehran.

It is conceivable that Iran could be persuaded to halt its nuclear program if stronger sanctions against imported refined gasoline were implemented. This is one proposal being investigated by US lawmakers. The 111th Congress introduced H.R. 2194: Iran Refined Petroleum Sanctions Act of 2009. In Section 3, Amendments to the Iran Sanctions Act of 1996, the following is found:

> PRODUCTION OF REFINED PETROLEUM RESOURCES—
> Except as provided in subsection (f), the President shall impose the sanctions described in section 6(b) (in addition to any sanctions imposed under subparagraph (A)) if the President determines that a person has, with actual knowledge, on or after the date of the enactment of the Iran Refined Petroleum Sanctions Act of 2009, sold, leased, or provided to Iran any goods, services, technology, information, or support that would allow Iran to maintain or expand its domestic production of refined petroleum resources, including any assistance in refinery construction, modernization, or repair.[377]

A similar tactic was considered and then rejected by the Bush administration. It was decided that trying to enforce a refined petroleum embargo would present a dangerous and complex challenge. Both Russia and China would have to be induced to join such an effort. Iran could retaliate by halting exports and bringing traffic in the Strait of Hormuz to a standstill.

That could prove to be a fiscal nightmare for an already susceptible world economy.

With H.R. 2194 on the table, Iran defiantly announced that it would end refined petrol imports. Seifollah Jashnsaz, managing director of National Iranian Oil Company, announced that Iran has planned the erection of nine refineries. He added that the country is currently constructing seven refineries. He indicated that the star in the refinery crown was "the biggest and most outstanding of all refineries being constructed in Iran and makes use of state-of-the-art technology…The said refinery, once fully operational, can produce 35 million liters of petrol on a daily basis. The production will not only satisfy Iran's demand for petrol but will also be sold at export markets."[378]

If Iran continues on its course of nuclear proliferation the US government must quickly take the extreme measure of a complete oil embargo, not allowing fuel to be sold by Iran or refined petroleum to be delivered to the country. This would collapse the economy of the Islamic terror state.

These are all things that could work against Iran: sanctions, engaging Russia and China, globalization techniques, and a refined oil embargo. They are tools that could be instrumental in intercepting the countdown to Armageddon and saving the West from an Iranian-induced apocalypse.

— 2 5 —

THE RED LINE

*"As the Iranians develop longer range, more accurate ballistic missiles,
it's not just Israel or other American allies in the region or American-
deployed forces that are at risk from an Iranian nuclear weapon."*[379]
—JOHN BOLTON, FORMER UN AMBASSADOR

MAHMOUD AHMADINEJAD HAS BEEN ANOINTED BY SUPREME LEADER Khamenei to continue his quest for nuclear arms. With the full backing of the cleric, the president can now proceed full-speed-ahead with nuclear proliferation. There is nothing to stop his march toward an apocalyptic event that would result in the supposed return of the Mahdi; nothing to prevent an attack on the US or Israel that would ignite World War III—and usher in the rule of the antichrist, who the Bible declares will head a worldwide government.

Reports from the IAEA indicate that nearly 3,000 centrifuges used in the production of nuclear fuel are buried underground near Qom, the supposed site of the reappearance of the Mahdi. The means to yield 20 percent—or medium grade—enriched uranium is at the fingertips of Iran's leaders. This is highly significant because the general concensus is that by late spring of 2013, Iran's Revolutionary Guard could have within its reach enough processed uranium to build one atomic bomb. It is at that point that Israel—and indeed the nations of the world—will have reached Prime Minister

Netanyahu's "red line". Then, a determination will have to be made on the proper action to halt Iran's nuclear progress.

This line could be reached based on production at Qom alone. If centrifuges in Natanz are added to the equation, it would be determined even more quickly. The Qom site is completely operational, which indicates that weapons-grade uranium could be produced more readily. The danger with Qom is the fear that it is impervious to an air assault by Israel or the US. Sanctions, while visibly slowing the economy has not halted the forward motion of the production of uranium. Threats and UN Security Council cajoling have not worked either. The IAEA and the UN are helpless and can only scold Iranian officials for not doing more to allay global fears about their nuclear pursuits.

Past declarations regarding their nuclear-related intentions have Iran's officials protesting that the 20 percent enriched uranium is strictly for medical purposes, nothing more. If that were true, the program could be shut down immediately as the country has already stockpiled enough of the type uranium for the foreseeable future. In the past, Iran has sought to ease concerns about its stockpile by converting some of its 20 percent uranium into a metal form that can't easily be turned into weapons-grade material.

In late March of 2011, the world received access to a 28½-minute video reportedly approved by the highest levels of the Iranian government for release to the nations of Islam. It is entitled, *The Coming Is Upon Us*. In it, Iranian clerics describe how the protests and revolutions of the "Arab Awakening" are all part of Islamic end-time prophecies according to the Hadith[380] (the most important set of Islamic writings after the Koran). The video mentions Egypt, Yemen, and other nations as specific examples. The Iranian leadership sees the governmental upheavals and civil war as signs that their ultimate victory is at hand—that the Twelfth Imam, the Mahdi, is at work and his appearance is imminent.

According to the video, it is foretold that in the last days Iran—"the people of the East"—will arise as a great power and begin the final jihad against non-Muslim nations, most notably Israel, the United States, and Western Europe. According to their interpretation, it was foretold that the US would attack Iraq as part of an overall war against Islam, that Iraq would become the center of world conflict, but that afterwards "it will serve as the capital of the world's governance by Imam Mahdi."[381] According to the Christian Broadcasting Network, the video also states:

> Iran's supreme leader, Ayatollah Khameini, and Hassan Nasrallah, leader of Iran's terrorist proxy Hezbollah, are hailed as pivotal end-times players, whose rise was predicted in Islamic scriptures.
>
> The same goes for Iran's President Mahmoud Ahmadinejad, who the video says will conquer Jerusalem prior to the Mahdi's coming.[382]

These men will "pass on the flag of Islam to the last messiah."[383] According to this teaching, the destruction of the Israeli regime and the liberation of Palestine will be the event that summons the return of the Mahdi and the beginning of a worldwide Islamic empire.

The video was released on the website of Reza Kahlil (a pseudonym), who once served as a CIA double agent within the Iranian Revolutionary Guard. According to Kahlil, the film was to be distributed throughout the Middle East with the hope of instigating further uprisings, all in pursuit of the Mahdi's soon return. The texts state:

> "The messiah will not arise unless fear, great earthquakes, and seditions take place,...The splitters will split and progress; the swift winged will attack,...Adultery will become common. Men will dress like women. Men will content themselves to men and woman to woman," and, "A Nation of the East will rise and prepare the way of the Coming of the Mahdi." [The video ends with the words:] "I can tell you with utmost confidence: the promise of Allah for The Coming and the establishment of a new Islamic civilization is on its way. . . . Victory is near. Good tidings to the believers."[384]

In the same sequence, the video quoted the Hadith text: "The worst kinds of humans will become leaders," and showed pictures of George W. Bush, Ariel Sharon, Benjamin Netanyahu, and Barak Obama. The video foretells that the Muslim Brotherhood will come to power and help in the work of the Mahdi, and that the current poor health of Saudi King Abdullah bin Abdul Aziz, an Iranian rival, is also a sign of the last days: "Whoever guarantees the death of King Abdullah of Saudi Arabia, I will guarantee the immediate appearance of the Mahdi." According to Mr. Kahlil:

> They show clearly in the movie that one of the most significant Hadiths that predicts this day calls for the destruction of Israel and the conquest of Jerusalem by Islamic forces as a last sign, which must take place before the Madhi reappears.[385]

We cannot afford to ignore the signs. The world is already in a battle between two books, two faiths, and a diabolically contradictory set of prophecies for what will happen in the coming years. As Benjamin Netanyahu once asserted in an interview:

> "I would be careful to make an analogy between Judeo-Christian traditions and prophecies and the radical Islamic traditions. . . The radical Islamists have a very violent tradition. In other words, it's not something that will happen, but it will happen by destruction *we* effect. . . . That is, we—the radical Muslims—should unsheathe our swords and embark on a great jihad of fire and blood. . . .
>
> [The Judeo-Christian tradition] is basically a benign conception of rebirth and redemption, as opposed to a very warlike cult of blood that seeks to destroy. It's construction versus destruction. It's peace versus war. It's beating your swords into plowshares as opposed to beating your plowshares into swords. And it's a very, very different conception."[386]

As we face the future, we must realize that Iran's vision of itself as the nation that must defeat Israel in order to facilitate the return of the Twelfth Imam is not simply some mad notion that will go away on its own; Iran has been arming itself for just such a clash of civilizations. It believes it is called by Allah to deliver the world from the Infidels, the Zionist regime, and their champions in the West. The proxies in Lebanon, Syria, and Gaza have primed for this coming war for years. With such antagonistic rhetoric flowing, it won't be long until Iran and Hezbollah take things into their own hands in order to be the instigators of the return of the Mahdi they have proclaimed.

If Iran is not stopped, what plays out will look exactly like Ezekiel 38:10-12, 14 (NKJV):

> "On that day it shall come to pass *that* thoughts will arise in your mind, and you will make an evil plan: "You will say, 'I will go up against a land of unwalled villages; I will go to a peaceful people, who dwell safely, all of them dwelling without walls, and having neither bars nor gates'— "to take plunder and to take booty, to stretch out your hand against the waste places *that are again* inhabited, and against a people gathered from the nations, who have acquired livestock and goods, who dwell in the midst of the land.
>
> Therefore, son of man, prophesy and say to Gog, 'Thus says the Lord GOD: "On that day when My people Israel dwell safely, will you not know *it?*

There are some telling conditions in the details of this prophecy that give us insight into how it will come about and just how close it might be. The first is that this will come in a time of relative peace and security for Israel, something the Jews haven't really known since the United Nations voted to partition Palestine into Jewish and Palestinian states in 1947. This is what has made some suggest that this attack will happen in the initial years of the Tribulation, soon after the peace accord engineered by the Antichrist, and that it is impossible any time before that. However, the initial years of the Tribulation don't appear to be any more secure than what Israel is experiencing now. Revelation tells us those years will be filled with natural disasters, wars, plagues, and famines that will kill a quarter of the world's population.[387]

There is no indication in Ezekiel's writings that this rest and security is something Israel experiences for a long period of time, though it must be long enough that Gog's coalition will see it as a window of opportunity in which to attack. A temporary settlement with the Palestinians could produce such a window, and one is perennially in the works. It could be forced on Israel at any moment as the ever-present, land-for-peace plan promoting Quartet (Russia, The U.N., The E.U., and the United States) that could unilaterally recognize Palestine as a state, with East Jerusalem as its capital. If the United States votes in favor of this move, it will pass. It will be interesting to see how this plays out in the months immediately ahead.

While Islamist animosity may seem enough to spur this attack, there is another reason for this invasion: Although the news has flown mostly under the radar, there are a handful of companies exploring for oil and natural gas in Israel and off its shorelines. Givot Olam Oil, which has been looking for oil in Israel since 1992, announced in August 2010 that it had discovered an estimated 1.525 billion barrels of oil accessible at its Rosh Ha'Ayin site, which is about ten miles inland from the coastline of Tel Aviv.[388] In November 2011, estimates were that the field was worth between $200 million and $900 million[389]—at that time oil was only about $80 a barrel, more than 25 percent less than it is as I write. Of course, these are just the initial estimates at one site, and they are reservedly optimistic at best. Givot Olam is also drilling at other sites in this general vicinity, searching for other deposits.

A May 2010 US Geological Survey report estimated there could be 1.7 billion barrels of recoverable oil and 122 trillion cubic feet of natural gas off the shoreline of the Levant Basin, most of which is within Israel's jurisdiction. The Levant Basin includes the Mediterranean trough off the coast of Israel, Lebanon, and Syria that goes almost all the way to the island of Cyprus. It also includes most of the Israeli mainland, the West Bank, western

Lebanon, and the Syria coastal regions. John Brown of Zion Oil and Gas, which has exploration rights to a good deal of that area, estimates there is $917 billion worth of oil and gas (again at 2010 prices) in the region controlled by Israel.[390]

Houston-based Noble Energy—working with several Israeli partner companies—recently confirmed the finding of what has been dubbed the "Leviathan" natural gas field off the coast of Israel. Experts speculate that the Leviathan has at least sixteen trillion cubic feet of natural gas,[391] worth around $45 billion.[392] It is one of the largest discoveries in the last decade and could supply *all* of Israel's energy needs for the next century. As Noble and its partners start to extract that gas, Israel will go from a country dependent on the foreign import of coal and natural gas to being a player in *exporting* natural gas to the Mediterranean region—a remarkable turn-around for a nation surrounded by oil and natural gas-rich neighbors who are ill-disposed to trade fairly with Israel.

The Israeli stock market surged to an all-time high in the spring of 2011, up 130 percent since November of 2008, despite continued tensions in the region. If these discoveries pan out, Israel will certainly be supplied with enough (as the prophet Ezekiel said) *"silver and gold . . . cattle and goods"* to make its neighbors envious!

Thus, the future is full of possibilities. As Israel begins to reap the benefits of these finds, its electrical plants will switch from burning coal to burning natural gas—a conversion that U.S. utility companies have found to be fairly straightforward—and end its dependence on foreign coal. And where does Israel get most of its coal? Seventy-one percent of Israel's coal comes from Russia.[393]

As the green revolution continues with the introduction of electric and natural gas vehicles, Israel could easily meet all of its own energy needs in the years just ahead. At the same time, it would likely begin to reap significant revenues from exporting these coveted resources. These exports would mean one of two things: 1) Israel could dramatically undercut the prices for these precious commodities to the chagrin of the other oil-rich states, or 2) Israel will see huge profits as prices continue to rise. Would Israel have enough of these resources to do this? Possibly. These are only estimates at this time, but considering that the concern for Libyan oil, which is only about 2 percent of the world's supply, sent prices over $100 a barrel as civil war began there, Israel's supplies could easily affect the world market. Similarly, even Israel's energy self-sufficiency would be enough to rock the boat. And with new discoveries in this vast region yet to be brought online, it won't be long before China and Europe start knocking on Israel's door, hungry to be better friends. Looking ahead to its future energy needs, China has left no stone unturned in negotiating deals for energy resources worldwide.

As for Russia, suddenly having an important consumer of its coal disappear and then finding it has to compete with that same tiny nation in selling "cleaner" natural gas resources to other nations will certainly sour that relationship even further. "*Magog*" will gain no new love for Israel. The time might finally come for Russia to deal with this nation that has been a thorn in its flesh.

As the world watches Iran's race to achieve nuclear arms status, the United States seems intent on losing the moral battle—a battle which began with three terrorist attacks during the 1960s, the assassinations of three men: John F. Kennedy, Robert Kennedy, and Martin Luther King. The murders of these three men were as devastating to that generation as was the attack on Pearl Harbor on December 7, 1941, or the attack on the World Trade Center Towers and the Pentagon on September 11, 2001.

Just as the bombing of Pearl Harbor plunged the US into a global fight for freedom so the murders of those three men signaled the end of the age of innocence that had been enjoyed by the American people. Almost overnight, we went from I Love Lucy, Leave it to Beaver, and Father Knows Best to the proclamation that God was dead and the advent of Woodstock. Social revolution in the arts that initially seemed harmless—the Beatles, Mick Jagger and his Rolling Stones, the LSD craze—soon became a full frontal assault against traditional family values and an American culture steeped in the tenets of the Bible.

The Bible says, "And you will know the truth, and the truth will set you free."[394] Rather than create freedom, the social revolution of the 60s enslaved. People became addicted to drugs, sex, pornography, and strange philosophical/"spiritual" beliefs. Values based on Judeo-Christian mores were left behind as people turned to Eastern religions and New Age practices for answers to life's biggest questions. Satanism saw a rise in practitioners, and we were subjected to the likes of Charles Manson and his demonic cult with a morbid fascination. Appetites dictated action, and nothing was sacred any longer. That is never truer than the days in which we live. As Timothy wrote in his second book, chapter 3, verse 3:

> But evil men and impostors will grow worse and worse, deceiving and being deceived.

— 26 —

THE ULTIMATE
SOLUTION

*"Now, today, this moment, is our chance to choose the
right side. God is holding back to give us that chance. It
will not last forever. We must take it or leave it."*[395]
—C. S. LEWIS

MOST CAN REMEMBER THE CLASSIC PAINTING OF JESUS standing outside a door waiting
to be allowed entry. That poignant portrayal of Christ on the outside, wanting to fellowship with His creation is never more powerful than it is today.
Prayer has been excised from schools; suits have been filed to force Congress
to remove "under God" from the *Pledge of Allegiance*; displays of the Ten
Commandments have been removed from public buildings; the motto "in
God we trust" is in danger of extinction. Teachers have been forbidden even
to carry a personal Bible in the view of students; Christian literature has been
removed from library shelves; religious Christmas carols have been banned
from school programs, and "spring break" has replaced Easter vacation.

When the worst tragedy in a US school took place at Sandy Hook,
Connecticut in December 2012, former Arkansas governor and presidential
candidate Mike Huckabee came under vitriolic attack for his comment:

"We don't have a crime problem, a gun problem or even a violence problem. What we have is a sin problem," Hucka-bee said on Fox News. "And since we've ordered God out of our schools, and communities, the military and public con-versations, you know we really shouldn't act so surprised ... when all hell breaks loose."[396]

In view of his statement, we can but ask ourselves: Are we better off today than we were in 1963 when, following a suit filed by Madelyn Murray O'Hare, the US Supreme Court in an eight-to-one decision voted to ban "coercive" prayer and Bible-reading from public schools in America? Are our schools safer? Are fewer kids on drugs? Are fewer kids engaged in promiscu-ous sex? Are fewer crimes committed by school-age children?

Battle after battle has slowly stripped Christians in the US of their rights. US courts that espouse such movements as gay rights, abortion rights, and even animal rights are now pursuing the right to be godless. I wrote in *The American Prophecies*:

> We have rejected the foundation of our culture that has traditionally held us together—God and the Holy Scrip-tures—and as our culture drifts away from that center, we . . . no longer hear His voice. As a nation, our innocence is being drowned. Things are falling apart. In our halls of justice, in our pulpits, and in the political arenas, those who would speak for God not only lack the conviction to be effective, they are being systematically silenced because of a perverted interpretation of "separation of church and state." First Amendment rights are denied to those who would speak for God, while those who fight for self, special inter-est, and immorality are passionately intense . . . as the "spirit of the world" takes over. . . . We have witnessed this spirit being more active in our world than ever before through the

"isms" of fascism, Nazism, communism, and terrorism—the greatest threats to human liberty we have ever faced.[397]

In the twenty-first century, the courts of our land protect perversion while chastising the Church. The writers of the Constitution would likely be amazed at the interpretation of the document over which they shed blood, sweat, and tears, and appalled at the lack of moral clarity in America today. The men who approved the purchase of Bibles with Congressional funds, the men who regularly called for national days of prayer and fasting, the men who appointed Senate chaplains, would mourn the path down which succeeding Congresses and Supreme Courts have taken this once-proud nation.

The social revolution of the '60s echoed Nietzsche's declaration, "God is dead." John Lennon proclaimed that the Beatles were more popular than Jesus. *Time* magazine reporter John T. Elson wrote: "There is an acute feeling that the churches on Sunday are preaching about the existence of a God who is nowhere visible in their daily lives,"[398] and questioned the dedication of professing Christians. According to Elson's article, God had been replaced by science, and the Church had become "secularized."

With the lack of moral clarity in the secularized Church, is there any wonder that the malaise has spread to the governing bodies of this nation? The bedrock foundation of the faith of our fathers has been replaced with shifting sands. The sacrifices of those who have gone before, from the War of Independence that birthed this nation to the War on Terror birthed on 9/11, have been diminished. The blood of dead soldiers, patriots from the past, cries to us from battlefields around the world. These men and women sacrificed all to insure freedom for all. Perhaps Dr. James Dobson summed it up most succinctly when he admonished: "We're at a pivotal point in the history of this country. Be a participant. Don't sit on the sidelines while our basic freedoms are lost."[399]

Internet pornography is a $57 billion industry worldwide, $12 billion in the US alone. According to *Internet Filter Review*, "US porn revenue exceeds the combined revenues of ABC, NBC, and CBS."[400] The report also indicates that the average age of a child exposed to pornography on the Internet is eleven, and a staggering ninety percent of eight to sixteen year olds have viewed pornography online.

Another favorite pastime of the morally decadent is to try to bring God down to their level. Taking the constitutional edict that "all men are created equal," they have applied it to religion and have declared that all religions are the same. "We are all going to the same place," they say. "We're just taking different roads to get there." Sin has been banished from our vocabulary; the cross of Christ has been reduced to costume jewelry (the gaudier the better); the blood of Christ has been counted as worthless. Religions that once elicited horror, Satanists and witches, are accorded equality with Judaism and Christianity, and are, in fact, featured in the Religion sections of your newspaper. And, who would have thought that Anton LeVey's Satanic Bible would have become a collector's item, with copies sometimes selling for as much as $1,000 each.

It has been said that human beings have a God-shaped hole in their hearts, a place that can only be filled with a relationship with their Creator. It is a spiritual law written on a tablet of flesh. Those who try to fill that void with everything imaginable—drugs, sex, pornography, alcohol, perversion, pagan religions—are only lying to themselves.

There is neither time nor space to fully discuss the divorce plague, fatherless families, the feminine mystique of Gloria Steinem, child abuse, and etc. All, however, have contributed to secular America's slide into depravity and debauchery. And, the starkest reality of all is that the secularized Church has often concurred. Isaiah 5:20 (NKJV) says:

> "Woe to those who call evil good and good evil, who put darkness for light and light for darkness, who put bitter for sweet and sweet for bitter."

We have clearly reached the point that the Apostle Paul expressed in his first letter to Timothy:

> "The Spirit clearly says that in later times some will abandon the faith and follow deceiving spirits and things taught

by demons. Such teachings come through hypocritical liars, whose consciences have been seared as with a hot iron."[401]

No? When did you last weep for an abuse victim; mourn the senseless death of an innocent and defenseless child; reach out to a battered wife; donate to a clinic that offers an alternative to abortion?

The genie of evil has been let out of the bottle. America has sown the wind, and is reaping the whirlwind. Babies die daily, sacrificed on the altar of self-interest. Abortion has become a valid means of birth control for many women. Have a one-night stand; get pregnant; no problem! Take a morning-after pill, or run down to the abortion clinic on the corner. After all, it's only "tissue," not a real baby. It's a fetus, not a child "fearfully and wonderfully made." Is there any wonder that Dr. Billy Graham said that if America failed to repent of her evil, God would have to apologize to Sodom and Gomorrah?

On September 11, 2001, America met evil head-on when nineteen Islamic fanatics commandeered four American airliners, piloted two into the World Trade Towers and a third into the Pentagon. The fourth airliner, likely headed for a target in Washington, DC, was retaken by passengers, and crashed into a field in Pennsylvania. It was our first taste of the hatred of *jihad* as preached by radical Islamic clerics.

Immediately following the attack, the politically correct were hard at work to avoid calling a terrorist a terrorist. Some objected to the use of the word "Islamic" or "Muslim" in describing these mass murders. While the American public was traumatized and paralyzed by the horrific events, members of the American press were locked in a debate over how not to offend a particular segment of society. A memo from the Reuter's news agency written by Stephen Jukes, admonished his group not to use the word "terrorist." He wrote: "one man's terrorist is another man's freedom fighter."[402] Never mind that Osama bin Laden had issued an edict calling on every *Muslim* to kill Americans.

Before the dust had settled over New York City and the fires were extinguished at the Pentagon, these spin doctors were outlining their campaign to thwart any attempt to hunt down those responsible for the carnage. What

followed in the weeks after 9/11 was a succession of anti-war demonstrations reminiscent of the Vietnam-era, a series of peace vigils, and other protests. America was declared guilty of aggression, having somehow deserved
the attacks due to some perceived ill against Islam and/or its adherents.
Those not blaming the US found another scapegoat in Israel. Why was it so
hard to place the blame precisely where it belonged, on a group of radical
Islamofascists spouting a hate-filled ideology and killing innocent people?

Lesbian writer, Susan Sontag wrote in defense of those who called the
hijackers "cowards":

> And if the word "cowardly" is to be used, it might be
> more aptly applied to those who kill from beyond the range
> of retaliation, high in the sky, than to those willing to die
> themselves in order to kill others. In the matter of courage
> (a morally neutral virtue): whatever may be said of the per-
> petrators of Tuesday's slaughter, they were not cowards.[403]

Not cowards? Nineteen men sauntered aboard four airlines loaded with
passengers—men, women and children—took control of those giants of
the air, murdered not only the passengers but thousands of other innocent
bystanders without ever looking them or their families in the eyes; and that
is not a cowardly act?

Yet another writer took Americans to task for the upsurge in patriotism
and the number of American flags that were raised in the days immediately
following the terrorist attack. The flag was purported to be a visual symbol
of bigotry, criminality, hatred, and even homophobia in America.

The novelist Barbara Kingsolver jumped into the mêlée with this liberal,
enlightened pronouncement:

> Patriotism threatens free speech with death. It is infuri-
> ated by thoughtful hesitation, constructive criticism of our
> leaders and pleas for peace. It despises people of foreign
> birth. It has specifically blamed homosexuals, feminists,
> and the American Civil Liberties Union. In other words, the

American flag stands for intimidation, censorship, violence, bigotry, sexism, homophobia, and shoving the Constitution through a paper shredder. Whom are we calling terrorists here?[404]

There has long been a fascination in the Islamic world with all things Hitler. In fact, the Arab states of Syria and Iraq, both Ba'ath Party regimes, were patterned after the Nazi leader's fascist concepts. Just as Hitler's vision was a world under the domination of his Nazi regime, so the vision of today's radical Islamic clerics is a world under the domination of Islamic, or Sharia, Law.

This was never more apparent than when the Ayatollah Ruhollah Khomeini launched his Islamic revolution even as the Shah of Iran was fleeing the country. It was Khomeini who dubbed the US "The Great Satan," and tagged our closest ally, Israel, "The Little Satan." Truthfully, these are the only two nations with the ability and the hope of the moral clarity needed to quench the flame of Islamic revolution before it ignites across the globe.

The liberal Left in the US took up the banner of the oppressed and downtrodden in Iran and ran with it. What followed was a litany of charges leveled against the US for her support of the Shah's regime, for supporting Israel locked in a life and death struggle with the Palestinians, for bombing Hiroshima and Nagasaki at the end of World War II, for Vietnam, etc. Palestinian terrorists became "freedom fighters" and the innocent victims of their atrocious acts became the instigators simply for daring to live in Israel. Suicide bombers who brought devastation to buses, restaurants, busy shopping malls, and even schools were given the religious designation of "martyrs."

Radical Islam has given birth to a weapon that truly cheapens human life: the suicide bomber. But this will be as nothing compared to the weapons of mass destruction under preparation in radical Islamist states; weapons whose targets may begin with Israel, but ultimately will be aimed at the world's greatest democracy.

The secular, liberal Left refuses to accept the very serious threat posed by the Islamic radicals. They refuse to accept the fact that every American, place of origin not withstanding; every Jew wherever found; every Muslim who disagrees with the particular philosophy of the Islamic fanatics is a target. University professors will not be spared simply because they have supported the radical any more than the Leftists siding with Khomeini were in deposing the Shah; erudite philosophers will not be spared because of their education; the religious Left will not be spared simply because of their worldview on religion. While their support is now welcomed and heralded globally by terrorist organizations, once the terrorists reach their goals, they will turn their guns on these as infidels just as they did following the Islamic Revolution of 1979. No, all will be required to conform to the doctrines and dictates of the mad mullahs that have hijacked an entire religion—or else.

Leftist groups that had once focused on social justice have turned their focus almost entirely on Palestine. The various wars that have occurred in the Middle East are over what is perceived to be skirmishes on the periphery of the current war on terror, and therefore completely separate from the *jihad* declared on the United States. It is easier, then, to view the terrorists as despairing victims and not the murderers and hate-mongers they are.

The Middle East conflict is not about land, nor about the establishment of a state for the Palestinian people. This has been offered and rejected various times—in 1939, in Oslo, at Camp David, and in Washington, DC. The conflict is about the destruction of the State of Israel and the annihilation of the Jewish people. The Palestinian Authority doesn't want Jerusalem divided, but rather it wants all of Jerusalem. They do not simply desire to occupy the West Bank, but *all* of Israel from the Jordan River to the Mediterranean Sea. It is not a matter of "land for peace;" it is a matter of using any means possible to rid the Middle East of the Jewish population altogether. They do not wish the subjugation of the Jewish people, they wish their destruction. This was Egyptian leader Gamal Abdel Nasser's agenda. It was Yasser Arafat's agenda. It is the agenda of Bashar al-Assad of Syria and Mahmoud Ahmadinejad of Iran.

Perhaps the late Yasser Arafat condensed the Arab-Israeli conflict into the most succinct statement of all when he said, "We shall oppose the establishment of this state to the last member of the Palestinian people, for if ever such a state is established it will spell the end of the whole Palestinian cause [the obliteration of Israel]."[405]

Attacks against the US spiritual and moral foundation have been cease-less during the past decades. Why has a largely Christian nation allowed the marketplace and the political arena to be stripped of everything godly? Why has abortion flourished? Why has God been taken out of schools while the distribution of condoms is allowed? Everything anti-Christian promoted, and Christians ridiculed? The desire to fit in has reduced the average Christian to a spineless jellyfish, afraid to speak up for fear of derision.

The Church, once a stronghold of everything good and right, has often become just another club where people gather to socialize. It, too, has fallen prey to the corruption of the secular, and has become a watered-down ver-sion of its former self, palatable to all, and effective for none.

Even so, the Church remains America's last hope in a hopeless world. And who, in this truth-challenged, politically-correct world will dare stand up and deliver the unadulterated truth according to God's Word? As I ask this question, I'm reminded again of the scripture in Romans 1:25 (kjv) that speaks of those "who change the truth of God into a lie."

The good news is that there is still a remnant. Not all Christians have bought into the secular, liberal Leftist agenda. It is because of these men and women, unnamed giants of the faith, prayer warriors all, that there is still hope. It is because they firmly hold to the truth in 2 Chronicles 7:14 (NKJV): "If my people, which are called by my name, shall humble themselves, and pray, and seek my face, and turn from their wicked ways; then will I hear from heaven, and will forgive their sin, and will heal their land."

The US doesn't have to reap the whirlwind; we do not have to get what we deserve; God has graciously made a way of escape. The answer is in humility: "Humble yourselves, therefore, under God's mighty hand, that he may lift you up in due time."[406] We, like the Apostle Peter after his denial of Christ, must become broken before the Lord in order to find forgiveness and restoration. Integrity must triumph over deception; the desire to do what is right must overcome the desire to conform to the mores of this world.

The Church must undergo the scrutiny of the Light. No longer can it tolerate the incursion of darkness; evil must be acknowledged and defined as such. The Church still has a choice. The words of Joshua ring in my spirit: "But if serving the Lord seems undesirable to you, then choose for yourselves this day whom you will serve. . . . But as for me and my household, we will serve the Lord."[407]

The choice is yours. As the prophet Elijah cried out to the people of Israel in I Kings 18:21 (NIV), "How long will you waver between two opinions? If the Lord is God, follow him..." It is time for the people of God to take up the banner of Jehovah Nissi—God our victory; God who fights our battles. The fields are white for harvest and in need of laborers. We are the generation of the final stand! Will we be content to hide within the walls of our churches and simply survive the coming events, or will we take the fight to the gates of Hell as Jesus said we could in Matthew 16:18? Will we raise the banner and challenge our Enemy, or will we cower in fear and failure?

I pray you can feel the urgency with which I write. Change is in the air in so many ways and whether that will be change for the better or for the worse is in our hands. The future of freedom in the Middle East and who wins between the Shia Twelvers of Iran and the democracies of the United States and Israel will not be put off for another decade. We must stand for what is right, pray for the peace of Jerusalem, bless and be a blessing to Israel, and then put into action the things God has placed in our hearts to do.

When the Master returns, will He find us faithful and wise, or will He catch us living the life of indulgence? Will we continue on the selfish, self-centered path that is lulling America to sleep as liberalism and debt swallow the liberties for which our forefathers fought? I pray not! I believe the prophets of God are sounding the alarm and His people are awakening. If only a remnant, we still must arise to shake off our flesh, fill our lamps with an abundance of oil, and stride forward to do God's will.

APPENDIX A

Additional Centrifuge Installation

Iran increased its enrichment capacity by installing additional centrifuges at its declared sites between August and November 2012. The hardened Fordow facility is now at maximum capacity (2,784 centrifuges). Of the 2,784, 696 centrifuges are currently enriching at Fordow and 696 are ready to begin enriching immediately. The IAEA also noted the addition of first-generation and advanced centrifuges, the latter undergoing testing, at the Natanz facility.

Increasing Enriched Uranium Stockpiles

Iran continues to produce low- (<5%) and medium-enriched (near 20%) uranium at historically high rates. It has now allocated roughly 40% of its medium-enriched uranium for conversion to reactor fuel plates; only a small fraction of the allocated material, however, has been packaged into fuel plates and placed into a reactor core as of August 2012.

Parchin Facility Inspection

Iran continues to deny the IAEA access to the Parchin facility, where the agency believes Iran conducted experiments related to nuclear weapons development. The IAEA noted that, even if it is given access to the site, its ability to "conduct effective verification will have been seriously undermined" by physical disruption and sanitization undertaken by Iran at the facility in 2012.

Weaponization

Iran continues to stonewall the IAEA regarding its weaponization activities. The agency reiterated its assessment of Iran's work on nuclear weapons development: "the information indicates that, prior to the end of 2003 the activities took place under a structured program; that some continued after 2003; and that some may still be ongoing."

Arak Reactor Timeline

Iran told the IAEA that it will begin operating the Arak heavy water reactor later than previously planned. The reactor, now scheduled for an early 2014 launch, will provide Iran with a separate pathway to acquiring fissile material for nuclear weapons in the form of weapons-grade plutonium.

Key Points

IRAN'S ENRICHMENT CAPABILITIES ARE NO LONGER THE PRIMARY BOTTLENECK IN A NUCLEAR BREAKOUT SCENARIO.

Iran can produce one bomb's worth of fissile material faster than it likely can deploy a functioning nuclear device. Tracking Iran's uranium enrichment activities now addresses only Iran's intentions and the size of its projected arsenal.

Obtaining fissile material in the form of weapons-grade uranium or plutonium is the most technically demanding step in acquiring a nuclear weapons capability. Designing an explosive device (consisting of non-nuclear components) and a delivery system for the device are comparatively less technically challenging. Those efforts can also proceed parallel to enrichment.

Iran has the infrastructure and material to produce weapons-grade uranium. It has enough enriched uranium to produce fuel for six nuclear weapons after conversion to weapons-grade levels. Its expanding enrichment activities have significantly reduced the time required for it to produce weapons-grade uranium. The key accelerants for this shrinking timeline have been its growing stockpiles of low- and medium-enriched uranium, which is 90% of the way to weapons-grade uranium, and an increasing number of centrifuges enriching.

Nuclear Program Expansion

Iran will likely have enough near-20% enriched uranium to rapidly produce fissile material for 2 nuclear weapons by late 2013 or early 2014.

Iran has installed many more centrifuges at the hardened Fordow facility than are now actually spinning, providing a reserve and/or surge capacity that will be difficult for Israel to destroy.

The installation of 2,088 additional centrifuges at Fordow since summer 2012 gives Iran the ability to:

- ✧ produce near-weapons grade uranium (20% enrichment level) in larger quantities faster, providing rapidly-convertible feedstock for a small arsenal of nuclear weapons;

- ✧ convert near-weapons grade uranium into nuclear weapons fuel in a shorter amount of time.

Iran's uranium enrichment is at historically high rates despite increasing sanctions and damage to the Iranian economy.

Iran told the International Atomic Energy Agency (IAEA) that it plans to begin operating the Arak heavy water reactor in early 2014 (it had previously planned commencement for mid-to-late 2013). This reactor will be capable of producing two warheads' worth of weapons-grade plutonium per year once operational.

Breakout Timelines

Time needed to produce fuel for 1 nuclear weapon:

- ✧ Iran needs 3.6 months to produce 25 kg of weapons-grade uranium and 1.9 months to produce weapons-grade uranium at the buried Fordow and pilot Natanz enrichment facilities.* It can cut these times significantly using the centrifuges installed but not yet operating at the Fordow facility.

✧ Iran needs 4-10.5 weeks to produce 25 kg of weapons-grade uranium and 1.5-5 weeks to produce 15 kg of weapons-grade uranium at the main Natanz enrichment facility.* The higher end of the range accounts for a three-step conversion process.

✧ Estimates of the time Iran needs to build a nuclear device to use this fissile material are generally longer than the timelines above.

✧ The existence of undeclared (covert) enrichment sites would have a significant impact on breakout estimates.

✧ Evidence of significant Iranian enrichment beyond 20% will strongly suggest not only that the decision to weaponize has been made, but also that the Iranians believe they have (or will shortly have) a viable warhead.[408]

ENDNOTES

1   Croesus, after being reprieved by Cyrus. (Herodotuemblys -The Histories, Bk 1, 87)
    http://members.ozemail.com.au/~ancientpersia/quotes.html, accessed July 2009.

2   The Circle of Ancient Iranian Studies; Cyrus, the Great, Father and Liberator; http://www.cais-soas.
    com/CAIS/History/hakhamaneshian/Cyrus-the-great/cyrus_the_great.htm, accessed June 2009.

3   Ezra 1:2-3 niv

4   Isaiah 44:28 niv

5   Cyrus Sorat, "Cyrus the Great," http://cyrusthegreat.net// ; accessed October 2012.

6   From Ancient Persia to Contemporary Iran—History of Iran Timeline; Ladjevard-
    ian, Reza, 2005; http://www.mage.com/TLgody.html, accessed June 2009.

7   Herodotus, Inscription, New York City Post Office, adapted from Herodotus
    Greek historian & traveler (484 BC - 430 BC), http://www.quotation-
    spage.com/quote/24166.html; accessed October 2011.

8   "Persia's Dark Power," Prophecy in the News, December 1, 2011, Gary Stearman, http://
    www.prophecyinthenews.com/persias-dark-power/; accessed October 2012.

9   Jeremiah 49:35-37, NIV

10 Ezra 1:1-2, NIV

11 Ezra 1:2-3, NIV

12 Daniel 5:2-6, NIV

13 Daniel 5:12, NIV

14 Daniel 5:23.28, NIV

15 "Historical Evidence for Belshazzar and Darius the Mede," http://www.biblehis-
    tory.net/newsletter/belshazzar_darius_mede.htm; accessed October 2012.

16 Daniel 9:4-19.

17 Daniel 10:10-13.

18 Daniel 11:32, nkjv.

19 Ezekiel 38:8, 11-12.

20 Sun Myung Moon (born January 6, 1920) is the Korean founder and leader of the worldwide Unifica-
    tion Church. Moon has said that he is the Messiah and the Second Coming of Christ and is fulfilling
    Jesus' unfinished mission. http://en.wikipedia.org/wiki/Sun_Myung_Moon; accessed July 2009.

21 Islam 101; http://www.islam101.com/dawah/pillars.html, accessed June 2009.

22 From Ancient Persia to Contemporary Iran—History of Iran Time-
    line; http://www.mage.com/TLgody.html, accessed June 2009.

23 Historical Setting, Pars Times, http://www.parstimes.com/history/his-
    toricalsetting.html#Rezashah, accessed June 2009.

24 Justice William O. Douglass, http://quotes.liberty-tree.ca/quote_blog/
    William.O..Douglas.Quote.8B96, accessed October 2012.

25 Manucher Farmanfarmaian and Roxane Farmanfarmaian, Blood & Oil: A Prince's Mem-
    oir of Iran, From the Shah to the Ayatollah (New York: Random House, 2005), p. 292.

26   Asadollah Alam, *The Shah and I: The Confidential Diary of Iran's Royal Court 1969-1977* (New York: St. Martin's Press, 1993), p. 540.

27   "Amir Taheri's Interview with Ardeshir Zahedi," cited in *Untold Secrets* by Ardeshir Zahedi, a compilation of original materials. Compiled by: Pari Abasalti, Editor in Chief, and Houshang Mirhashem, Publisher of Rah-e-Zendegi Journal, February 2002, p. 15.

28   Manucher Farmanfarmaian and Roxane Farmanfarmaian, p. 266.

29   Dwight D. Eisenhower, *Mandate for Change, 1953-1956: The White House Years* (Garden City, NY: Doubleday, 1963), p. 165.

30   "Heroes and Killers in the 20th Century," Mohammad Mossadegh, Hero File, http://www.moreorless.au.com/heroes/mossadegh.html; accessed May 2008.

31   White House Transcript, "Remarks at Millennial Evening: the Perils of Indifference," April 12, 1999; http://www.historyplace.com/speeches/wiesel-transcript.htm, accessed July 2008.

32   Amir Tahiri, "Iran and the US: Who Should Apologize and Why?" (Cited in *Untold Secrets* by Ardeshir Zahedi; a compilation of original materials. Compiled by: Pari Abasalti, Editor in Chief, and Houshang Mirhashem, Publisher of Rah-e-Zendegi Journal, February 2002, p. 43.)

33   Personal Interview with Dr. Parviz Mina, Paris, France, April 18, 2008.

34   Houchang Nahavandi, *The Last Shah of Iran*, translated from the French by Steve Reed (France: Editions Osmonde, 2004), p. 97.

35   Barbara Walters, *Audition* (New York: Alfred A. Knopf, 2008), p. 201.

36   Houchang Nahavandi, p. 30.

37   Neil Farquhar, "Persepolis Journal; Shah's Tent City, Fit for Kings, May Lodge Tourists," *The New York Times,* September 7, 2001; http://query.nytimes.com/gst/fullpage.html?res=9C06E6DB1039F934A3575AC0A9679C8B63, accessed July 2008.

38   US Subcommittee Hearings 1973:507.

39   Henry Kissinger, *White House Years* (Boston: Little, Brown, 1979), p. 1261.

40   David Harris, *The Crisis* (New York: Little, Brown and Company, 2004), p. 47.

41   Clair Apodaca, *US Human Rights Policy and Foreign Assistance: a Short History*; Ritsumeikan International Affairs, Vol. 3, p. 64. (The paper was presented at the "Global Governance" project at a seminar held by the Institute of International Relations and Area Studies, Ritsumeikan University, March 8, 2004.)

42   Ryszard Kapuscinski, *Shah of shahs* (New York: Vintage Books, a division of Random House, 1985), p. 137.

43   Barbara Walters describes Ambassador Zahedi: "The ambassador was an imposing figure, tall and dark with a great head of hair, a prominent nose, a ready smile, and a glad hand for everyone. He was also smart, shrewd, and the Shah's most trusted adviser in the United States." She described the Iranian Embassy as "the Number one Embassy when it came to extravagance and just plain enjoyment...large parties with hundreds of guests, flowing champagne, mounds of fresh Iranian caviar, and a bulging buffet..." Barbara Walters, *Audition* (New York: Alfred A. Knopf, 2008) pp.248-249.

44   Personal Interview with Ardeshir Zahedi, June 2008.

45   Ardeshir Zahedi interview, June 2008.

46   Asadollah Alam, p. 500.

47   National Security Archive, Memo from Henry Kissinger, July 25, 1972; http://www.gwu.edu/~nsarchiv/NSAEBB/NSAEBB21/03-01.htm; accessed April 2008.

48   Mike Evans, *Israel: America's Key to Survival* (Plainfield, NJ: Logos International), p. ix.

49   Cited by Slater Bakhtavar, "Jimmy Carter's Human rights Disaster in Iran," *American Thinker.com,* August 26, 2007; http://www.americanthinker.com/2007/08/jimmy_carters_human_rights_dis.html, accessed June 2008.

50   Marvin Zonis, *Majestic Failure: The Fall of the Shah of Iran* (Chicago: University of Chicago Press, 1991), p. 60.

51   *New York Times*, April 20, 1979, p. 12.

52   Cited by Dariush Zahedi in *The Iranian Revolution Then and Now* (Boulder, CO: Westview Press, 2000), p. 155.

53   Asadollah Alam, p. 500.

54   Ibid, p. 484

55   Dariush Zahedi, pp. 39-40

56   Dr. Parviz Mina interview, April 19, 2008, Paris France.

57   Comptroller General of the United States. "Iranian Oil Cutoff: Reduced Petroleum Supplies and Inadequate US Government Response." Report to Congress, General Accounting Office, 1979.

58   US Senate Department briefing paper, May 15, 1977, Declassified. Document found in Archived in Chadwyck-Healy Volume, *Iran: The Making of US Foreign Policy 1977-190*, Alexandria VA 1990.

59   Asadollah Alam, The Shah and I: the Confidential Diary of Iran's Royal Court, 1968-1977 (London: I.B.Tauris, 2008), p.542.

60   CIA Report: Iran in the 1980s, pp. 1-3, Declassified. Archived in Chadwyck-Healy Volume, *Iran: The Making of US Foreign Policy 1977-190*, Alexandria VA 1990.

61   Annabelle Sreberny-Mohammadi and Ali Mohammadi, *Small Media, Big Revolution: Communication, Culture and the Iranian* (Minneapolis: University of Minnesota Press, 1994), p. 139.

62   Confidential Document, US Embassy to Secretary of State, "Opposition Views." January 1978. Declassified.

63   Iran: Chronology of Revolution, 1978; http://ivl.8m.com/Chronology2.htm; accessed July 2008.

64   Eric Rouleau, *Le Monde*, "Khomeini's Iran," Fall 1980, http://www.foreignaffairs. org/19800901faessay8148/eric-rouleau/khomeini-s-iran.html; accessed February 2008.

65   US State Department telegram Sullivan to Vance, April 25, 1978, Declassified. Archived in Chadwyck-Healey, *Iran: The Making of US Policy 1977-1980*, Alexandria VA 1990.

66   US State Department Telegram Christopher to Sullivan, April 26, 1978, Declassified. Archived in Chadwyck-Healey, *Iran: The Making of US Policy 1977-1980*, Alexandria VA 1990.

67   Confidential Telegram, US Embassy Tehran to Secretary of State, "Opposition lawyers capture Bar Association and plan closer scrutiny of political court cases," June 19, 1978. Declassified.

68   Personal interview with Her Majesty Farah Pahlavi, March 28, 2008.

69   William H. Sullivan, Dateline Iran: the Road not Taken; *Foreign Policy* No. 40, pp. 175-186.

70   Zbigniew Brzezinski, *Power and Principle* (New York: Farrar, Straus, Giroux, 1983), p. 252.

71   Mohammad Reza Shah Pahlavi, *Answer to History* (New York: Stein and Day, 1980), p. 165.

72   Ardeshir Zahedi interview, June 2008.

73   Michael Ledeen and William Lewis, *Debacle: the American Failure in Iran* (New York: Alfred A. Knopf, 1981), p.163.

74   Cyrus Vance, *Hard Choices* (New York: Simon and Schuster, 1983), p. 316.

75   Zbigniew Brzezinski, p.357.

76   "His Imperial Majesty Interview with Kayhan," *Kayhan International*, September 17, 1977.

77   Cyrus Vance, *Hard Choices* (New York: Simon and Schuster, 1983), p. 321.

78   Joseph Kraft, "Letter from Iran," *New Yorker*, December 18, 1978; http://www.newyorker.com/arch ive/1978/12/18/1978_12_18_138_TNY_CARDS_000324558?printable=true; accessed January 2008.

79   Fouad Ajami, "A History Writ in Oil," *New York Times,* Thursday, June 5, 2008;
     http://query.nytimes.com/gst/fullpage.html?res=940DE5DB1638F93BA35756
     C0A96E948260&sec=&spon=&pagewanted=3; accessed June 2008.

80   Mustafa Alani, "Probable Attitudes of the GCC States Towards the Scenario of a Mili-
     tary Action Against Iran's Nuclear Facilities," Gulf Research Center, 2004, p. 11.

81   James A. Bill, *The Eagle and the Lion: The Tragedy of American-Iranian Rela-
     tions* (New Haven: Yale University Press, 1988), p.204.

82   H. E. Chehabi, *Iranian Politics and Religious Modernism: the Liberation Movement of Iran
     under the Shah and Khomeini* (Ithica: Cornell University Press, 1990) p. 12.

83   M. Parsa, *The Social Origins of the Iranian Revolution* (Bruns-
     wick, N.J.: Rutgers University Press, 1989) p. 172; and

84   Central Intelligence Agency National Foreign Assessment Center, December 21, 1978, "Oppo-
     sition Demonstrations in Iran: Leadership, Organization, and Tactics." Declassified.

85   Department of State Telegram, From the Embassy in Tehran to US Embassies worldwide. Declassified.

86   Ibid.

87   Dr. Parviz Mina interview, Paris, France, April 18, 2008.

88   Personal Interview with Uri Lubrani, May 2008.

89   Cited by Dariush Zahedi in *The Iranian Revolution Then and Now* (Boul-
     der, Co: Westview Press, 2000), p. 136.

90   Ibid, p. 136.

91   Ryszard Kapuscinski, *Shah of shahs* (New York: Vintage Books, a divi-
     sion of Random House, 1985), p. 74.

92   Jahangir Amuzegar, *The Dynamics of the Iranian Revolution* (Albany:
     State University of New York Press, 1991), p. 259.

93   Chadwyck-Healey, *Iran: The making of US Policy 1977-1980*, Alex-
     andria VA 1990, Organizations Glossary, p. 151.

94   Misagh Parsa, *The Social Origins of the Iranian Revolution* (Bruns-
     wick, NJ: Rutgers University Press, 1989), p. 217

95   Cited by Ofira Seliktar in *Failing the Crystal Ball Test* (Westport, CT: Praeger Publishers, 2000), p. 133.

96   Clive Irving, Sayings of the Ayatollah Khomeini (The astonishing beliefs of
     the man who has shaken the Western World); http://baytulhikma.wordpress.
     com/2008/08/10/strange-sayings-of-ayatollah-khomeini/; accessed July 2009.

97   The Museum of Broadcast Communications, http://www.museum.tv/archives/
     etv/V/htmlV/vietnamonte/vietnamonte.htm; accessed July 2008.

98   Houchang Nahavandi in *The Last Shah of Iran,* translated from the French
     by Steeve Reed (France: Editions Osmonde, 2004), p. 242

99   http://www.indymedia.org.uk/en/2008/01/388699.html

100 BBC Persian Service Archives, program for the 65th anniver-
     sary of the Service, produced by Shahryar Radpoor

101 The BBC Persian Service, 1941-1979, http://www.indymedia.org.
     uk/media/2008/01//388700.pdf; accessed 2010.

102 Naraghi, Ehsan, Des Palais du Chah, Aux Prisons de la Revolution, *Edi-
     tions Balland* 1991 Translated from the French by Nilou Mobasser

103 The BBC Persian Service, 1941-1979, http://www.indymedia.org.
     uk/media/2008/01//388700.pdf, accessed 2010.

104 Azarbardin interview, June 2008.

105 Robert E. Huyser, *Mission to Tehran* (New York: Harper and Row, 1986), pp. 31-32.

106 *The New York Times*, April 6, 1977, June 7, 1977, June 8, 1977, July 13, 1977.

107 *The New York Times*, June 20, 1977

108 *The New York Times*, June 17, 1977

109 *The New York Times*, November 6, 1977

110 *The New York Times*, November 8, 1977

111 *The New York Times*, December 14, 1978

112 *The New York Times*, December 29, 1978

113 US State Department Memorandum Stempel to State, September 25, 1978, Declassified. Archived in Chadwyck-Healey, *Iran: The Making of US Policy 1977-1980*, Alexandria VA 1990.

114 Personal Interview, Valery Giscard d'Estaing, April 2008.

115 US State Department Telegram Sullivan to State Department, October 1978. Archived in Chadwyck-Healey, *Iran: The Making of US Policy 1977-1980*, Alexandria VA 1990.

116 Barry Rubin, *Paved with Good Intention* (New York and Oxford: Oxford University Press, 1980), p.220.

117 Mir Ali Asghar Montazam, *The Life and Times of Ayatollah Khomeini* (London: Anglo-European Publishing Limited, 1994), p. 169.

118 Michael A. Ledeen, *The War Against the Terror Masters: Why it Happened, Where we are now, and How We'll Win* (New York: McMillan, 2003), pp. 14, 20.

119 Personal Interview with Charles Villeneuve, journalist on Khomeini's flight to Tehran, Paris, France, April 19, 2008.

120 Charles Villeneuve interview, April 2008.

121 William Shawcross, *The Shah's Last Ride* (New York: Simon and Schuster, 1988), p. 26.

122 Uri Lubrani interview, May 2008.

123 *The New York Times*, December 29, 1978

124 *The New York Times*, January 7, 1979

125 Iran Politics Club, http://iranpoliticsclub.net/politics/hostage-story/index.htm; accessed May 2008.

126 *The New York Times,* January 14, 1979

127 "Tearful Shah Leaves Iran," *Gulfnews* Report, January 17, 1979, http://archive.gulfnews.com/indepth/onthisday/january/10182356.html; accessed March 2008.

128 Mohamed Heikal, *Iran: The Untold Story* (New York: Pantheon, 1982), pp. 145-146.

129 Brainy Quotes, Alexander Haig, http://www.brainyquote.com/quotes/authors/a/alexander_haig.html; accessed March 2008.

130 Dr. Ahmed Tehrani interview, June 12, 2008.

131 Houchang Nahavandi, *The Last Shah of Iran*, translated from the French by Steeve Reed (France: Editions Osmonde, 2004), p. 91.

132 Ardeshir Zahedi interview, June 2008.

133 Department of State Telegram, Charles W. Naas, Director, Officer of Iranian Affairs, Bureau of Near Eastern and South Asian Affairs, Department of State, August 17, 1977.

134 Gary Sick, *All Fall Down: America's Tragic Encounter with Iran* (Lincoln, NE: *iUniverse.com*, 1986, 2001) p. 258.

135 Mohamad Heikal, pp.191.

136 BBC World Service, "My Century...," Transcription, December 24, 1999, http://www.bbc.co.uk/worldservice/people/features/mycentury/transcript/wk51d5.shtml; accessed January 2008.

137 Lt. General Shapur Azarbarzin interview, June 2008.

138 William R. Polk, "The United States and Iran: A Tragic Friendship," p. 6; http://www.william-polk.com/pdf/2007/The%20United%20States%20and%20Iran.pdf; accessed May 2008.

139 BBC; On This Day: 1979, "Exiled Ayatollah Khomeini Returns to Iran." http://news.bbc.co.uk/onthisday/hi/dates/stories/february/1/newsid_2521000/2521003.stm; accessed January 2008.

140 General David Ivry interview, May 20, 2008.

141 Newsweek, February 12, 1979, p.44.

142 Wikipedia, William H. Sullivan, http://en.wikipedia.org/wiki/William_H._Sullivan; accessed April 2008.

143 Samuel Segev, The Iranian Triangle (New York: Free Press, 1988), p. 109.

144 US Congress, Committee to investigate the Iran-Contra Affair, 1987, p. 171.

145 Eric Schechter, C4ISR Journal, January 4, 2007, "Desert Duel"; http://www.c4isrjournal.com/story.php?F=2245036; accessed April 2008.

146 Samuel Segev, pp. 110-111.

147 Mohamed Heikal, Khomeini and his Revolution, Les Editions Jeune Afrique, 1983 (Translated from French), pp. 180-181.

148 Lt. General Shapur Azarbarzin interview, June 2008.

149 Nadar Entessar, "Israel and Iran's National Security," Journal of South Asian and Middle Eastern Studies 4 (2004), p. 5.

150 Ibid, p. 4.

151 David Menashri, Post-Revolutionary Politics in Iran (London: Frank Cass, 2001), p. 266.

152 Milton Viorst, In the Shadow of the Prophet: The Struggle for the Soul of Islam (Boulder, CO: Westview Press, 2001), p. 195.

153 Ofira Seliktar, Failing the Crystal Ball Test (Praeger: Westport, CT, 2000), p. 128.

154 Personal Interview with General Yitzhak Segev, June 2008.

155 Extract from Le Pouvoir et le Vie, Part 3, Chapter 6, V. Giscard d' Estaing, 2006; translated in Paris for Dr. Evans with permission from Mr. d'Estaing in May 2008.

156 Said Arjomand, The Turban for the Crown: the Islamic Revolution in Iran (New York: Oxford University Press, 1988), p. 190.

157 Jihad Watch, "D.C. Imam Glorifies Khomeini, Justifies Suicide Bombing, Preaches Islamic Supremacism," http://www.jihadwatch.org/archives/015242.php; accessed March 2008.)

158 Ahmed Taheri, Holy Terror, The Inside Story of Islamic Terrorism (London: Sphere Books, Hutchinson Ltd, 1987), pp. 95-100.

159 Mohamed Heikal, p. 20-23.

160 Cyrus Vance, Hard Choices (New York: Simon and Schuster, 1983), p. 345.

161 Dr. Abdol Majid Majidi interview, April 2008.

162   Margaret Talbot, "The Agitator, Oriana Fallaci Directs her fury toward Islam" The New Yorker, June 5, 2006; http://www.newyorker.com/archive/2006/06/05/060605fa_fact' accessed July 2008.

163 Ibid.

164 Dr. Parviz Mina interview, April 2008.

165 Department of State Telegram, Declassified, October, 1978, From the American Embassy Paris to American Embassy Tehran., signed "Hartman."

166 Mohammad Reza Pahlavi, The Shah of Iran, Answer to History (Briarcliff Manor, NY: Stein and Day, 1980), p. 182.

167 Postscripts, "Iran: Imminent Threat or Paper Tiger?" November 1, 2007, http://notorc.
     blogspot.com/2007/11/iran-imminent-threat-or-paper-tiger.html; accessed April 2008.

168 Confidential Memo, American Embassy in Tehran, L. Bruce Laingen, Charge
     d'Affaires, to State Department, October 15, 1979. Declassified.

169 Farah Pahlavi interview, March 2008.

170 Council on Foreign Relations; State Sponsors: Iran; August 2007, http://
     www.cfr.org/publication/9362/#5; accessed February 2008.

171 "Proxy Power: Understanding Iran's use of Terrorists"; Brookings Institution; http://
     brookings.edu/opinoins/2006/0726iran_byman.aspx; accessed February 2008.

172 "Iran: US Accuses Iran of extending its support for Mideast terror groups,"http://www.glo-
     balsecurity.org/wmd/library/news/iran/2005/iran-050311-rferl03.htm; accessed July 2009.

173 AP and JPost.com staff, "EU official: Hamas responsible for Gaza," Jeru-
     salem Post, (January 26, 2009); accessed November 2012.

174 NBC news staff, November 26, 2012, http://worldnews.nbcnews.com/_
     news/2012/11/26/15454998-gazans-move-quickly-to-rebuild-bombed-tunnels-to-
     bring-in-food-weapons?lite&ocid=msnhp&pos=1; accessed November 2012.

175 "Iran, Hezbollah, Hamas, and the Global Jihad: A New Conflict Paradigm for the
     West" 2007; Brig. Gen. (Ret.) Dr. Shimon Shapira and Daniel Diker, "Iran's Sec-
     ond Islamic Revolution: Strategic Implications for the West," Jerusalem Cen-
     ter for Public Affairs; p. 41; http://www.jcpa.org/; accessed January 2008.

176 Peter Schweizer, Victory: The Reagan Administration's Secret Strategy that Hastened the Col-
     lapse of the Soviet Union (New York: The Atlantic Monthly Press, 1994), page xv.

177 Ibid, page 140.

178 Ibid, pp. 141-143.

179 Ibid, pp. 234.

180 From all sources, 2,977 died in the attack; twenty-four remain listed as "missing in action." Resource:
     http://en.wikipedia.org/wiki/Casualties_of_the_September_11_attacks; accessed January 2013.

181 Find the Data, http://cia-world-fact-book.findthedata.org/q/261/129/How-
     much-oil-does-did-China-consume-in-2011; accessed January 2013.

182 The statistics on China's oil consumption in this paragraph and the next are drawn from the
     US Department of Energy, Energy Information Administration (EIA), "China: Country Analy-
     sis Brief," from the EIA website at the following Internet reference: http://www.eia.doe.gov/
     emeu/cabs/china.html The EIA last updated the China Country Brief in August 2005.

183 The statistics on Iran's oil industry come from the EIA website, "Iran: Country Brief" http://www.
     eia.doe.gov/emeu/cabs/iran.html. The EIA last updated the Iran Country Brief in March 2005.

184 Agence France Presse (AFP), "China signs $70 billion oil and LNG agreement with
     Iran," reported in Lebanon's The Daily Star, October 30, 2004. http://www.dai-
     lystar.com.lb/article.asp?edition_id=10&categ_id=3&article_id=9713

185 BBC News, "China to develop Iran oil field," Nov. 1, 2004. http://
     news.bbc.co.uk/2/hi/business/3970855.stm

186 John C. K. Daly, United Press International, "UPI Energy Watch," printed in The Washington
     Times, July 7, 2004. http://washingtontimes.com/upi-breaking/20040706-110750-8628r.htm

187 Iran's nationalized control of the country's oil and national gas resources are docu-
     mented on the "National Iranian Oil Company" section of the Ministry of Petro-
     leum's website: http://www.nioc.org/subcompanies/nioc/index.asp

188 "Norwegian firms among bidders on Iranian oil field," archived on the Inter-
     net at the following address: http://www.alahwaz.info/new002.htm; the source
     of the Internet report is the Democratic Solidarity Party of Al-Ahwaz.

189 M.K. Bhadrakumar, "India finds a $40bn friend in Iran," *AsianTimesOn-Line*, Jan. 11, 2005. http://atimes.com/atimes/South_Asia/GA11Df07.html

190 China Business InfoCenter, "Economy and politics of Sino-Russian oil deals," Jan. 13, 2005. http://www.cbiz.cn/news/showarticle.asp?id=2208

191 "Yukos at a glance," on the English version of the Yukos website at the following URL: http://www.yukos.com/About_us/yukos_at_a_glance.asp

192 Ibid.

193 Associated Press, New Dehli, "India, Pakistan to build Iranian pipeline," reported in *BusinessWeekOnLine*, Dec. 19, 2005. http://www.businessweek.com/ap/financialnews/D8EIBUQG2.htm?campaign_id=apn_home_down&chan=db

194 Ministry of Foreign Affairs of the People's Republic of China, "China and Russia Issue a Joint Statement, Declaring the Trend of the Boundary Line between the Two Countries has been Completely Determined," Oct. 14, 2004. http://www.fmprc.gov.cn/eng/wjdt/2649/t165266.htm

195 David Francis, "How Iran and Russia Could Cause an Oil Shock," *The Fiscal Times*, March 5, 2012, www.thefiscaltimes.com/Columns/2012/03/05/How-Iran-and-Russia-Could-Cause-an-Oil-Shock.aspx#7Ky7wxKSWu8Gqo3r.99.

196 Reuters, UK, "Iran says does not need permission for nuclear work," Dec. 26, 2006. http://today.reuters.co.uk/news/newsArticle.aspx?type=worldNews&storyID=2005-12-26T124448Z_01_FLE645877_RTRUKOC_0_UK-NUCLEAR-IRAN.xml&archived=False

197 For a statement of this argument against America's War on Terrorism, see: Stephen J. Sniegoski, Ph.D., "America's 'War on Terror': A Prescription for Perpetual War," in *Current Concerns*, Dec. 25, 2005. http://www.currentconcerns.ch/archive/2005/06/20050601.php

198 Jephraim Gundzik, President of Condor Advisors, "The Ties that bind China, Russia, and Iran," published in *AsiaTimesOnLine*, June 4, 2005. http://www.atimes.com/atimes/China/GF04Ad07.html

199 Mahmoud Ahmadinejad quotes, http://thinkexist.com/quotation/anybody-who-recognizes-israel-will-burn-in-the/667654.html; accessed December 2012.

200 Jim Lobe, "Asia the world's top arms importer," *Asia Times* online, September 2, 2005, http://www.atimes.com/atimes/South_Asia/GI02Df02.html; accessed January 2013.

201 Radio Free Europe/ Radio Liberty, "Russia: Moscow: Beijing Conclude War Games, as Region Looks On with Interest," August 25, 2005. http://www.globalsecurity.org/wmd/library/news/russia/2005/russia-050825-rferl01.htm

202 The Russian Topol-M missile deployment was announced on the Internet as a special report of *The Drudge Report*, Dec. 26, 2005. See also: Fraser Nelson, Political Editor, "Putin's show of strength triggers fear of fresh nuclear arms race," The Scotsman, Dec. 26, 2005. http://thescotsman.scotsman.com/international.cfm?id=2459162005

203 "UN Wipes Israel Off the Map—Photos. November 29, 2005 UN Day of Solidarity with the Palestinian People," on the website of *EyeOnTheUN.org*, at the following Internet address: http://www.eyeontheun.org/view.asp?l=21&p=142 The website shows photographs of the UN map without Israel that was used in the public meeting, as well as photographs of the meeting itself.

204 Anadolu News Agency, Cihan News Agency, Tehran, "Visits to Ankara Disturb Tehran," *ZamanOnLine*, Dec. 27, 2005. http://www.zaman.com/?bl=international&alt=&hn=27965

205 Press Release, "Cicek: 'CIA Head's Visit is a Natural Outcome of Developments," *TurkishPress.com*, Dec. 27, 2005. http://www.turkishpress.com/news.asp?id=89033

206 The PKK is profiled on the website of the Federation of American Scientists, at the following web address: http://www.fas.org/irp/world/para/pkk.htm

207 "Iran accused of aiding Turkey Islamic violence," *IranMania.com*, Dec. 19, 2005. http://www.iranmania.com/News/ArticleView/Default.asp?NewsCode=38929&NewsKind=Current%20Affairs See also: Michael Riazaty, "Iran's Qods Operations in Turkey," reported by Gary Metz on *RegimeChangeIran.blogspot.com*, on Dec. 19, 2005. http://regimechangeiran.blogspot.com/2005/12/irans-qods-operation-in-turkey.html

208 Iran Republic News Agency (IRNA), "Rafsanjani underlies need to bolster ties with Turkey," Dec. 27, 2005. http://www.irna.ir/en/news/view/line-24/0512252842164857.htm Also: Kumar Choudhary, "Iran-Turkey cooperation promotes regional stability: Rafsanjani," *KeralaNext.com*, Dec. 26, 2005. http://www.keralanext.com/news/?id=481260

209 Cumali Onal, Cairo, "Gul: There is No Demand from US to Support Iran," *ZamanOnLine*, Dec. 27, 2005. http://www.zaman.org/?bl=international&alt=&hn=28013

210 "World should focus on Israel's nukes," http://edition.presstv.ir/ detail/126944.html; accessed November 2012.

211 "Iran Tells Turkey to Change Tack or Face Trouble," *Hurriyet Daily News*, Tehran, Iran, September 10, 2011, http://www.hurriyetdailynews.com/default.aspx?pageid=438&n=iran-tells-turkey-change-tack-or-face-trouble-2011-10-09; accessed November 2012.

212 "Clinton Warns Iran over US Presence in Turkey, *Hurriyet Daily News*, Tehran, Iran, October 24, 2011, http://www.hurriyetdailynews.com/default.aspx?pageid=438&n=clinton-warns-iran-over-us-presence-in-turkey-2011-10-24, accessed November 2012.

213 Ian O. Lesser, "Turkey, Iran, and Nuclear Issues," in Henry Sokolski and Patrick Clawson (Editors) *Getting Ready for a Nuclear-Ready Iran* (Carlisle, PA: The Strategic Studies Institute, October 2005), pages 89—112, at page 89.

214 Mahmoud Ahmadinejad quotes, http://thinkexist.com/quotation/anybody-who-recognizes-israel-will-burn-in-the/667654.html; accessed December 2012.

215 Human Rights Watch, "Introduction: Ministers of Murder: Iran's New Security Cabinet." http://hrw.org/backgrounder/mena/iran1205/1.htm#_Toc121896786

216 Associated Press, "Iran Government Shuts Down Newspaper, Magazine," reporting from Tehran, Jan. 3, 2006. http://www.breitbart.com/news/2006/01/03/D8ETIBGOP.html

217 Iran Focus, "Iran's new Foreign Minister 'was involved in terrorism,'" *IranFocus.com*, Aug. 24, 2005. http://www.iranfocus.com/modules/news/article.php?storyid=3460

218 Iran Focus, "Iran's president criticizes détente foreign policy," *IranFocus.com*, Jan. 3, 2006. http://www.iranfocus.com/modules/news/article.php?storyid=5117

219 Iran Focus, "Iran President says anti-Israel comments 'awakened' Muslims," *IranFocus.com*, Jan. 3, 2006. http://www.iranfocus.com/modules/news/article.php?storyid=5123

220 Iran Focus, "Iran says anti-Israel diatribe is 'deliberate strategy," *IranFocus.com*, Jan. 3, 2006. http://www.iranfocus.com/modules/news/article.php?storyid=5138.

221 Iran Press Service, "Iran Government Urging the Hidden Imam to Help," *Iran-Press-Service.com*, October 21, 2005. http://www.iran-press-service.com/ips/articles-2005/october-2005/jamkaran_211005.shtml.

222 Richard Ernsberger, Jr., with Ladane Nasseri and Alan Isenberg, "Religion Versus Realith: Who is this man—a mystic, a bumbling political novice or an imminent threat to Iran's established order?" Archived on the website of KRSI Raydio Sadaye Iran at the following URL: http://www.krsi.net/news/detail.asp?NewsID=1603.

223 Alan Peters, "Mullahs' Threat Not Sinking In," *FrontPageMag.com*, Nov. 4, 2005. http://www.frontpagemag.com/Articles/ReadArticle.asp?ID=20065

224 Kenneth R. Timmerman, "Is Iran's Ahmadinejad a messianic medium?" posted on *DailyStar.com*, Dec. 30, 2005. http://www.dailystar.com.lb/article.asp?edition_id=10&categ_id=5&article_id=21113.

225 Behnam Majidzadeh, "The Shadow in Ahmadinejad's Office," posted on RoozOnLine.com at the following URL: http://roozonline.com/11english/011280.shtml

226 Information on the background of Mahmoud Ahmadinejad in this and the following paragraph is drawn from "Mahmoud Ahmadinejad's Biography," on *GlobalSecurity*.org at the following URL: http://www.globalsecurity.org/military/world/iran/ahmadinejad.htm.

227   As quoted by Felice Friedson, Iranian Crown Prince: Ahmadinejad's regime
      is "delicate and fragile", August 12, 2010, http://www.rezapahlavi.org/
      details_article.php?article=459&page=2; accessed January 2013.

228   These points were vividly made on an Independent Television News report. See: "An important video
      report on the hidden Imam," *RegimeChangeIran.blogspot.com*, Dec. 8, 2005. http://regimechangeiran.
      blogspot.com/2005/12/important-video-report-on-hidden-iman.html. The link to view the video is
      available at *Panahjoo.com* at the following URL: http://www.panahjoo.com/viewtopic.php?t=995.

229   Samira Simone, "Feared Basij militia has deep history in Iranian conflict," June 22, 2009; http://
      www.cnn.com/2009/WORLD/meast/06/22/iran.basij.militia.profile/; accessed July 2009.

230   R. Nicholas Burns, Under Secretary of Political Affairs, US Department of State, "US Policy Toward
      Iran," a speech given at the John Hopkins University Paul H. Nitze School of Advanced International
      Studies, Washington, D.C., November 30, 2005. http://www.state.gov/p/us/rm/2005/57473.htm.

231   N. Janardhan, "In the era of Ahmadinejad, do Iran's youth offer a future of
      boom or bust?" *The Daily Star,* Dec. 13, 2005. http://www.dailystar.com.
      lb/article.asp?edition_id=10&categ_id=5&article_id=20706.

232   "Iran imports worth of $4.5b dollars gasoline," *Persian Journal*, July 29, 2005.
      http://www.iranian.ws/iran_news/publish/article_8323.shtml

233   Peter Ackerman and Ramin Ahmadi, *International Herald Tribune*, "Iran's Future?
      Watch the Streets," reported on *Iranvajahan.net*, January 4, 2006. http://www.
      iranvajahan.net/cgi-bin/news.pl?l=en&y=2006&m=01&d=04&a=10.

234   "Iran: New Limits on Travel Abroad," reported on *Adnkronos International*, Dec. 19, 2005.
      http://www.adnki.com/index_2Level.php?cat=Politics&loid=8.0.241132494&par=0.

235   "Iran: Tehran's Stock Exchange Risks Closure," reported on *AdnkronosInternational*, October 5,
      2005. http://www.adnki.com/index_2Level.php?cat=Business&loid=8.0.215506356&par=0

236   "Iran: New Stock Exchange Head Named," reported on *Adnkronos International*, Nov. 22, 2005.
      http://www.adnki.com/index_2Level.php?cat=Business&loid=8.0.231524454&par=0

237   Iran Focus, "18 of Iran's 21 new ministers hail from Revolutionary Guards, secret police," Iran-
      Focus.com, Aug. 14, 2005; http://www.iranfocus.com/modules/news/article.php?storyid=3315

238   BBC News, "Iran president bans Western music," BBC.co.uk, Dec. 19, 2005.
      http://news.bbc.co.uk/1/hi/world/middle_east/4543720.stm

239   Student Movement Coordinating Committee for Democracy in Iran (SMCCDI),
      "Hundreds of Bassji and militiamen in Shiraz," Dec. 31, 2005. http://www.
      daneshjoo.org/publishers/currentnews/article_2978.shtml

240   Student Movement Coordinating Committee for Democracy in Iran (SMCCDI),
      "Female students injured by Islamists using acid," Jan. 4, 2006. http://
      www.daneshjoo.org/publishers/smccdinews/article_4486.shtml

241   Student Movement Coordinating Committee for Democracy in Iran (SMCCDI), "Soc-
      cer game leads to another political action in Tehran," Dec. 30, 2005. http://
      www.daneshjoo.org/publishers/currentnews/article_2968.shtml

242   Student Movement Coordinating Committee for Democracy in Iran (SMCCDI), "Students slam repres-
      sive rule in Iran," Dec. 13, 2005. http://www.daneshjoo.org/publishers/smccdinews/article_4456.shtml.

243   "Iran's crackdown on internet," reported on *News24.com*, June 22, 2005. http://
      www.news24.com/News24/World/News/0,,2-10-1462_1725138,00.html.

244   Scott Peterson, "Waiting for the rapture in Iran," *The Christian Science Monitor,* Dec. 21,
      2005. http://www.csmonitor.com/2005/1221/p01s04-wome.html?s=widep. See also:
      Scott Peterson, "True believers dial messiah hotline in Iran," *The Christian Science Moni-
      tor*, Jan. 4, 2006. http://www.csmonitor.com/2006/0104/p07s02-wome.html.

245   Ehud Olmert, Quotes on Iran, http://www.brainyquote.com/quotes/key-
      words/iran_2.html#qfpcYiZdIJLqSSJf.99; accessed December 2012.

246 David Horowitz, "The second Islamic Revolution," *The Jerusalem Post*, June 26, 2009, p.24.

247 Roger Cohen, "The end of the beginning," *The New York Times Global Edition*, June 24, 2009, p. 7.

248 Christopher Dickey, "The Supreme Leader," *Newsweek*, June 29, 2009, p.36.

249 Reuel Marc Gerecht, "The Koran and the ballot box," *International Herald Tribune*, June 22, 2009, p. 6.

250 Professor David Menashri, Director at The Center for Iranian Studies, Tel Aviv University, Tel Aviv, Israel, Phone conference with The Israel Project; accessed June 28, 2009.

251 Ibid.

252 Martin Fletcher, "Iran clerics declare election invalid and condemn crackdown," *Times* Online; http://www.timesonline.co.uk/tol/news/world/middle_east/article6644817.ece; accessed July 2009.

253 Oliver Javanpour, "The global Muslim theocracy movement is worried," *The Jerusalem Post*, June 24, 2009; www.jpost.com/servlet/Satellite?cid=12451849203 48&pagename-JPost%2FJPArticle%2FPrinter; accessed June 2009.

254 Borzou Daragahi, "Intent of show trial puzzles Iranians," *Houston Chronicle*, August 9, 2009; p. A29.

255 Neil Macfarquhar, "Crackdown Across Iran shows power of new elite," *International Herald Tribune*, June 26, 2009, pp. 1,4.

256 Simon Tisdall, "Iran has been isolated by Arab spring," The Guardian, May 17, 2011, http://www.guardian.co.uk/commentisfree/2011/may/17/iran-arab-spring; accessed December 2012.

257 Henry Kissinger, *Does America Need a Foreign Policy? Toward Diplomacy for the 21st Century* (New York: Simon & Schuster, 2001), page 197.

258 Cited by Mark Silverberg, featured writer, *The New Media Journal*.us; "The Strategy of Defeat"; December 27, 2007; http://www.therant.us/staff/silverberg/12272007.htm' accessed January 2008.

259 David Limbaugh, "Ashamed of America," *Townhall.com*, July 11, 2008, http://townhall.com/Columnists/DavidLimbaugh/2008/07/11/ashamed_of_america; accessed August 2008.

260 Ahmadinejad Threatens to send US to the 'Morgue', July 11, 2011, http://in.news.yahoo.com/ahmadinejad-threatens-send-us-morgue-013326973.html; accessed November 2013.

261 "Iran, Hizbullah, Hamas and the Global Jihad: A New Conflict Paradigm for the West" 2007; Gen. (Ret.) Moshe Yaalon, "The Second Lebanon War: From Territory to Ideology," Jerusalem Center for Public Affairs; p. 16; accessed January 2008.

262 Jonathan Steele, "Lost in Translation," *Guardian*, June 14, 2006, http://commentisfree. guardian.co.uk/jonathan_steele/2006/06/post_155.html; accessed March 2008.

263 Michael Evans, *The Final Move Beyond Iraq: The Final Solution While the World Sleeps* (Lake Mary, FL: Front Line, 2007) p. 210.

264 "Iran: Holocaust Conference Soon in Tehran," reported by *AdnkronosInternationa.com*, Jan. 5, 2006. http://www.adnki.com/index_2Level.php?cat=Politics&loid=8.0.246551760&par=0#

265 Louis Rene Beres and Tsiddon-Chatto, Col. (res.) Yoash, "Reconsidering Israel's Destruction of Iraq's Osiraq Nuclear Reactor," *Temple International and Comparative Law Journal 9 (2)*, 1995. Reprinted in *Israel's Strike Against the Iraqi Nuclear Reactor 7 June 1982*, Jerusalem: Menachem Begin Heritage Center, 2003, p.60.

266 Rafael Eitan, "The Raid on the Reactor from the Point of View of the Chief of Staff," *Israel's Strike Against the Iraqi Nuclear Reactor 7 June, 1981*, Jerusalem: Menachem Begin Heritage Center: 2003, 3133.

267 Maj. Gen. (res.) David Ivry, "The Attack on the Osiraq Nuclear Reactor—Looking Back 21 Years Later," *Israel's Strike Against the Iraqi Nuclear Reactor 7 June, 1981*, Jerusalem: Menachem Begin Heritage Center, 2003, p. 35.

268 Yitzhak Shamir, "The Failure of Diplomacy," *Israel's Strike Against the Iraqi Nuclear Reactor7 June, 1981*, Jerusalem, Menachem Begin Heritage Center: 2003, p. 16-17.

269 On *GlobalSecurity.org*. This Internet site contains an extensive discussion of Iran's nuclear facilities, including a site-by-site description, reached by navigating through the following

sequence: Iran > Facilities > Nuclear. The discussion of Iran's uranium mines is drawn from this site: http://www.globalsecurity.org/wmd/world/iran/mines.htm; accessed 2006.

270 Saghand Mining Department, Atomic Energy Organization of Iran. http://www.aeoi.org.ir/NewWeb/Recenter.asp?id=26 See also: National Geoscience Database of Iran (NGDIR), "Mineral Resources of Iran." http://ngdir.ir/GeoportalInfo/SubjectInfoDetail.asp?PID=54&index=67; accessed 2005.

271 "AP: Iran to Extract Uranium in Early 2006," News Max wires, at *NewsMax.com* September 6, 2004. http://www.newsmax.com/archives/articles/2004/9/5/115634.shtml; accessed 2005.

272 "Esfahan/Isfahan. Nuclear Technology," *GlobalSecurity.org*, at: http://www.globalsecurity.org/wmd/world/iran/esfahan.htm; accessed 2006.

273 "Revealed: Iran's Nuclear Factory," *The Sunday Times-World*, May 1, 2005, archived at *Timesonline.co.uk* at: http://www.timesonline.co.uk/article/0,,2089-1592578,00.html; accessed 2005.

274 "Iran renews nuclear weapons development," *Daily Telegraph*, September 12, 2008; http://tehran-watch.blogspot.com/2008/09/iran-renews-nuclear-weapons-development.html; accessed July 2009.

275 "Natanz," at *GlobalSecurity.org*. http://www.globalsecurity.org/wmd/world/iran/natanz.htm

276 Louis Ferdinand Celine quotes (French writer and physician, 1894-1961), http://thinkexist.com/quotes/with/keyword/transparency/; accessed December 2012.

277 "Iran resumes nuclear research activities," reported by the Islamic Republic News Agency, Jan. 10, 2006. http://www.irna.ir/en/news/view/line-24/0601106548122559.htm.

278 "Iran plans 'small scale' nuclear fuel work: IAEA," Reuters, Jan. 10, 2006. http://today.reuters.com/news/newsArticle.aspx?type=worldNews&storyID=2006-01-10T143019Z_01_KNE030810_RTRUKOC_0_US-NUCLEAR-IRAN.xml&archived=False.

279 "EU powers to mull Iranian nuclear efforts," *Haaretz*, February 9, 2004. http://www.haaretz.com/hasen/pages/ShArt.jhtml?itemNo=472862&contrassID=1; accessed 2006.

280 "Iran confirms uranium-to-gas conversion," a report published in the *China Daily*, May 10, 2005. http://www.chinadaily.com.cn/english/doc/2005-05/10/content_440631.htm

281 Ibid.

282 Tom Baldwin, "Iran faces sanctions after reactivating nuclear plant," *TimesOnLine.com*, August 9, 2005. http://www.timesonline.co.uk/article/0,,251-1727066,00.html See also: Seth Rosen, "Iran restarts its nuclear activities," *The Washington Times*, August 9, 2005. http://www.washtimes.com/world/20050809-120112-3017r.htm; accessed 2006.

283 AFP, "Iran Develops Uranium Separation Technology," Jan. 1, 2006. http://news.jpn.co.jp:8080/htmldb/news.article?P=Iran_Develops_Uranium_Separation_Technology_20060101.html

284 "Iran Rejects U.N. Resolution," CBS News, September 25, 2005. http://www.cbsnews.com/stories/2005/09/25/world/main882946.shtml; accessed 2006.

285 Remarks on UN reform, the Human Rights Council, and other Issues, Ambassador John R. Bolton, US Permanent Representative to the United Nations, On-The-Record Briefing, January 25, 2006, Washington, D.C.; http://www1.umn.edu/humanrts/unreform-remarks.html; accessed July 2009.

286 "Iran enriches uranium. Iran starts converting new uranium batch, diplomat says," *Reuters*, November 27, 2005. http://www.blog.ca/main/index.php/boris-newz/2005/11/17/iran_enriches_uranium~315692; accessed 2006.

287 "Russia plan could end Iran talks impasse—ElBaradei," *Reuters*, December 6, 2005. http://today.reuters.co.uk/news/newsArticle.aspx?type=worldNews&storyID=2005-12-06T173520Z_01_DIT663295_RTRUKOC_0_UK-NUCLEAR-IRAN-ELBARADEI.xml; accessed 2006.

288 Quoted in *Taheri, Holy Terror*, p. 24.

289 See: Taheri, *Nest of Spies*, page 271.

290 Yehezkel Dror, "The New Ruler," Global Leadership for the 21st Century, Conference on the Future of the Jewish People, May 2008, Jerusalem Israel; The Jewish People Policy

Planning Institute, http://www.jpppi.org.il/JPPPI/Templates/ShowPage.asp?DBID=1&LNG ID=1&TMID=105&FID=452&PID=0&IID=510, p. 133; accessed August 2009.

291 Information provided by the National Council of Resistance of Iran, US Representative Office. "Information on Two Top Secret Nuclear Sites of the Iranian Regime (Natanz and Arak)," December 2002. The Report is available on the website *IranWatch.org* at the URL: http://www.iranwatch.org/privateviews/NCRI/perspex-ncri-natanzarak-1202.htm;   accessed 2006.

292 National Council for Resistance in Iran, "Disclosing a Major Secret Nuclear Site under the Ministry of Defense," Press Release, November 14, 2004. Archived on the website of *GlobalSecurity.org* at: http://www.globalsecurity.org/wmd/library/report/2004/new-nuke-info.htm; accessed 2006.

293 "Implementation of the NPT Safeguards Agreement in the Islamic Republic of Iran," Report by the Director General, International Atomic Energy Agency (IAEA) Board of Governors, GOV/2006/67, September 2, 2005. http://www.globalsecurity.org/wmd/library/report/2005/iran_iaea-gov_2005-67_2sep05.htm; accessed 2006.

294 "Questioning Iran's Pursuit of the Nuclear Fuel Cycle—Iran's Nuclear Fuel Cycle Facilities: A Pattern of Peaceful Intent?" US Department of State, September 2005. http://www.globalsecurity.org/wmd/library/report/2005/iran-fuel-cycle-brief_dos_2005.pdf; accessed 2006.

295 Ibid.

296 Ibid.

297 Ibid.

298 Ibid.

299 Ibid.

300 "Abdul Qadeer Kahn 'Apologizes' for Transferring Nuclear Secrets Abroad." The statement is archived on the Federation of American Scientists website, *www.fas.org*, at the following URL: http://www.fas.org/nuke/guide/pakistan/nuke/aqkhan020404.html; accessed 2006.

301 Attachment A. Unclassified Report to Congress on the Acquisition of Technology Relating to Weapons of Mass Destruction and Advanced Conventional Munitions, 1 July Through 31 December 2003. The report can be found on the Internet on the website of the Central Intelligence Agency at the following URL: http://www.cia.gov/cia/reports/721_reports/july_dec2003.htm; accessed 2005.

302 Ibid.

303 "Iran Claims Solid Fuel for Missiles Achieved," *NewsMax.com*, July 27, 2005. http://www.newsmax.com/archives/articles/2005/7/27/104439.shtml; accessed 2006.

304 Anthony H. Cordesman, Arleigh A. Burke Chair, Center for Strategic and International Studies. *Iran's Developing Military Capabilities: Main Report Washington, D.C. Center for Strategic and International Studies.* Working Draft: December 14, 2004. The discussion of the shahab-3 missile is drawn from pages 25-27.

305 "Nuclear Weapons development—2006," *Global Security*.org, http://www.globalsecurity.org/wmd/world/iran/nuke2006.htm; accessed July 2009.

306 "Iran's nuclear program status," Congressional Research Service, November 20, 2008; p. CRS-10, http://www.fas.org/sgp/crs/nuke/RL34544.pdf; accessed July 2009.

307 HR282, Iran Freedom Support Act, US House bill, April 27, 2006. http://www.theorator.com/bills109/hr282.html; accessed July 2009.

308 Dudi Cohen, "Israel will soon disappear," *Ynetnews*, October 10, 2006, http://www.ynetnews.com/articles/0,7340,L-3317417,00.html; accessed July 2009.

309 Michael Goldfarb, editor, "Ahmadinejad: World has lost its will," *Weekly Standard*, November 14, 2006; http://www.weeklystandard.com/weblogs/TWSFP/2006/11/ahmadinejad_world_has_lost_its_will_.html; accessed July 2009.

310 "Iran determined to master nuclear fuel cycle," *Iran Daily*, November 15, 2006; http://iran-daily.com/1385/2708/html/index.htm; accessed July 2009.

311 "Key judgments from a National Intelligence Estimate on Iran's nuclear activity," *The New York Times,* December 4, 2007; http://www.nytimes.com/2007/12/04/washington/04itext.html?pagewanted=2&_r=2; accessed July 2009.

312 Ali Akbar Dareini, "Iran says it now runs more than 5000 centrifuges," *Associated Press,* November 26, 2008; http://www.google.com/hostednews/ap/article/ALeqM5jG7bnyWWJfgaYD-JwcqmImlpRujwD94MND800; accessed July 2008.

313 David Albright and Jacqueline Shire, "IAEA Report on Iran," Institute for Science and International Security, 19 February 2009.

314 "Responsible leadership for a sustainable future," 2009 G8 Summit, L'Aquila, Italy, July 8-10, 2009; http://www.g8italia2009.it/static/G8_Allegato/G8_Political_issues_FINAL_2240%5b3%5d.pdf; accessed July 2009.

315 James Hider, "Middle East desire for nuclear power could trigger an arms race," *Times Online,* June 24, 2009, http://www.timesonline.co.uk/tol/news/world/middle_east/article6565549.ece#cid=OTC-RSS&attr=797093; accessed July 2009.

316 Shashank Bengali, "IAEA reports no progress on access to Iran's nuclear facilities, *Los Angeles Times,* December 7, 2012. http://articles.latimes.com/2012/dec/07/world/la-fg-iran-nuclear-20121207; accessed December 2012.

317 Radio Free Europe, "IAEA seeks Parchin Access; Iran says No, January 15, 2013, http://www.rferl.org/content/iaea-iran-parchin-access/24824662.html; accessed January 2013.

318 Benjamin Netanyahu, *Terrorism: How the West can Win,* (New York, NY: Garrar, Straus, Giroux, 1986), p. 181.

319 Jim Wolf, "Gates reassures Israel on US-Iran strategy," *Reuters,* July 27, 2009; http://www.reuters.com/article/topNews/idUSTRE56Q0QK20090727. (Access August 2009)

320 Ibid.

321 James Hider, Richard Beeston, Michael Evans, "Iran is ready to build an N-bomb—its just waiting for the Ayatollah's order," *The Times Online,* August 3, 2009; http://www.timesonline.co.uk/tol/news/world/middle_east/article6736785.ece#cid=OTC-RSS&attr=797093; accessed August 2009.

322 Brainy Quotes, http://www.brainyquote.com/quotes/keywords/weapons_2.html; accessed August 2009.

323 Ibid.

324 Daily Inspirational Thoughts, *Kindle Podcast.com*; http://retirementwitha-purpose.com/quotes/quotesprayer.html; accessed August 2009.

325 Benjamin Netanyahu, *Terrorism: How the West can Win,* (New York, NY: Garrar, Straus, Giroux, 1986), p. 14.

326 Ecclesiastes 3:1,8 (NKJV)

327 *ThinkExist.com,* George Washington, http://thinkexist.com/quotes/like/there_is_nothing_so_likely_to_produce_peace_as_to/262864/; accessed August 2012.

328 Ronald Reagan, Message to the Congress Transmitting Proposed Legislation To Combat International Terrorism, April 26, 1984; http://www.reagan.utexas.edu/archives/speeches/1984/42684a.htm; accessed August 2009.

329 "Iranian nuclear challenge must be tackled in 2013: Netanyahu," *The Peninsula,* December 11, 2012, http://thepeninsulaqatar.com/middle-east/217603-iranian-nuclear-challenge-must-be-tackled-in-2013-netanyahu.html, accessed December 2012.

330 For technical descriptions and photographs of the Popeye Turbo cruise missile, see: "Popeye Turbo," on the website *IsraeliWeapons.com.* http://www.israeli-weapons.com/weapons/missile_systems/air_missiles/popeye_turbo/Popeye_Turbo.html.

331 "Israeli Submarines," on the website of the Federation of American Scientists (FAS), at the following URL: http://www.fas.org/nuke/guide/israel/sub/index.html.

332 Sammy Salama and Karen Ruster, "A Preemptive Attack on Iran's Nuclear Facilities: Possible Consequences," a CNS research story on the website of the Center for Nonproliferation Studies, archived at the following URL: http://www.cns.miis.edu/pubs/week/040812.htm.

333 "F-16I Soufa fighter and Ground Attack Aircraft, Israel," featured on the website of *Airforce-Technology.com* at the following URL: http://www.airforce-technology.com/projects/f-16i/. In addition to technical specifications, the website also has photographs of the F-16I.

334 For technical specifications and photographs of the F-16I, see Israeli-Weapons.com at the following URL: http://www.israeli-weapons.com/weapons/aircraft/f-15i/F-15I.html This site also provides technical specifications and photographs for the F-16I at http://www.israeli-weapons.com/weapons/aircraft/f-16i/F-16I.html.

335 This point is made by Anthony Cordesman, a senior researcher at the Center for Strategic and International Studies in Washington, D.C. Cordesman is quoted in: "Iran's military called no match for U.S. but its missiles pose treat to Israel, *GeoStrategy-Direct.com*, week of January 4, 2005. URL reference: http://www.geostrategy-direct.com/geostrategy-direct/secure/2005/1_04/1.asp. See also: Anthony H. Cordesman, Arleigh A. Burk Chair, *Iran's Developing Military Capabilities, Main Report.* Washington, D.C.: Center for Strategic and International Studies, Working Draft December 14, 2004, referred to hereafter as the *CSIS Report*.

336 "US to give thousands of 'bunker-buster' bombs," *YNetnews.com*, Decembe 12, 2012, http://www.ynetnews.com/articles/0,7340,L-4318508,00.html; accessed December 2012.

337 *CSIS Report*, pages 39-40.

338 Ibid. (For additional Internet reports concerning Iran purchasing Sunburn cruise missiles, see: "A Weapons Analysis of the Iran-Russia-US Strategic Triangle," on *TBRnews.org*, at URL: http://www.thetruthseeker.co.uk/print.asp?ID=2439. Also, see: Mark Gaffney, "Iran a Bridge Too Far?" archived on the Information Clearinghouse website at URL reference: http://www.informationclearinghouse.info/article7147.htm.)

339 Kenneth M. Pollack, The Persian Puzzle: The Conflict Between Iran and America (New York: Random House, 2004), pages 196-197.

340 "Netanyahu: Clear 'red line' needed to stop Iran's nuclear program," *FoxNews.com*, http://www.foxnews.com/politics/2012/09/27/netanyahu-will-never-be-uprooted-again/; accessed December 2012.

341 Senator Lindsey Graham: No Defense Cuts until Iranian Nuclear Threat Ends," http://abcnews.go.com/blogs/politics/2012/12/sen-lindsey-graham-no-defense-cuts-until-iranian-nuclear-threat-ends/; accessed December 2012.

342 James Earl Carter, Jr., State of the Union Address 1981; http://www.let.rug.nl/usa/P/jc39/speeches/su81jec.htm; accessed February 2008.

343 Bret Stephens, "How to Stop Iran without Firing a Shot"; May 15, 2006; http://www.opinionjournal.com/wsj/?id=110008382; accessed February, 2008.

344 "Obama holding talks with Iran excluding Israel," Jerusalem Post, December 11, 2012, http://www.jpost.com/IranianThreat/News/Article.aspx?id=295560; accessed December 2012.

345 "Iran congratulates North Korea on rocket launch," YahooNews, December 12, 2012, http://uk.news.yahoo.com/iran-congratulates-north-korea-rocket-launch-145452352.html; accessed December 2012.

346 Dante Alighieri, http://thinkexist.com/quotation/the_hottest_places_in_hell_are_reserved_for_those/169930.html; accessed December 2012.

347 "Arabs like Saddam, Hugo Chavez, more than Obama," December 13, 2012, http://education-views.org/arabs-like-saddam-hugo-chavez-more-than-obama/; accessed December 2012.

348 List of Current ships of the US Navy, http://en.wikipedia.org/wiki/List_of_current_ships_of_the_United_States_Navy; accessed October 2012.

349 Websites of the military installations discussed are as follows: Ft. Rucker, Alabama, at http://www-rucker.army.mil ; Hulburt Field, Florida http://www.hurlburt.af.mil/index2.shtml ; http://www.29palms.usmc.mil/ The authors are acknowledge an

unpublished paper by Paul L. Williams, "U.S. Invasion of Iran Now 'Imminent,'" as identifying the importance of these bases in preparing for a U.S. military attack on Iran.

350 Iran's nuclear facilities are detailed at GlobalSecurity.org, including in many instances satellite photographs. http://www.globalsecurity.org/wmd/world/iran/nuke-fac.htm

351 NTI, "Iran Profile: Iran Missile Facilities," NTI.org, at the following URL: http://www.nti.org/e_research/profiles/Iran/Missile/3876_4104.html

352   See, for Instance, Global Security.org at the following URL: http://www.globalsecurity.org/military/world/iran/

353 Robert Coram, Boyd: The Fighter Pilot Who Changed the Art of War (Boston: Little, Brown and Company, 2002), page 42.

354 Described in Bijal Trivedi, "Inside Shock and Awe," National Geographic Channel, posted to the website on Feb. 14, 2005, at the following URL: http://blogs.nationalgeographic.com/channel/blog/2005/03/explorer_shockawe.html

355 Robert Tait, "Iran issues stark warning on oil price," The Guardian, Jan. 16, 2006. http://www.guardian.co.uk/frontpage/story/0,16518,1687381,00.html

356 Then Prime Minister of Israel, speaking before the US House of Representatives Government Reform Committee on September 20th, 2001.

357 "Ayatollah Ali Khamenei says Iran, Israel on 'collision course'," Ramin Mostaghim and Borzou Daragahi, Los Angeles Times, September 20, 2008; http://articles.latimes.com/2008/sep/20/world/fg-iran20; accessed July 2009.

358 Patrick Devenny "Hezbollah's strategic threat to Israel," Middle East Quarterly, Winter 2006, pp. 31-38; http://www.meforum.org/806/hezbollahs-strategic-threat-to-israe; accessed July 2009.

359 Foreign Broadcast Information Service—Daily Reports, July 20, 1994; Source—Radio Iran; Quoted in "The Islamic Republic of Iran and the Holocaust: Anti-Semitism and Anti-Zionism," Meir Litvak, The Journal of Israeli History, V. 25, No. 1, March 2006, PP. 267-284, 271.

360 Comment by Mahmoud Ahmadinejad, March 1, 2007, Quoted in "Zionist regime offspring of Britain, nurtured by US—Ahmadinejad," Islamic Republic News Agency (IRNA), http://www2.irna.ir/en/news/view/line-20/0703015352005938.htm; accessed July 2009.

361 Personal interview with Benjamin Netanyahu, 2007.

362 Ibid.

363 David Ignatius, "The Spy who wants Israel to talk," Washington Post, November 11, 2007; http://www.washingtonpost.com/wp-dyn/content/article/2007/11/09/AR2007110901941.html; accessed July 2009.

364 Mahmoud Ahmadinejad, United Nations, September 17, 2005 speech; http://www.globalsecurity.org/wmd/library/news/iran/2005/iran-050918-irna02.htm; accessed July 2009.

365 Golnaz Esfandiari, "Iran: President Says Light Surrounded Him During UN Speech," Radio Free Europe/ Radio Liberty, November 29, 2005. http://www.rferl.org/featuresarticle/2005/11/184CB9FB-887C-4696-8F54- 0799DF747A4A.html RegimeChangeIran.blogspot.com provides a link to a news broadcast where the videotape of Ahmadinejad's conversations with the mullahs over tea can be seen and heard: http://regimechangeiran.blogspot.com/2005/12/important-video-report-on-hidden-iman.html See also, Scott Peterson, "Waiting for the rapture in Iran," Christian Science Monitor, 21 December 2005.

366 "Iran: Part of the Axis of Evil," April 22, 2006; http://www.zionism-Israel.com/log/archives/00000042.html; accessed July 2009.

367 LookLex Encyclopedia, "Twelvers," http://i-cias.com/e.o/twelvers.htm; accessed July 2009.

368 Truth and Justice, "Let this land…go up in smoke," http://seektruthandjustice.blogspot.com/2011/01/let-this-landgo-up-in-smoke.html; accessed December 2012.

369 Financial Times Enforcement Network, USA Patriot Act, Section 311, http://www.fincen.gov/statutes_regs/patriot/section311.html; accessed August 2009.

370 David Ignatius, "US Sanctions with Teeth," *Washington Post,* February 29, 2007; http://washingtonpost.com/wp-dyn/content/article/2007/02/07/27/AR2007022701157_p; accessed July 2009.

371 Stuart E. Eizenstat, "Mega-Trends in the Next Five Years Which Will Impact on World Jewry and Israel," Conference on the Future of the Jewish People, May 2008, Jerusalem Israel; The Jewish People Policy Planning Institute, http://www.jpppi.org.il/JPPPI/Templates/ShowPage.asp?DBID=1&LNGID=1&TMID=105&FID=452&PID=0&IID=510. pp. 67-68; accessed August 2009.

372 Jamie Glazov, "The China-Russia-Iran Axis," *FrontPageMagazine.com,* January 22, 2008, http://www.frontpagemag.com/readArticle.aspx?ARTID=29604; accessed August 2009.

373 Trudy Rubin, "Hold Off Engaging Iran," *Miami Herald,* July 23, 2009; http://www.miamiherald.com/opinion/other-views/v-fullstory/story/1153627.html; accessed August 2009.

374 "What is Globalization?" http://www.globalization101.org/What_is_Globalization.html?PHPSESSID=e54636b5a846c31e34b20315060d2a71; accessed August 2009.

375 Benjamin Netanyahu, Translation, Prime Minister's Office, July 28, 2009; http://www.pmo.gov.il/PMOEng/Communication/PMSpeaks/speechmabal280709.htm; accessed August 2009.

376 Jim Kingsdale's Energy Investment Strategies, "Iranian oil production verging on disaster," June 2008; http://www.energyinvestmentstrategies.com/2008/06/25/iranian-oil-production-verging-on-disaster/; accessed August 2009.

377 Full Text of H.R. 194 (111th) : Comprehensive Iran Sanctions, Accountability, and Divestment Act of 2010, 111*th* Congress, 2009–2010. Text as of Aug 25, 2010 (Passed Congress/Enrolled Bill), http://www.govtrack.us/congress/bills/111/hr2194/text; accessed September 2010.

378 "Iran to end petrol import," Press TV, August 1, 2009; http://www.presstv.com/detail.aspx?id=102237&sectionid=351020102; aaccessed August 2009.

379 John Bolton: Iranian Nukes Threaten Russia, *Newsmax.com,* http://archive.newsmax.com/archives/ic/2006/3/10/03021.shtml; accessed January 2013.

380 The Shia and Sunni Hadiths differ in content, which is largely why the prophecies of the Twelfth Imam are Shia and not Sunni beliefs—nor do all Shia interpret these scriptures as the leaders of the current Iranian regime do.

381 *The Coming Is Upon Us*, streaming video, "Iran Leaders: The Coming is Upon Us—Israel Shall be Destroyed! (Watch the Video)" A Time to Betray website (March 28, 2011), http://atimetobetray.com/blog/iran-leaders-the-coming-is-upon-us---israel-shall-be-destroyed-watch-the-video/.

382 Erick Stakelbeck, "Iranian Video Says Mahdi is 'Near'," *CBN News* Website (March 28, 2011), http://www.cbn.com/cbnnews/world/2011/March/Iranian-Regime-Video-Says-Mahdi-is-Near-/.

383 *The Coming Is Upon Us*, video.

384 Ibid.

385 Reza Kahlil, interview with Joel Rosenberg presented during "Assessing the Threat of Radical Islam in the Epicenter," streaming video, Epicenter Conference 2011 (May 16, 2011), http://www.epicenterconference.com/.

386 Rosenberg, *Epicenter 2.0,* 333-334.

387 See Revelation 6:1-8, *New American Standard Bible.* Copyright © 1960, 1962, 1963, 1968, 1971, 1972, 1973, 1975, 1977, 1995 by The Lockman Foundation. Used by permission, *www.Lockman.org.*

388 Adrienne S. Gaines, "Company Claims 1.5 Billion Barrels of Oil Found in Israel," *Charisma News* online (August 19, 2010), http://www.charismamag.com/index.php/news/29124-company-claims-15-billion-barrels-of-oil-found-in-israel.

389 Lev & Yoni Kempinski, "Meged Field May Be a (Black) Gold Mine for Israel," *Arutz Sheva* (November 29, 2010), http://www.israelnationalnews.com/News/News.aspx/140899.

390 Gaines, "Company Claims 1.5 Billion Barrels of Oil Found in Israel."

391 Ethan Bronner, "Gas Field Confirmed Off Coast of Israel," *The New York Times* (December 30, 2010), http://www.nytimes.com/2010/12/31/world/middleeast/31leviathan.html?_r=2.

392   Susan Kraemer, "Israel's Leviathan Gas Find Will Have Widespread Repercus-
      sions for World Power," *Green Prophet* (December 31, 2010), http://www.green-
      prophet.com/2010/12/leviathan-gas-israel-balance-of-power/.

393   Ibid.

394   John 8:32, ESV.

395   C.S. Lewis, *The Case for Christianity*, Quoted at *Good Reads.com*, http://www.
      goodreads.com/quotes/tag/end-of-the-world; accessed January 2013.

396   Mike Huckabee: Newtown Shooting No Surprise, We've 'Systematically Removed God' From
      Schools, The Huffington Post, December 15, 2012, http://www.huffingtonpost.com/2012/12/14/
      mike-huckabee-school-shooting_n_2303792.html; accessed December 2012.

397   Michael D. Evans, *The American Prophecies* (Nashville: Warner Faith, 2004, p. 21.

398   John T. Elson, "Toward a Hidden God," *Time* Magazine, April 8, 1966, http://www.time.
      com/time/magazine/article/0,9171,835309,00.html; accessed November 10, 2006.

399   "Dr. Dobson urges: Head to Alabama," *WorldNetDaily.com*, August 26, 2003, http://www.
      worldnetdaily.com/news/article.asp?ARTICLE_ID=34267; accessed November 11, 2006.

400   "Top Ten Reviews," *Internet Filter Review*, http://internet-filter-review.toptenreviews.
      com/internet-pornography-statistics.html; accessed November 10, 2006.

401   1 Timothy 4:1-2, NIV.

402   "To Put it Another Way," *Washington Post*, October 7, 2001, B.03.

403   Susan Sontag, "The Talk of the Town," *The New Yorker*, September 24, 2001, http://www.
      msgr.ca/msgr-3/talk_of_the_town_susan_sontag.htm; accessed December 11, 2006.

404   Barbara Kingsolver, *Milwaukee Journal Sentinel*, September 27, 2001, http://www.
      rightwingnews.com/quotes/left.php; accessed November 11, 2006.

405   David Horowitz, *Unholy Alliance: Radical Islam and the American Left* (Wash-
      ington, DC: Regnery Publishing, Inc, 2004), 135-136.

406   1 Peter 5:6, KJV.

407   Joshua 24:15, NIV.

408   Maseh Zarif, Iranian Nuclear Program: Timelines, Data, and Estimates V5.0 from
      AEI's Critical Threats Project, http://www.irantracker.org/nuclear-program/zarif-
      timelines-data-estimates-november-23-2012; accessed January 2013.

BOOKS BY: MIKE EVANS

Israel: America's Key to Survival

Save Jerusalem

The Return

Jerusalem D.C.

Purity and Peace of Mind

Who Cries for the Hurting?

Living Fear Free

I Shall Not Want

Let My People Go

Jerusalem Betrayed

Seven Years of Shaking: A Vision

The Nuclear Bomb of Islam

Jerusalem Prophecies

Pray For Peace of Jerusalem

America's War: The Beginning of the End

The Jerusalem Scroll

The Prayer of David

The Unanswered Prayers of Jesus

God Wrestling

Why Christians Should Support Israel

The American Prophecies

Beyond Iraq: The Next Move

The Final Move beyond Iraq

Showdown with Nuclear Iran

Jimmy Carter: The Liberal Left and World Chaos

Atomic Iran

Cursed

Betrayed

The Light

Corrie's Reflections and Meditations (Booklet)

GAMECHANGER SERIES:
GameChanger
Samson Option

THE PROTOCOLS SERIES:
The Protocols
The Candidate

The Revolution

The Final Generation

Seven Days

The Locket

Living in the F.O.G.

COMING IN 2013:

The History of Christian Zionism

GameChanger: The Four Horsemen

Born Again: Israel's Rebirth

Jerusalem

Ten Boom

**TO PURCHASE, CONTACT: ORDERS@TIMEWORTHYBOOKS.COM
P. O. BOX 30000, PHOENIX, AZ 85046**